CHIARA LUBICH
Prophet of Unity

CHIARA LUBICH
Prophet of Unity

a biography by
MAURIZIO GENTILINI

New City Press

Published by New City Press (English Translation)
202 Comforter Blvd., Hyde Park, NY 12538
©2020 New City Press

Original title: *Chiara Lubich: La Via Dell'unità, Tra Storia e Profezia*

Cover design and layout by Miguel Tejerina

Library of Congress Cataloging-in-Publication Data
Chiara Lubich: *Prophet of Unity*

Library of Congress Control Number: 2020941546

ISBN: 978-1-56548-131-2 (Paperback)
ISBN: 978-1-56548-150-3 (e-book)

CONTENTS

FOREWORD 11
INTRODUCTION 13

Part I
THE BEGINNING OF A STORY

TRENT AND SURROUNDING AREAS, 1920 27
    Between Austria and Italy 27
    A region and a Church on the borders 28
    The time of Celestino Endrici 33
    Time of war 38
    The post-war period 45
    The beginning of the "long vigil" 47

THE LUBICH FAMILY 49
    Family history 49
    Family places 52
    Luigia, Luigi ... and the others 58

FORMATION BETWEEN THE TWO WARS 63
    A little child to the child Mary 63
    At school in 1926 64
    At high school 67

FROM CATHOLIC ACTION TO THE THIRD ORDER 72
    Trent: Church and fascism 72
    Propagandist 76
    Teacher in the mountains and in the city 83
    Tertiary 86

Part II
THE FINGER OF GOD

LIGHTING THE HOME FIRES (FOCOLARES) 93
    Bombs on the City 93
    7th December 1943 "Give yourself completely to me" 95
    The first companions 97
    Jesus Forsaken 99
    Stars and Tears 103

THE LITTLE HOUSE 106
    Piazza Cappuccini 106
    The birth of the Ideal 107
    The Word of Life 110
    Meetings 113

CHIARA AND THE FATHER BISHOP 117
    Protocol 117
    The first doubts 118
    Bishop Carlo 119
    The period after the war 123
    The first meeting and the finger of God 127

ORGANIZING UNITY 129
    Focolare and Catholic Action 129
    Towards the first statute 133
    Forty–eight 136
    A special guest 139
    Charges and defenses 140
    Where two or three are gathered 141
    Prospects of unity 143

IN THE ETERNAL CITY 145
    Friend Foco 145
    At the threshold of St. Peter's 149
    Focolarino and (future) priest 152

PARADISE '49 155
   On earth as it is in heaven: mysticism and prophecy 155
   The Pact of unity 156
   Perspective '49 160

Part III
A DIFFICULT JOURNEY

ENCOUNTERS AND CHALLENGES 167
   Unity in the era of divisions 167
   Challenges and encounters 169
   Facing the Holy Office 172
   The dark night of the soul 177
   The foundations of the castle 181
   "Into your hands ..." Resignation without detachment 185

INSIDE AND OUTSIDE THE WALLS 188
   The Secretariat of State 188
   Meeting the successor of Peter 196
   Chiara and De Gasperi: two minds for unity 201
   The summer Mariapolis 206
   The great attraction 210

BEYOND THE WALLS 213
   Religious and theologians 213
   Light and darkness New sufferings and new horizons 219
   A particular consecration 227
   The drive towards the East 231
   Speaking with "God's microphone" 238
   From the Vatican to the Italian Bishops Conference... and back 242
   Expansion, towards the world 248

SPRINGTIME OF THE CHURCH AND THE MOVEMENT 257
   Gaudet Mater Ecclesia 257
   The birth of the Work of Mary... *ad experimentum* 262

Part IV
LOVE IN AND FOR THE WORLD

WHAT KIND OF LOVE ... ? 269
    The bond of love of the Trinity 269
    Agape 275
    Light and colors 278
    Jesus in the midst 280
    Love and justice 283
    Mary, *Theotókos* and *Hodegetria* 284

AFTER THE COUNCIL 291
    Nostra aetate 291
    Lay people in the Church and in the world 303
    The woman Mary 308
    Shalom – Peace 312
    New generations 320

IN DIALOGUE 327
    the sources of the charism of unity 327
    Unity among Christians 335
    Dialogue between religions 346
    Dialogue with humanists 353

WITHOUT BORDERS
THE GLOBALIZATION OF LOVE 357
    The city-world 357
    In dialogue with culture 367
    The Economy of Communion 372
    Coming out of the temple 377
    Memory, communications and the future 385

EPILOGUE 399
    The final night 399
    March 14, 2008 400

BIBLIOGRAPHY 409
  History of Christianity and the Catholic Church,
  encyclopedias, atlases, dictionaries 409

Part I & II
The beginning of a story
The finger of God 410

Part III
A difficult journey 412

Part IV
Love in and for the world 413

Books by or about Chiara Lubich. 416

Other sources for Focolare movement and its activities 421

FOREWORD

The Passion of Saint John the Baptist

The responsorial psalm for today's Mass of the Martyrdom of Saint John the Baptist, Psalm 71, proclaims *"For you are my hope, O Lord; my trust, O God, from my youth. On you I depend from birth; from my mother's womb you are my strength."*

These words certainly characterize, as I have come to know it, the life and the call of Chiara Lubich in bringing to birth the "Work of Mary."

In 1981, the late Bishop Joseph A. McNicholas of Springfield, Illinois, sent me to study Canon Law at the *Angelicum* in Rome: but he exhorted me to not stay in my room at the Casa Santa Maria dell' Umiltà. So I went out for walks and ministry, coming to know and love Rome and Italy and its people. These walks and ministry eventually led me to meet the Focolare and hear the story of Chiara Lubich. Over the years I have been blessed to come to know Focolare, its members, and its history even more profoundly.

All who read *Chiara Lubich: Prophet of Unity* will find their own journeys of life and Faith reflected here – like a mirror that reflects to us the presence and the word of God. Especially in our very fractured and politicized and polarized world, this work is a God-given and providential gift: extending and bringing forth Chiara's life as a "Prophet of Unity" in this challenging time.

The following words from the Introduction set the stage for us:

Only God remains. Silvia experienced God as love and discovered him as her father. This was the inspiring spark that illuminated her life and that turned into a call from God, so much so that on December 7 of the same year she decided to give her life to him. *She consecrated her life to God in the local Capuchin Church. Silvia, fascinated by the evangelical radicalism of Clare of Assisi, took the name Chiara (Clare) and chose to base her life on putting the Gospel into practice.*

I pray that this publication be that inspiring park for us in the world today to put the Gospel into practice in our lives and those whom the Lord sends to us.

+Kevin W. Vann
Bishop of the Diocese of Orange, California
August 29, 2020

INTRODUCTION

The cover of this book portrays Chiara Lubich in a familiar pose. She is speaking into a microphone to a listening and attentive audience, which is probably quite numerous. The picture has several levels, with a marked depth of field and "eloquence." Like any good shot, this one captures several nuances that confirm the words of Diane Arbus, the well-known photographer, "I really believe there are things nobody would see if I didn't photograph them."

We see Chiara, as in thousands of other shots, with her typical hairstyle, her sober and well-groomed attire, her hand raised as if to emphasize the importance of her words, her lively and penetrating gaze and her open smile illustrating how the face is always the portrait of the soul, and the eyes its interpreter.

Her body language appears totally in tune with the words she is saying, her composure expressing a harmony between content and form, and between what is being said and how it is being said. It is an attitude that demonstrates how much "communicating," rather than just "speaking," is about helping others to understand a message.

It is easy to guess the topic of the conversation: the "spirituality of unity." It's an idea that comes from Jesus' prayer to the Father in John's Gospel (17: 21), which marked Chiara's charism and God's plan for her. It inspired and guided her whole life, with the aim of bringing everyone together into one family and creating a new humanity.

For someone like Chiara Lubich (Trent, 1920 – Rocca di Papa, 2008), one hundred years since her birth and more than ten years since her death is sufficient time to begin to recount her story and attempt a critical evaluation and interpretation of her work, making use of a wide ranging bibliography.

She was born in a frontier land, in a city that had been part of the Austro-Hungarian Empire and, at the time of her birth, had recently become part of the Kingdom of Italy after the tragedy of the First World War. It was a land where, since the end of the nineteenth century, social Catholicism had redeemed entire generations from poverty and taught them the importance of the laity and of the common good. It had also formed a ruling class that had produced a statesman of international standing, Alcide De Gasperi.[1]

Chiara's baptismal name was Silvia. Her father Luigi was a printer who favored socialist ideas, while her mother Luigia was a woman of deep Catholic faith. There were two younger sisters, Liliana and Carla, and a brother, Gino, who became a partisan and communist, a medical student and journalist.

Though poor, they lived a serene childhood. When she left school, Silvia studied to become a primary school teacher and joined Catholic Action.[2] She always felt drawn to the spiritual life and to a passionate search for truth. She started her career as a primary school teacher, first in the mountain valleys, then in the city of Trent, with the orphans of the college of the Capuchin Fathers.[3] The desire to continue her studies at university was frustrated, first by the family's lack of money and then by the Second World War. She then focused her research on Jesus – the way, the truth, and the life – and on following him.

In September 1943 Trent was hit by Allied bombs. Faced with death and destruction, in a climate of hopelessness, the biblical warning resounded: "Vanity of vanities! All is vanity" (Eccles. 1: 2).

---

1. Alcide De Gasperi (1881-1954) prime minister of Italy from 1945 to 1953.
2. Catholic Action was the name of many groups of lay Catholics who were attempting to encourage a Catholic influence on society.
3. Capuchins are one of three main orders or distinct religious institutes in the Catholic Church which trace their origin to St Francis of Assisi. The three are: Order of Friars Minor, the Conventuals and the Capuchins.

Only God remains. Silvia experienced God as love and discovered him as her father. This was the inspiring spark that illuminated her life and that turned into a call from God, so much so that on December 7 of the same year she decided to give her life to him. She consecrated her life to God in the local Capuchin church. Silvia, fascinated by the evangelical radicalism of Clare of Assisi, took the name Chiara (Clare), and chose to base her life on putting the Gospel into practice. She chose the way of life of the first Christian communities, where no one was in need, as the model for herself and her first companions. They lived the virtue of charity with a deep desire to renew the social fabric of the city, which had disintegrated through war and poverty.

They went to live in a little house near the convent, putting everything in common so as to distribute it to the poor. They gave witness to the truth of the Gospel promise "Give, and it will be given to you" (Lk. 6: 38) "... Ask, and it will be given to you" (Mt. 7: 7). Their way of life became contagious and involved many other people. A community was born on the model of the family of Nazareth: the "focolare" (hearth). It was a model that was to give life to small communities of lay people, men and women, devoted to God and called to "generate," spiritually, the presence of Jesus, based on his words: "For where two or three are gathered in my name, I am there among them." (Mt. 18: 20). It was a new vocation in a Church that was still rooted in the norms and the theology of the Council of Trent of four centuries earlier. But it was also a Church that was beginning to feel the first tremors of the breath of the Spirit that, in a few years, would swell the sails of Peter's boat, giving life to the ecclesial renewal of the Second Vatican Council.

Chiara understood that the moment when Jesus suffered most was on the cross, when he cried out in desperation, seemingly abandoned by the Father. It was an invitation to embrace the pain of humanity. In the air-raid shelters, Chiara and her first companions carried with them only the Gospel, where they meditated on the passage of Jesus' testament: "That they may all be one" (Jn 17: 21). Unity with God and the unity of the human family became the purpose of their lives.

The suffering of Jesus crucified was also evident in the criticisms they received and in the misunderstandings that were soon to be manifested in the Church and in society. That group of young people who tried to live the Gospel to the letter was accused of being "Protestants"; the communion of goods was an opportunity to accuse them of being inspired by communist doctrines. Their response was, however, evangelical: the grain of wheat must die to bear fruit. After the war, the Archbishop of Trent, Carlo de Ferrari, wanted to get to know Chiara and the Focolare Movement. He gave his approval to their spirituality and lifestyle, commenting: "Here is the finger of God."

The charism of prophecy, a gift of the Spirit, is always unfathomable. Chiara Lubich lived an intense mystical experience in the summer of 1949, during a holiday period in the Dolomite mountains. She lived and shared it with Igino Giordani,[4] a Catholic intellectual and politician, and with her first companions: "Outside of us remained what is created. We had entered into the uncreated. The risen Jesus became present in unity, he opened to us a deeper understanding of God, of Mary, of humanity, and of the future of what was being born." That experience came to be known as "Paradise '49."

The spirituality of unity as understood in that period, marked Chiara's soul deeply, and revealed itself as the vital principle of her every intuition and action, capable of transforming the lives of people of every age, ethnicity, culture and creed. It was a spirituality deeply rooted in the relationship of love that

---

4. Igino Giordani (1894-1980) was a noted Italian lay theologian, prolific writer, journalist, newspaper editor, and politician. From 1928 to 1944 he worked in the Vatican library.

exists between the persons of the Trinity. This proved to be in tune with the spirit of the Second Vatican Council and with the spirituality of communion that developed in the Church on the threshold of the third millennium. After centuries of subtle theological reflections and abstract hermeneutics, Chiara seems to give an "empirical" value to the Trinity. She affirms that we are made for relationship and encounter, that God – Father, Son and Spirit – by creating us in his own image has impressed on us this desire for communion, and that we need this relationship of love to become new people and fully part of humanity.

The ideal of unity was to become a unifying current capable of transforming diversity into creative richness, of making the seeds of truth and love, present in people of different cultures, religions and beliefs, germinate. And all this without any form of syncretism or proselytism, fully respecting everyone's convictions. Dialogue was to become the privileged way to help compose the human family through mutual trust, precisely at a time when it seemed most threatened by individualism, nihilism, fragmentation, fundamentalism, and the clashes of civilizations.

The focolares[5] were at the heart of a movement that grew rapidly – albeit with many difficulties because official recognition by the Church was only given in 1964 with the approval of the statutes of the *Work of Mary*[6]. It was the birth of an adventure that would mark the history of Christianity and humanity, of the Church and society of the twentieth century, and which proved to be full of vitality, even after the death of the founder, with a capacity to renew itself spiritually, to engage with cultures and

---

5. The consecrated single men and women of the Focolare Movement live in separate communities called "focolares" (hearths), which are at the core of the Movement.
6. *Work of Mary* is the official name under which the Focolare Movement has been approved by the Catholic Church.

religions, and to take up so many challenges posed by globalized, post-modern and post-secular society.

The impression that Chiara often aroused in the outside observer was that of a woman who is both gentle and severe, empathetic with individuals and with the crowds but also somewhat detached, capable of grasping deeply the most intimate problems. She always seemed to see things from a global point of view and had a passionate conviction of what she was saying. Simplicity, clarity, capacity for synthesis and constant reference to the witness of the Gospels were the hallmarks of her charism. It is a charism capable of penetrating cultural spheres and religious dimensions, of meeting with popes and spiritual and political leaders on an equal footing.

Anyone who listened to her soon realized that her vision was based on the coherence between God and the created world, "on earth as it is in heaven," and that her vision that saw beyond history, was formed by a total inner freedom, the fruit of a radical experience of and relationship with God. Her clarity and self-assuredness, rather than being the fruit of intuition and intellectual reasoning, seemed to be an expression of direct knowledge, of having drawn from the divine.

Piero Coda, theologian and a spiritual son of Chiara, recalls how "in her there was an opening, which often disarmed you, to the disruptive power of the Holy Spirit." He describes her capacity, and the prophetic aspect of her charism, as a way of "being in God where God is needed, working in a hidden way." He says that she reminds him of the role of the biblical prophet, who speaks in the name of JHWH and manifests his plans, indicating to Israel the path to be taken in history. Or even that of Jesus himself in his relationship with God "in spirit and truth," as the mediator of revelation.

In this regard, a scholar of spirituality, Jesús Castellano Cervera, wrote that "in Chiara there coexists a very profound mystical vision with a deep sense of what is real. Her acting was inseparable from the mystical impetus, transforming something now into a future that already begins here. In this way existence itself becomes the epiphany of a God who is love."

Various biographies of Chiara Lubich describe the period till the mid-1960s, the time that saw the definitive approval of the statutes of the Focolare Movement and the celebration of the Second Vatican Council. For the periods that followed, there are also some well-researched studies which, however, only partially illuminate the person and work of Lubich.

The structure of this book is presented in two distinct narratives. The first follows the chronological development of Chiara's life, from her birth to the early 1960s. The second deals with some themes considered particularly significant to illustrate her life in relation to her spiritual leadership and her leadership of a great ecclesial movement committed to evangelization, ecumenism, and inter-religious dialogue. It also includes her promotion of peace and human rights, and the development of new solutions and new ways in economy and politics.

It is a story that in any case requires a twofold point of view. To use an expression that Giorgio La Pira[7] employed to explain history, it is necessary to have both a "physical eye" (that of the lay-person, based on method and where possible on science) and a "theological eye" (i.e. one that is open to perceive the "finger of God" operating in history). Another difficulty is that this is a story that requires the continuous passage from the eye of the portrait painter (made of close-ups) to the eye of the landscape painter (with "wide-angle" shots). The fact, the perception of the

---

7. Giorgio La Pira was an Italian anti-fascist politician who served as deputy of the Christian Democrats Party and participated in the assembly that wrote the Italian Constitution following World War II. He served as Mayor of Florence for 10 years between 1951 and 1964.

fact and the narration of the fact, are all elements to be carefully and constantly taken into account in order to place a person in the contexts in which he or she has worked, and vice versa.

Ideally, a biography such as this should reference as many and varied sources as possible to make a critical comparison. I have only been able to do this in a limited way and only in a few sections.

The numerous quotations from Chiara's writings and talks in the text are taken from published works, especially *Essential Writings* and other anthologies listed in the bibliography.

This book therefore is a rather surface level and partial recount of Chiara's biographical itinerary. It was written many years after the events took place, at a time when memory starts to become history, and where some eyewitnesses are still alive, but whose accounts have to blend in with other sources.

However, "memory" can be quite "slippery"... The presence of witnesses is an extraordinary richness, but also a potential danger. They can direct, propose partial visions, and object, according to their personal experiences. The accuracy of the reconstruction or the precision of the facts is not, for the most part, in question. What is in question is usually the interpretation offered to historical analysis.

History is a great teacher of complexity. It depends on the questions that are asked of it, and the questions are always new for contemporary readers. So, in fact, it offers more questions than answers.

So often in the Bible there is the invitation to listen: from the "Shemà Israel: listen O Israel" (Dt. 6: 4) to King Solomon who asks God for "a God-listening heart" (1 Kings 3: 9 MSG). The Gospels explain how the disciple is first of all the one who listens to Jesus to fulfill his greatest commandment (Mk 12: 29), loving God and neighbor.

I have tried to listen to Chiara Lubich's testimony and message. I found in that testimony and in that message not "spoken words," but "speaking words," that is, authentic, meditated and suffered words. Chiara's words are the fruit of a correspondence between gestures and words, between words and actions and between promises and fulfillments. It is a correspondence between what we, by the grace of God, want to be and what we manage to be in our daily lives. It is clear that every subject Chiara has addressed is incarnated in the light of the Holy Spirit who makes every Christian a free, courageous and different person, who opens the doors wide and invites us to bear witness to Jesus.

I was also able to observe how so many of Chiara's intuitions, which took root in Trent during the bombings of the Second World War, have only now come to maturity at the level of the Magisterium of the Church.

I am thinking, for example, of the great stimulus of Pope Francis' *Evangelii gaudium,* to return to being an "outward-looking Church," on the road, on the way (in the direction indicated by the Council). We are reminded of the maxim "Reality is more important than ideas," which is nothing other than the Lord's criterion: to start from reality, that is, from the suffering of humanity. This doesn't mean we have to deny principles, but to put them into practice, to give them a value of real fecundity for the life and hope of people.

Let us consider the criterion inspired by love and mercy which must always guide the application of a law, contained in *Amoris laetitia,* with its invitation to rediscover the charism of spiritual discernment.

Let us consider courageous experiments in the social sphere such as the economy of communion[8], born to create an alternative

---

8. The "economy of communion" is an initiative of the Focolare, initiated in

to the "market god" and which is compatible with dignity, humanity, and the safeguarding of creation. Then there is the virtue of meekness, which presents itself as a true revolution and a solution, because through it we enter into communion with others and are able to welcome the other in his otherness.

As Cardinal Carlo Maria Martini loved to say, "Christianity is young," and so we must always turn with confidence to the future, making Isaiah's prophecy (43: 19) our own: "I am about to do a new thing; now it springs forth, do you not perceive it? I will make a way in the wilderness and rivers in the desert."

Thank you

This book on Chiara Lubich's life came about when I received an unexpected request from Alba Sgariglia and João Manoel Motta, directors of the Chiara Lubich Centre in Rocca di Papa. My surprise at the request and for their trust (which I immediately considered to be extremely misplaced) gave way, as time went by, to amazement for their willingness to deal with my questions, their advice on sources and for the total freedom with which I was able to carry out the research and formulate my reflections. I owe equal gratitude to the "cenacle" – equally competent and available – which gravitates around the Centre, composed of Donato Falmi, Lucia Abignente, Maria Caterina Atzori, Anna Maria Rossi, Giuliano Ruzzier and Florence Gillet.

A heartfelt thanks also to the group of historians and friends from the region of Trent who have given me excellent ideas and indications: Bishop. Luigi Bressan, Fr. Giovanni Dalpiaz, Franco de Battaglia, Giovanni Delama, Giuseppe Ferrandi and Paolo

---

1991, which seeks to address social problems by creating businesses, operated according to the principles of unity, which direct profits to sustainability, to aid those in need and toward nurturing a "culture of giving."

Marangon. To them should be added Nino Carella and Ilaria Pedrini, who are both attentive scholars and also witnesses of the charism of unity. A grateful thought goes to Katia Pizzini and Claudio Andreclli, from the Diocesan Archive of Trent, who put me on the trail of the origins of the Lubich family. Various traces and hypotheses have been transformed into precise data with the help of Otto Werth, of the parish of Anterivo in the province of Bolzano.

Beyond the borders of Trent (and any other kind of border), my gratitude goes to Victória Gomez, Vincenzo Buonomc and Pasquale Ferrara, who were able to offer important elements of understanding and new perspectives of reading Chiara and her work. I am equally grateful to Massimo Naro for his theological advice. A special thanks to Antonio and Sara Foresi, for their testimony – with an extremely precious secular point of view – on the activity of the Movement and the person of the co-founder Pasquale Foresi. Thanks also to Bernardino and Antonio Stedile, brother and nephew of Aldo Stedile, one of Chiara's first companions. For help with various themes and aspects of the book, I am indebted to Vittorio Alberti, Giorgio Butterini, Gregorio Moggio, Giuseppe Sangiorgi and Livio Sparapani.

I am also grateful to the publishing house Città Nuova, particularly Luca Gentile, for publishing this book in one of its prestigious series, and to the editorial staff as a whole.

And last but not least, thanks to Gabriella, for the careful and patient rereading and revision of the texts.

M.G.

Part I

THE BEGINNING OF A STORY

TRENT AND SURROUNDING AREAS, 1920

Between Austria and Italy

Chiara Lubich was born in Trent on January 22, 1920, the second of Luigi and Luigia's four children. The birth took place – as usual in those days – at home, with the help of the midwife Domenica Pegoretti, and the child was baptized on February 1with the name of Silvia Maria Elvira, in the parish church of St. Mary Major.

The registration of the baptism, attended by her uncle Silvio as godfather, was inscribed on page sixty-two of volume XXIV (1908-1920). She was baptized by Fr. Giovanni Battista Fedrizzi, who, by virtue of the Austrian legislation – at the time still in force in Trent – also held the function of civil registrar. This function would shortly afterwards pass under the jurisdiction of the civil authorities of the Kingdom of Italy. Following the outcome of the First World War and the peace treaties between belligerent powers the province of Trent had become part of Italy only a few months earlier.

This baptism registration with its juridical nature reveals in part the specific geographical, civil, ecclesial, social, and cultural context in which Chiara's life began.

All historical reconstructions – first and foremost a biographical profile – need to be seen within the context and climate of its period. They should then be compared with the events that frame them, to give meaning and add nuances and details to the story. In order to understand the influences that these contexts may have had on Chiara Lubich's life and work, it may be appropriate to mention the historical background and to refer to some of the circumstances in which her story began.

A REGION AND A CHURCH ON THE BORDERS

Silvia Lubich's childhood and youth are set in a period in the history of Trent which was particularly dense with various events and interruptions.

One of the elements that define the features and the geographical identity of the province of Trent consists in its being a borderland... in particular a political and cultural border between the Mediterranean basin and the Central European area. Its identity has been defined for many centuries[9] by its status as an "episcopal principality," with the bishop administering the territory also in *rebus temporalibus* (in the affairs of the world), linked to the Holy Roman Empire. After the Napoleonic period, the principality was suppressed (even though the title of prince-bishop was formally maintained) and, until the First World War, the diocesan territory was included in the Austrian Empire.

Although faithful subjects of the Habsburg government, the bishops maintained a resilient attitude towards attempts at being assimilated by the state. They always demanded some autonomy for the Church and the local administration, and were influenced by both the Italian and German speaking worlds present in their territory, especially with regard to the social question[10].

The civil and ecclesial structures were characterized by relations based on mutual recognition and a general tendency of the

---

9. From the 11th to the beginning of the 19th
10. The social question means certain evils and grievances affecting the wage-earning classes and calling for removal or remedy.

state to have control over the church. This political approach had marked the government of the Empire throughout the nineteenth century, and which – in many respects – considered the Church a component of the state. Symbolic of that situation was the choosing of bishops, an imperial prerogative granted by the Holy See to the sovereigns of the so-called "Catholic" states since 1822. The profiles and the actions of the bishops of Trent during the 19th century demonstrate that the right of nomination by the civil authorities was generally exercised in a far-sighted manner and attentive to the size and pastoral problems of the dioceses. While not ignoring fidelity to the crown, which inevitably led them to be considered officials of the state, bishops were usually chosen because of their spiritual and moral qualities, their knowledge of the territories, and their socio-political situations. They were also chosen for their pastoral concern and their ability to govern. This way of appointing bishops produced a series of prelates who were particularly attentive to the care of souls and dedicated to the direction and management of their churches and the needs of the people.

By the end of the century, the general economic situation, social conditions and all the problems of life in a mountain and border region, were far more pressing pastoral problems than the pure theological disputes and the defense of the temporal prerogatives of the pope and the Church. Much of the local economy was based on smallholdings and subsistence farming. There was widespread poverty and disease, as well as natural disasters and a high rate of emigration. The Church's disagreement with the united Italian State[11] and, in lesser ways with liberal European regimes (sanctioned in 1870 with the end of the temporal power of the popes) were felt in the territories of the Empire in a much less traumatic way.

---

11. From 1861 and in subsequent stages until 1918.

The first wave of industrialization introduced the social question and caused socialist ideas to enter civic debate. The arrival of the railways and the birth of mountain tourism imported hitherto unknown elements of modernity. In those years there was a clear gap between the Church and the political participation of Italian Catholics within the united and liberal State imposed by the *Non expedit*,[12] a situation that had little effect on Trent's Catholic movement.

During this period, one of the symbolic initiatives of the social action of the Church in Trent was the foundation of the cooperative movement. It was a series of initiatives born with the intention of improving the living conditions of the people. It started in September 1890 with its constitution and the first cooperative society, founded by Fr. Lorenzo Guetti. The main objective of the cooperative was to finance the rural world and to limit the retail prices of food both in the countryside and in the cities. Another aim was to increase the bargaining power of the farmers, who were committed to selling their products on the market and to offer a job to agricultural workers, who were the poorest and most affected by the great economic depression of those years. With these activities the Catholic world, and directly the clergy too, entered fully into the economic system of the province of Trent, organizing and controlling the agricultural, artisan, consumer and credit cooperatives and helping develop the cooperative movement.

During the last decade of the century and with the support of the teachings of Leo XIII (in particular his encyclical *Rerum Novarum*), the anti-liberal (and, increasingly, anti-socialist) struggle of the Catholic movement became explicit in the flower-

---

12. "It is not expedient" were the words with which the Holy See enjoined upon Italian Catholics the policy of abstention from the polls in parliamentary elections.

ing of activities that responded to existing and emerging social needs. The development of trades unions, of Catholic youth and professional societies, of the various articulations of the cooperative world and of the press, was largely based on the fabric of the diocese and the parish. Many of the ideas were taken from the experiences of the German Catholic movement in the second half of the nineteenth century. Regarding the social question, these ideas emerged from the Bishop of Mainz, Wilhelm Emmanuel von Ketteler, as well as the *Catholic Centre Party* in Germany, started in 1870 under the leadership of Ludwig Windthorst, was perhaps the main model for dealing with the social question, with a program for the defense of Christian principles and the rights of the Church, and with a new vision of the laity.

The clash with the different currents of modern thought within the life of the Church at the end of the nineteenth century was always taken seriously in Trent, but with an eye on the local institutional and political context, as well as its social and economic situation. In Trent as in Rome, by its printed condemnations, accusations, and excommunications the Church set itself apart from Protestantism, liberalism, indifferentism, socialism, and Freemasonry, digging an ever-deeper furrow between itself and the culture of the modern world. The Church and the Catholic movement took a critical position towards modernity, rejecting its principles, aims and products. But, to bring this criticism to fruition and maximize its results, they used the means typical of modernity itself (associations, trades unions and democratically regulated party organizations, promotion and wide use of the media...).

Newspapers were the main instrument of propaganda, debate, debate, training, and the spreading of ideas and programs. The local press offered multiple points of view, summarized by many newspapers: *La Voce Cattolica* represented, since 1865, the position of the diocese of Trent and the Catholic world, decidedly in the majority; *Il Trentino* (1871-1875), organ of Trent's National Liberal Association founded in 1871, and the liberal-national *Alto Adige* (1886) summarized the positions of the liberal forces. Socialist thought was represented by *Il Popolo* (1900), edited by Cesare Battisti, and *L'Avvenire del Lavoratore* (first printed in Vienna in 1895), which began to come out regularly in Trent at the beginning of the new century (1901-1914).

The Catholic world of Trent and its political and cooperative movement followed the guidelines proposed in Italy within the Opera dei Congressi[13] on the instigation of Leo's papacy aimed at regaining society for the Church through social action. The driving force behind this renewed direction was the Diocesan Committee of Catholic Action, created in 1898. For decades to come it would be the inspiring and organizing body of the difficult path taken by the Catholic movement of winning over society through an autonomous and creative system capable of giving a positive orientation to the people. It was a path that threaded its way between the need to adapt to the modern world and that of radical opposition to it. This model was designed by some young and brilliant priests, trained in Rome and at the same time sensitive to the experiences in the social setup beyond the Alps. Two such men were Celestino Endrici and Guido de Gentili. The former was a teacher of moral and social theology in the seminary, the other, editor of *La Voce Cattolica*. Both were motivated by a strong passion for the presence of the Church in history; a Church marking its own path by facing the challenges of the

---

13. The *Opera dei Congressi* or *Work of the Congress* was a Roman Catholic organization that promoted Catholic ideas and culture. It was created in 1874, and observed of the positions of the Catholic Church, particularly *Non Expedit*. It began as a non-political group but moved into protesting against the imprisonment in the Vatican of the pope. It fought against anticlerical legislation and the many divorce bills that were introduced by successive Liberal governments (1861-1922).

time. They were forerunners of the concept of "practical living" developed a few years later by Romano Guardini, a fundamental way of overcoming the detachment between thought and reality introduced by modernity.

The time of Celestino Endrici

On January 3, 1904 the Austrian government proposed, as Bishop of Trent, the young moral teacher Celestino Endrici (1866 – 1940). Papal confirmation was given on February 5 and on March 13 the episcopal consecration was presided over by the new Secretary of State, Rafael Merry del Val. The bishop took his position as bishop of the diocese on March 19. During his long episcopate, Endrici faced one of the most complex and troubled periods of Trent's history, at least from a social, political-institutional, and ecclesial point of view. In his first years, Endrici found himself managing a period that saw the transformation of an empire of peoples into an empire of national political communities, something extremely challenging to manage within a modern constitutional form. It was increasingly difficult to keep together the legacy of the old empire, which was undermined by nationalism, and had little by which to keep things together: an overweight bureaucratic apparatus, the army, and the charismatic and mythic figure of the emperor.

In those years, scientific thinking in anthropological, social, and historical matters, all tended to replace worldviews based on metaphysical references and were in competition with traditional religions, ethical systems and established social models. To the massive spread of cultural approaches inspired by Marxism, socialism and rationalism, the Church opposed "Christian philosophy" expressed by the neo-Thomistic school. This seemed to offer a systematic and alternative vision to that of secular thinking, while welcoming many aspects of the scientific method, especially in sociology, economics, and ethics.

Endrici's cultural and doctrinal approach, together with his energy and activism, led the Church in Trent to redefine its vision and pastoral action. He worked vigorously to modernize and reorganize the old diocesan structure, which had a wealth of institutes and jurisdictions, but not under episcopal control. With the watchword "re-Christianizing society," he started to organize both the ecclesial structures and the laity in relation to social commitment and to the political-economic changes taking place in that period. He started to rethink the concept of the care of souls and the establishment of autonomy regarding the structures of the state apparatus. The implications of the Concordat[14], with the imperial right to select new bishops and, more generally, the plan to use religion as an instrument of consensus with respect to the existing order, weighed the Church down with "golden chains," to use Endrici's expression. However, the shine of the gold could not hide the fact that the Church was being controlled by civil institutions. He was determined to re-establish the autonomy of the Church.

The turmoil in the Italian Catholic world at the beginning of the century in Trent was manifested in various ways. The political and ecclesial climate was marked by the divisions that had arisen within the Opera dei Congressi (and its suppression by papal edict), the demands of the Christian Democrats and the political-religious reforms of Romolo Murri.[15] Added to these

---

14. Concordat of 1855 with the Austrian Empire.
15. Romolo Murri: (1870 – 1944) was an Italian politician and priest. He was suspended for having joined the party Lega Democratica Nazionale and is widely considered in Italy as the precursor of Christian democracy.

was the modernist crisis and the ideas of Luigi Sturzo,[16] with his reflections on democracy, which contrasted with the concept of the liberal state.

In the German-speaking part of the diocese – whose pastoral administration was entrusted to a vicariate – there was a much more conservative attitude, as in the rest of Tyrol. The different ecclesial currents participated in various ways in the debates that were most salient in the society in Trent. There was debate on nationality, discussions on autonomy and the Italian university, and the issues regarding dual language schooling. There was conflict between the German associations such as the *Schulverein Südmark* and the *Tiroler Volksbund* on the one hand, and the opposing *Pro Patria* and *Lega Nazionale* on the other. The Church in Trent was moving from uncritical imperial loyalty (or at least of political neutrality) to positions more inclined to the recognition of the autonomy and rights of the people of Trent.

In October 1904, the People's Political Union of Trent was founded, allowing Catholics to enter the political arena with all their organizational strength, but keeping the purely religious sphere distinct from the social one and definitively leaving the orbit of Austrian Catholicism. In short, the electoral victories confirmed the success of the strategy and the organizational commitment, taking 70% of the votes in the 1907 elections, with the election of seven out of nine MPs. Catholic politicians from Trent (first and foremost Alcide De Gasperi) maintained a position that was always critical of irredentist[17] demands. Aware of the historical ties that had united Trent and Austria

---

16. Luigi Sturzo (1871 – 1959) was an Italian Roman Catholic priest and prominent politician. He was known in his lifetime as a "clerical socialist."
17. Irredentism is any political or popular movement that seeks to claim or reclaim and occupy a land that the movement's members consider to be a "lost" (or "unredeemed") territory from their nation's past.

for centuries, they did not claim "liberation" and union with Italy. In a context of loyalty to the crown and within the multinational empire, the claims to the central government in Vienna concerned the right to remain Italian, in terms of cultural and linguistic identity, and administrative autonomy. It was a strong position that placed the intransigent defense of the Italian nationality of Trent within the institutional framework of the empire. The Catholic group saw the nationalist positions of the liberals and socialists led by Cesare Battisti[18] as a threat to the European political-institutional structure and consequently to peace. In their international political vision, there was firm support for the "Threefold system,"[19] because it was precisely this alliance that constituted the necessary guarantee of the internal balance that they supported.

In 1906 the name of the newspaper *La Voce Cattolica* was changed and, entrusted by the bishop to the young De Gasperi. It became *Il Trentino*, with the specific aim of "reconstituting the moral unity of Trent, on the triple basis of religion, the national spirit and democracy." The new paper covered a wider range of topics and had a more secular slant. It reported the important role played by the Diocesan Committee for Catholic Action with respect to all other ecclesial organizations and promoted the advocates of Christian-social thought as well as the teaching of the Magisterium. It also gave space to the organized participation of the Catholic laity in political life, the Italian character of the population of Trent, and the autonomy and free exercise of the bishop's pastoral care in the face of the obstacles posed by the laws of the Habsburg Empire.

---

18. Cesare Battisti (1875 – 1916) was an Italian patriot, geographer, socialist politician and journalist of Austrian citizenship, who became a prominent Irredentist at the start of World War I.
19. the triple basis of religion, the national spirit and democracy

After the bitter contrasts that had characterized the end of the 19th century, Trent's Catholic intellectual world decided to pursue less radical strategies with regard to modern culture, avoiding polarization and condemnation. It also tried to harmonize the scientific debate by recognizing what was consistent with the truths of faith. The main sources of this new attitude were the Catholic University Association of Trent and the *Rivista Tridentina*. The conflict between secular neo-idealist philosophy and Christian doctrine inspired by Thomism had deeply engaged the intellectual forces of the clergy and laity.

From the early years of the 20th century, the environment of Trent's Catholic culture was strongly influenced by Fr. Emilio Chiocchetti.[20] This Franciscan philosopher followed a particularly free and open style of education. Although the teaching of Antonio Rosmini was not "officially" accepted by the Church, Chiocchetti drew on it. He also studied the various forms of Idealism, specially the one developed by Benedetto Croce[21]. He tried to compare Croce's thought with neo-Scholastic Christian philosophy, seeking and finding theoretical points of contact and encouraging the consolidation of a dialectical method, which avoided the polarization of debate and positions. This allowed the Catholic student and intellectual component of Trent to acquire an autonomy and maturity unknown elsewhere.

---

20. Emilio Chiocchetti (1880 – 1951)
21. Benedetto Croce (1866 – 1952) was an Italian idealist philosopher, historian and politician. In most regards, Croce was a liberal, although he opposed laissez-faire free trade. Croce was President of PEN International, the worldwide writers' association, from 1949 until 1952. He was nominated for the Nobel Prize in Literature sixteen times.

Time of War

In 1914 the election of Benedict XV coincided with the outbreak of the European war. At the beginning of the conflict, the Italian government, presided over by Antonio Salandra, proclaimed neutrality. Italy accused Austria of failing to fulfil its commitment under the treaty of the "Triple Alliance" to inform its allies in the event of military initiatives by one of the signatory powers. Within Italy, a strong confrontation developed between different positions regarding the war. The political forces, the press, and public opinion were divided into opposing fronts, the neutralists and the interventionists, within which the motivations and reasons for the choice were influenced by various factors.

The approach of the Catholic world was more nuanced: condemnation of the war, with Benedict XV (in line with the encyclical *Ad Beatissimi Apostolorum* of November 1, 1914), and loyalty to the homeland in the event of danger. There was widespread support for Belgium, which had been neutral and an example of compatibility between Christianity and democracy. It had now been occupied and devastated by the Germans, as denounced by Cardinal Mercier. There was sympathy also for threatened France, where a Catholic minister was present in the government and Catholic Action there had close contacts with the Italian one. A decidedly anti-war attitude was manifested by socially committed Catholics. Some personalities, such as Filippo Meda,[22] moved to pro-war positions after the German attack on Belgium, claiming that the violation of international law required Italian intervention to reaffirm law and justice.

---

22. Filippo Meda (1869 – 1939) Italian banker, journalist and politician, protagonist of the Catholic movement.

"To my peoples." Thus began the proclamation with which Franz Josef announced the outbreak of the war that would dissolve his empire. He gave the impression of an atmosphere of harmony, of different nationalities peacefully coexisting in a multi-national state, guarantor of individual cultures. In reality, the Habsburg Empire was undermined by national hatreds: relations between Austrians and Hungarians and their customs war; the massive representation of Slavic peoples in parliament; relations between Hungarians, Slovaks and Croats, Italians and Slovenes, Ruthenians and Poles were in fierce conflict.

Within the territories of the Habsburg monarchy, the outbreak of the conflict was generally welcomed with enthusiasm, including the ecclesial authorities who blessed the war effort unconditionally. This attitude was reinforced by the favor that had been shown by Pope Pius X towards Franz Josef, who had considered him to be the last great Catholic monarch in Europe. Only the Bishop of Trent, Celestino Endrici, did not manifest patriotic and favorable attitudes towards entering the war. He went so far as to accuse the Austrian episcopate of an uncritical stance towards politics, a legacy of the season of the so-called Josephism,[23] and little aware of the dangers and suffering that the conflict would entail.

On July 31, 1914 came the imperial proclamation of mobilization. In Trent, out of 360,000 Italian-speaking inhabitants, 60,000 were enlisted in the Austro-Hungarian army and sent on the eastern front, in Galicia and the Carpathians, against Russia. In this way Trent was deprived of the heads of families with a paralyzing impact also on work and production.

The Catholic daily newspaper *Il Trentino*, edited by Alcide De Gasperi, entitled the leading article on August 6, "The Hour of

---

23. Josephism was a term for the collective domestic policies of Joseph II, Holy Roman Emperor (1765–1790).

God," and followed with realism and trepidation the developments of the conflict. The hope that the situation would not be rushed, and the efforts to avoid the worst, lasted until May 14, 1915. It first counted on the neutrality of Italy and then on the prospect of a short war. On March 16, 1915, De Gasperi met Foreign Minister Sidney Sonnino in Rome. The prospect of the transfer of the province of Trent to Italy in a peaceful manner through diplomatic negotiations or, in the case of their failure, through recourse to war, was by now a concrete one and partly public knowledge. In the conversation with Sonnino, De Gasperi addressed political and economic issues, even in detail, like the destiny of agricultural production in the face of Italian competition; the question of the wages and salaries of the clergy; the question of municipal autonomy; the discharge of the soldiers who came from Trent. Even considering the political loyalty of the people of Trent to Austria, consensus on the state of war began to break down. This was caused by the massacres on the Galician front, the prolonged distance of the military from their families, the stagnation of productive activities, and the hardships caused in civil society worsened by the climate of suspicion in the Italian part of Tyrol. De Gasperi pressed for a peaceful transfer of the province of Trent, sharing the efforts being made by the German ambassador to Italy, Prince von Bülow, who since December 1914 was committed to the arduous task of ensuring Italian neutrality. The attitude of the government in Rome was different. It was urged on by the prospect of siding with the powers of the Entente[24] and reneging the alliance that united Italy with the central empires, with the aim of conquering the northern territories claimed in the course of Italian Unification. Pope Benedict also attempted to mediate by trying to convince the imperial government to concede the disputed territories.

---

24. The Triple Entente: France, Russia and Great Britain. *Entente* (French) meaning agreement, co-operation or understanding.

The diplomatic initiatives remained ambiguous until April 26, when Salandra and Sonnino, without consulting the Chamber of Deputies, signed the London Treaty with the representatives of Great Britain, France, and Russia, committing themselves to go to war within a month. On May 23, Italy sent the declaration of war to Austria (but not to Germany, with which war would not be declared until August 25, 1916). On May 24, Trent became a zone of military operations with all the devastating effects on the population and the territory.

Within the Church, among the clergy of Trent, a moral view of the tragedy was unfolding. They saw the war as nothing other than a confirmation of the failure of modernity, experienced as divine punishment for the deviant moral decline of Europe. And they recognized in it a mysteriously providential opportunity for repentance and a way of atonement and regeneration. Bishop Endrici, in his pastoral letters, refused to exploit religion for patriotic purposes and in the service of government propaganda, firm in his own concept of the Church's freedom within the State. The war provoked the enactment of exceptional provisions on public order and censorship, the progressive tightening of relations between civil administration and military government, and the gradual narrowing of opportunities for political activity. Among the people – especially the rural population – the Church recorded a decisive strengthening of its moral authority, in virtue of the great help provided by priests for the care of the people.

But the real test to which the Church in Trent and the clergy were subjected at the outbreak of hostilities with Italy, was the epic of the exodus of civilians from the combat zones, ordered by the Austrian government at the end of May 1915. The 70,000 civilians who were transferred (1,700 for political reasons) to the central provinces of the monarchy, Austria, and Bohemia, became "displaced people." With the refugees, also 234 diocesan priests, forty men religious (Franciscan Friars Minor and Capuchins) and 80 women religious left. In the southern areas, occupied by the Italian army, 35,000 civilians were transferred to Italy (from Piedmont to Sicily), with 30 priests and 15 religious. Due, above all, to their role as spiritual leaders of their people, 32 priests from Trent were interned in the Katzenau camp in Upper Austria. The real suffering of the elderly, and of women and children began. Many of them had never left the valley or the country where they were born. It was their first experience of travelling and their first contact with a train. In July 1915, the Central Committee for Refugees of the South was set up, which included some local politicians and churchmen. An essential instrument of the Committee was the "Bulletin," a weekly newspaper which was small, but precious for the information, news, and indications it could give to the displaced people.

The clergy of Trent, at times, appeared to be the only structure able to maintain a network of connections, acting as a link between the refugees and the authorities, setting the political line of the "Bulletin" itself, so as to influence the mentality and morale of those displaced. Thanks to the work undertaken by the diocesan secretariat, it was possible to open Italian-language schools and social and recreational structures like those left behind in Trent. Bishop Endrici closely followed the fate of the internees. He protested the unjustified threat of retaliation against the population. He clearly refused any declaration or act that meant support for the war, disappointing the political and military circles that asked him this in the name of loyalty to the state. The tension grew to the point that he had to retire to the bishop's suburban villa in San Nicolò, where from March 1, 1916, he lived formally confined by order of the supreme military command, which took away all communication with the outside world. In May, through intervention of the nuncio he moved to Vienna, to answer to the Austrian government for his position. Considered by then politically unreliable, he was denied permission to return to Trent and formal steps were taken with Vatican authorities for his dismissal. From that moment until the end of the war the bishop remained confined to the abbey of Heiligenkreuz, near the Austrian capital. In October 1917, after the reopening of parliament in Vienna, Alcide De Gasperi condemned both the treatment given to the bishop and the condition of the refugees, speaking of people who "were evacuated or, to put it better, deported."

In 1916, in addition to the ups and downs of the military operations and the movement of the front, Trent was the scene of a drama of great political and symbolic significance. Between July 10 and 12 of that year, the death of Cesare Battisti filled the headlines. A lieutenant in the Italian army, he was captured by the Austrians on the Pasubio front. He was transferred to Trent, tried for high treason, and sentenced to death by hanging. The sentence was carried out immediately in the moat of the Buonconsiglio castle. The tragedy of the Great War had swallowed up his existence. Battisti was a living symbol, but after his death he became a martyr for Italy and a traitor for Austria. Cesare Battisti has been discussed and is still being discussed today because symbols unite and divide. He was a geographer, essayist, journalist, socialist, political activist, and member of parliament for Trent in Vienna. He was an emblematic figure of a country where different cultures and languages coexisted. He dreamed of a Europe of peoples and brotherhood as a principle of coexistence, but he was overwhelmed by the immense catastrophe. When in 1914 the European states decided to resolve national conflicts with weapons, he too took part in the war like millions of other men, choosing to fight for Italy against the empire of which he was a citizen and parliamentarian. But his story goes far beyond his person and speaks of the sunset of an era and the end of a world.

1917 was perhaps the most tragic year of an exhausting and destructive war. In the face of the "patriotic" positions of the majority of the Italian Church, the pope showed increasing concern for the fate of the conflict, expressing his sorrow for the unheard appeals in the face of the peoples' increasingly acute desire for peace. Diplomatic anxiety led Benedict XV to write the note of August 1 to the leaders of the warring powers, a document best known for defining the conflict as "useless slaughter." Strengthened by hope in his power to arbitrate, the pope reaffirmed the absolute impartiality of the Holy See and, voicing the "aspirations of the peoples," made proposals ranging from the simultaneous reduction of arms, the "freedom and common use of the seas," the total and reciprocal condemnation of the evils of war and the restitution of occupied territories.

Between June and September 1918, the counter-offensive of the Allied forces in France and the Italian counterattack, which culminated in the battle of Vittorio Veneto, forced Austria-Hungary to surrender. On November 3, the armistice was signed at Villa Giusti near Padua, while the Italian soldiers entered Trent and Trieste. On November 11, the general armistice with the Allies came into force, marking the end of the war. It was an end that closed the political cataclysm caused by the dissolution of the empires of Central and Eastern Europe. Czechs and Slovaks, Poles, "Southern Slavs," "Italians of Austria" (including the province of Trent), saw the two-headed Habsburg eagle disappear, to be replaced by other icons, symbols, and flags. From one day to the next they had new national identities. In November 1918, the area of Trent counted 11,400 dead, 14,000 wounded and 12,000 prisoners. The war was estimated to have cost four million Italian lire. The territory was devastated and the economy had to be rebuilt, all of that within the framework of a complex institutional transition into Italy.

On November 13, 1918 bishop Celestino Endrici returned to his diocese after the long months of confinement imposed by the Austrian government. He was welcomed triumphantly by the Italian military authority and by a large crowd of citizens.

The post-war period

The peace treaty of Saint-Germain (September 10, 1919) ceded to Italy the entirety of the Tyrolean region south of the Brenner Pass. The new-born Republic of Austria was left with the rest of the land. The economic problems, connected to the devaluation of the Austrian currency and the collapse of the public debt contracted by the Austro-Hungarian monarchy during the years of the conflict, made the immediate post-war period extremely difficult. The end of the war was perhaps the most challenging time for the civilian population. Trent experienced a period of great anxiety concerning health, transport, and supplies. The return of those displaced in 1915 was particularly problematic given the conditions of the territory. Trent had a population of about 61,000, including 15,000 refugees who had no sources of food. The difficulty of the military being quartered alongside citizens compromised the public order, causing looting, damage to the countryside and private property, the theft of animals and other robberies. The epidemic known as "Spanish flu," which struck with deadly timing throughout Europe in the years immediately following the conflict, was particularly virulent in the valleys around Trent.

During the years of the military governorship of General Guglielmo Pecori Giraldi (1918-1919) and then of the civil administration led by Commissioner General Luigi Credaro (1919-1922) it was hoped that the minority of 220,000 people within the Kingdom of Italy could at least maintain some linguistic and cultural rights. A key point in the region's transition from Austria to Italy was replacing existing legislation with that of the Kingdom. In this area there were delays in applying the law of annexation and establishing the extraordinary administrative bodies and the central and peripheral commission to plan the regional, provincial, and municipal autonomous structures. In this context, the Italian governors worked prudently, aiming at dialogue and understanding of local issues, sharing the autonomous system, and respecting the legitimate rights of the German-speaking minority. Bishop Endrici and his diocese dedicated themselves to a material and moral reconstruction of enormous proportions, while the complex social and political structures were immediately reconstituted.

In directives sent to the clergy of the diocese on July 24, 1919, he wrote: "We should be certain that without people being organized in every town we cannot lead nor win the battles that will take place in the social, political and educational fields" and that "therefore every healer of souls must have at his side a good organization of the people."

On November 23, 1918 the newspaper *Il Nuovo Trentino*, edited by De Gasperi, was published. The People's Party of Trent was reconstituted, which had to take charge of the needs and demands most felt by the population in the new regime. The Worker's Union, the structures of the cooperative movement and the apparatus of Catholic associations, articulated under the guidance of the diocesan committee, were reconstituted. The Catholic party, with over 50% of the consensus, was in tune with the action of the Italian people and was officially inaugurated in January 1919 under the guidance of Fr. Luigi Sturzo. Alcide De Gasperi immediately became its leader. At the first political elections held in Trent, in 1921, he was elected as an MP.

In 1918, Endrici renewed the proposal for the transfer of the ten German-speaking deaneries under the rule of Trent (which occupied a large part of the current territory of Alto Adige) so that in 1922 the Holy See decreed their transfer to the diocese of Bressanone. However, due to opposition from the Italian government, the decision was not executed. After 1920 the diocese of Trent no longer belonged to the metropolitan district of Salzburg, but became *immediate subiecta*[25] (and in 1929, after the Lateran Pacts, it acquired the title of archbishopric).

The beginning of the "long vigil"

1922 saw the advent of Fascism, which gradually disrupted the organization of Catholics and finally, in 1926, seized with brutal violence the structures that supported it. This meant taking control of the economic and organizational institutions at the roots of Trent society, and that represented the main instruments of social progress and redemption from poverty.

De Gasperi, who became national secretary of the People's Party in 1924, was opposed more and more by the regime until his arrest in 1927 and his removal from public life to a humble post at the Vatican Library (thanks to the intercession of Bishop Endrici and the mediation of his friend Igino Giordani, who worked there).

These were the years during which the ruling class, formed in the last decades of the Habsburg period and strongly active in the post-war period – mostly Christian-Democratic in inspiration – was fought more and more, and eventually defeated and excluded from social life in Trent under the Fascist regime's plan to occupy every sphere of civil life. The region's administrative autonomy, a principle strongly defended by Trent's political representatives in Rome, collapsed, erasing any trace of the administrative and institutional heritage left by Austria.

By the end of 1926 the dense web of cooperative organizations set up within society with the support of the Church was

---

25. Directly linked to papal authority.

disrupted, the newspaper editorial offices devastated by the Fascist squads were reduced to silence. The banks and economic institutions were occupied by men who sympathized with Fascism.

The "three-fold" system, set up at the beginning of the century by the pastoral action of bishop Endrici and accepted and organized by a large part of the clergy and Catholic laity, was lost.

After this date any possibility of political and institutional opposition vanished and the organized presence of Catholics was limited to militancy in the ranks of Catholic Action. Although strictly controlled and at times threatened with dissolution, Catholic Action was allowed to continue its traditional role of educating young people. It also encouraged an attitude of independence and moral resistance to the regime. This attitude became the cultural ground within which, during the "long vigil" (De Gasperi's expression) of almost twenty years, the civil conscience of many free and strong spirits would be nurtured, who in the end would defeat the dictatorship and contribute to the democratic rebirth of the country.

THE LUBICH FAMILY

Family History

The surname Lubich is not common in Italy, nor was it in the area of Trent where Chiara was born, so much so as to suggest that its origin is not Italian. Research by Gino Lubich, Chiara's elder brother, into the origins of the family name has been included in numerous biographies and essays dedicated to the founder of the Focolare. According to Gino, the Lubich family had Slovenian origins and had moved to Trent because of the cattle trade, probably during the first half of the 19th century.

This is quite likely, as the surname Lubich (with some variations) is common in the Balkan area between eastern Croatia (Zagreb and Slovenia) and southern Hungary. At that time those areas were part of the Austro-Hungarian Empire. However, research of personal data available in the region of Trent has made it possible to trace Silvia's ancestry back at least five generations before her birth and to identify the family's places of origin.

Documents registering the administration of the sacraments in parish archives have made it possible to retrace the family's movements. Silvia's father and grandfather – both named Luigi – were born in Trent. Her great-grandfather Vincenzo Stefano was born on April 5, 1816 in Calliano, an agricultural village by the Adige River, a few kilometers south of the capital.

Vincenzo's father, Matteo, married Marianna Topainer, originally from Merano, on January 10, 1803. At the time of the wedding, they both lived in Calliano and worked for Mr.

Ignazio Hecchel. Matteo's marriage certificate– the first of the series of documents mentioned so far, drafted in Latin – refers to Anterippo Flemmarum, or Anterivo in Val di Fiemme.

Anterivo (*Altrei* in German, *Fåltrúi* in the dialect of the southern valleys of South Tyrol, *Antereu* and *Nantarù* in the Fiemme vernacular) – strongly dependent on the Romance Ladino[26] language, typical of that area – is a little village situated 1,200 meters above sea level. It lies on a small hill between the mountains that divide the Adige Valley from the Fiemme and Cembra Valleys. It currently has 390 inhabitants, almost all of whom are engaged in mountain farming and breeding livestock. It is part of the autonomous province of Bolzano (its southernmost tip), and it belongs to the diocese of Bolzano-Bressanone and to the deanery of Egna (Neumarkt).

The history of this settlement has been documented since 1321, when Duke Henry of Carinthia gave his vassal Gottschalk of Bolzano the right to settle ten farmsteads in Anterivo, to be entrusted to Tyrolean settlers. At the time of Matteo's birth – born to Pietro and Anna Amorth on September 9, 1767 in the hamlet Guggal – the village was under the secular and pastoral government of the Prince-Bishop of Trent. The civil administrative functions were exercised (by delegation of the bishop) by the Magnifica Comunità di Fiemme[27] and the canonical ones by the parish church (Pieve) of Cavalese. By far the most illustrious citizen of Anterivo was Johann Baptist Zwerger (1824-1893), professor of theology at the bishop's seminary, dean of the cathedral and vicar general of the diocese of Trent. In 1867 he was appointed Archbishop of Graz-Seckau and in 1870 participated in the First Vatican Council.

---

26. Ladino is a Romance language mainly spoken in the Dolomite Mountains in Northern Italy in the provinces of South Tyrol, Trent, and Belluno, by the Ladino people.
27. An institution established in the 12th century, which was given an independent administration by the Bishop of Trent.

According to this brief research, the surname Lubich is the result of a series of transcriptions and errors made by priests in the registration of the sacraments given to the ancestors of the founder of the Focolare. The documents in Trent register Silvia's grandfather as "Luigi Lubick." Fr. Paolo Ciola, curate in Calliano, who baptized his great-grandfather Vincenzo, wrote "Lutbigh"; and when marrying Matteo and Marianna, Vincenzo's parents, that same Fr. Ciola also recorded the groom's surname in the register as "Lutbigk." In the volume that records the baptisms from 1705 to 1805 in the parish dedicated to Sts. Catherine and James in Anterivo, Matteo is registered with the surname "Ludwig" (one of the most widespread names in the village). The same name was recorded for the marriage of his father Pietro to Anna Amorth on September 24, 1752 by the parish priest Giovanni Battista Savoi.

It therefore seems legitimate to say that the origins of Chiara Lubich's family can be traced back to this small village on a political and linguistic border, made up of many "focolares" (fireplaces; home fires) such as the mountain farmsteads, where the sense of unity (family and community), solidarity and the administration of common goods is codified in the customs and institutes of law. This sense of cooperation and various forms of solidarity-based economy have been rooted and practiced there for centuries. They were based on the needs arising from poverty and the harshness of the territory, but which have also penetrated the hearts and customs of the people, both resisting and adapting to the times and to the processes of globalization.

A further note on the form of the surname concerns the period immediately after Silvia's birth. Following the promulgation of Royal Decree-Law no. 17 of January 10, 1926 (*The transfer into Italian of the surnames in the province of Trent*) could have resulted in an official change of their surname, with further effects on the graphic variants of their genealogy.

The first article of the law stated that any "original Italian or Latin surname translated into other languages or misrepresented by foreign handwriting or with the addition of a foreign suffix," had to return to its original form. Equally "the surnames named after places, whose names had been translated into another language, or misrepresented by foreign handwriting, and also the name particles which noblemen translated into foreign form" had to be returned to the Italian form.

This policy of Italianization desired by the Fascist regime, which affected the area of Trent and above all South Tyrol, had negative effects on the names of Germanic and Ladino origin, with social and political repercussions that have been felt until recent years. Probably, Silvia's family did not undergo this revision, as in the province of Trent it was conducted by authorities with less diligence than elsewhere.

Family places

Many of the places that provide a background to the early years of Silvia Lubich's life have a more interesting and symbolic meaning than her actual life story does. The links between places and identities are always complex. A "sense of place" often helps give meaning to the world. And if it is true that the place is a physical fact, it is also true that it helps shape individual personalities and social interactions. It is a structure that expresses feelings and is a center of meaning. At the same time, it is the people who "make the place," who constitute the image, the narrative, and the representation; who provide its meaning.

The urban context of Trent within which this biography begins is strongly influenced by the religious history of the city, but also linked to some great events and important paths that have marked the history of the Catholic Church and Christianity in its different periods.

Silvia was born in a house at the "civic," at number 11 Via Prepositura. The term "civic," typical of the legal context of the Ambrosian[28] Church, means the office of a parish priest ("preposito" or provost) invested with certain special prerogatives and privileges. In reality, in the ecclesial context of the area of Trent, the provost is the second most important person (after the dean, and before the archdeacon) of the Cathedral Chapter, the college of canons who, since the 12th century, supported the bishop in governing the local Church. Trent was the only diocese south of the Alps where for centuries, not only in the Middle Ages but also during the modern age, bishops had effective power in civil affairs, and for a long time the canons retained the right to elect them. The provost owned and administered large estates, many of which were located in the town center and in the area where the Lubich family lived.

Silvia's baptism was celebrated in the parish church of St. Mary Major, located a few steps from her birthplace. This place and the building are significant in the history of the Church, both local and universal. St. Mary's was the oldest church with the rights of spiritual and economic-patrimonial jurisdiction. This place of worship was built on the remains of the old Roman forum of *"Tridentum"* (meaning "three teeth," the three hills on which Trent is built), and where the foundations of the first Episcopal Chair of the diocese of Trent are found. The *Passio Sancti Vigilii* (Acts of St. Vigilius), an eighth century hagiography

---

28. The Ambrosian Rite is a Catholic Western liturgical rite named after Saint Ambrose, a bishop of Milan in the fourth century. Today it is confined to about 5 million people in the Milan region, but in earlier centuries encompassed a much larger area.

which combines history and legend, attributed the foundation of the church to St. Vigilius. He was the third bishop and patron saint of Trent, at the end of the 4th century and the time of the first evangelization of the region. Recent archaeological excavations have confirmed its early Christian origins and its status as the first *Ecclesia* of Trent.

The present church was built during the 1520's by Bernardo Clesio, prince-bishop and imperial councilor, who was commissioned to prepare a great council with the intention of reforming the Church and rebuilding the division with the Protestant world. The choice of architecture and the style of the décor also reflect political factors and were therefore in keeping with the cultural trends of the Italian Renaissance. It intentionally differs from the Gothic style and more closely resembles the courts and Central European cathedrals.

St. Mary Major was the church of the Council of Trent, one of the greatest events of doctrinal, pastoral, and organizational revision in the history of the Catholic Church. It was there that the preparatory meetings for the entire third session of the Council (the one at which the most important decisions were taken) took place, from April 1562 to December 1563.

This event, in the following centuries, affected the whole of European society and the rest of the world, including the genesis and development of the modern state, the transformation of ecclesiastical structures, public and private customs and morals, art and culture. It redefined many of the paradigms for reading European history and modernity. It determined the relations between Church, empire, and principalities. It shaped and clarified the renewal of the territorial organization of the Church and its instruments of governance, pastoral care, liturgy, and religious life. It started new models of missionary activity and renewed the discipline of the sacraments, the role of the new orders, and the way of venerating ancient and new saints. It separated the internal and external forum[29] and established new expressions and styles of language, architecture, painting, and music.

On the façade of St. Mary Major, in the center of the portal, there is a bas-relief representing the coat-of-arms of the prince-bishop and the cartouche with the inscription *Bernardo Clesio Praesule ac Prince Tridentino Auctore MDXX*.[30] The coat of arms, with the bishop's miter above, is formed by a bundle of seven rods tied with a ribbon bearing the motto *Unitas* (unity). In heraldry such an emblem is called a "canting arm": a sign that, through symbolic representations and words, brings to mind and sums up a typical characteristic, a wish, a function, a mission, a program (even political) of the person or family to which they refer.

For Bernardo Clesio, the most illustrious and influential among the Tridentine bishops of his century and of the preceding and subsequent periods, that coat of arms meant unity of the family, of the territory administered by him, and of the Church. It also meant unity between the ideals of civil humanism and Christian humanism – particularly with respect to the need for peace, both political and religious – according to the teachings of his friend and tutor Erasmus of Rotterdam. Clesio received the cardinal's "red hat" and was a candidate for the papal throne in the conclave of 1534.

The *Unitas* coat of arms would become one of the most widespread symbols in the city of Trent at the time of the Council, painted and sculpted on the major civil and religious buildings, engraved on the statutes and documents testifying to the prerogatives and privileges of the principality, printed on the bindings of the books of the imposing library of the bishop and carved on many items of furniture.

---

29. In Catholic canon law a distinction is made between the internal forum (the realm of personal conscience) and the external forum where an act is public and verifiable.
30. Bernard Clesic Bishop and Prince of Trent builder 1520.

It is a logo and a motto that still characterizes the Federation of Cooperatives, one of the main associations of the province of Trent. At the end of the 19th century the first logo of the Federation and of the rural banks was that of "shaking hands." But since the beginning of the twentieth century the *Unitas* trademark appeared in the advertising and documents of the Agricultural Industrial Union of Trent (SAIT), created with the aim of "making it easier for families of the cooperative to purchase goods, machinery, and other necessary objects."

The Lubich home in Via Prepositura overlooks what, from 1831 to 1835, was the headquarters of the Institute of Charity, founded by Antonio Rosmini,[31] one of the greatest philosophers of nineteenth-century Europe. He founded and gave life to that center of spirituality, study, and training, which was later to be closed on the bishop's authority due to the hostility of the Austrian government.

After many misunderstandings and excommunications, Rosmini was beatified a few years ago and is beginning to be recognized among the great witnesses of that "courageous search between philosophy and the Word of God," of which humanity and the Church today have such a great need.[32] His life and that of his disciples were long weighed down by ecclesial prohibitions and censures; he not only received the most solemn declarations of esteem but also malicious judgments, hostility and censorship. His was a destiny typical of all prophets...

Although coming from very different periods and in very different social and ecclesial contexts, Antonio Rosmini and Chiara

---

31. Antonio Rosmini (1797 – 1855) was an Italian Roman Catholic priest and philosopher. He founded the Rosminians, officially the Institute of Charity. He pioneered the concept of social justice and was a key figure in Italian liberal Catholicism.
32. John Paul II's encyclical *Fides et Ratio* places Rosmini alongside John Henry Newman, Jacques Maritain, Étienne Gilson, and Edith Stein.

Lubich both have founded spiritual currents destined to make a dramatic impact on the time in which they lived: the Institute of Charity and the Focolare Movement. These reveal common roots and interesting historical links, still largely to be explored. Both found connections with personalities who would strengthen and spread their message. The most significant of these public figures are, respectively, Clemente Rèbora and Igino Giordani.

The same building that, in the first half of the nineteenth century, had housed the first Rosminian religious was later used as an oratory of the parish of St. Mary Major.

Although in strikingly different forms from those of Rosmini, in the following decades that place again became, a center of formation and spirituality, exploring new models of pastoral care and the administration of charity. Thanks to the clergy and laity who animated it from the last decades of the nineteenth century onwards, the oratory of St. Mary Major represented a center of particular social importance for the heart of the city. In addition to the usual activities of catechesis and entertainment for the youth, there was a soup kitchen where minestrone was cooked for all the needy of the city and facilities and initiatives for welcoming girls whose families had abandoned them. Courses were held there as well as workshops (especially sewing) to alleviate poverty, to protect them from exploitation and prostitution, and to give each one prospects for the future.

Franco de Battaglia[33] called the oratory of St. Mary Major "a vibrant center of moral and material solidarity," where "the approach was 'feminine,' intensely feminine, also in practice and this was the great resource and the great ecclesial novelty of the oratory."

---

33. Born in Trent, 1943, journalist and writer of many books regarding Trent and the Dolomites. He was for a time director of the daily newspaper "Alto Adige."

Several women's religious institutes were active in the parish of St. Mary and had a profound impact on the religious history of the city. Among them were the Daughters of the Sacred Heart, the Sisters of the Child Mary, and the lay Ursulines of Casa Sant'Angela Merici, all dedicated to the education of youth and the care of the sick and destitute.

This was an environment that the little Silvia Lubich undoubtedly frequented, and she would have experienced this atmosphere during the first years of her Christian upbringing, as did her family. Her mother Luigia was a woman of deep faith and piety; but in all probability the culture of her father Luigi was more secular, albeit deeply marked and inspired by ideals and values of solidarity and equality typical of socialism.

Luigia, Luigi ... and the others...

In her writings and talks, Chiara Lubich often speaks of transmitting faith through two channels: "witness" and "attraction." It means putting your heart completely into your faith in Jesus Christ and transmitting to humanity your most precious treasure. It is a way far removed from any mechanical and rational teaching of faith.

The transmission of faith through the generations often has a female imprint, passing through the voices and facial expressions of mothers and grandmothers, in an atmosphere that emanates love. It is a creed whose words are learned, but which, to be understood, needs to be backed up by gestures, caresses, tenderness, even by knowing the dialect. Witnessing in everyday life what we believe in (and which makes us righteous in the eyes of God) and being consistent with what we say by the way we live, arouses the curiosity of those around us. This curiosity represents a seed of the Holy Spirit who transmits faith. Probably these were the ways and examples that Luigia Marinconz offered to her four children – Gino, Silvia, Liliana, and Carla.

Luigia was born on July 7, 1881 and her family was originally from Coredo, in Val di Non. Her father Germano had moved to Trent to work as a coachman, and he used a horse-drawn carriage to carry the travelers who arrived in the capital by rail (built in 1860 by the Austrian government). In May 1908 Luigia married Teobaldo Nardelli, who died after not even a month. The marriage with Luigi Lubich was celebrated on August 15, 1916 – the feast of the Assumption – at the height of the war. They had met at their workplace, the printing house where the newspaper of the Trent Socialist Party "Il Popolo," directed by Cesare Battisti, was printed.

Luigia is described as a person with a deep religious sensibility, but also as being strong and determined in everyday life, sensitive to the suffering of those close to her, and able to live the many trials she faced in life with dignity and optimism. She had a deep faith and a spiritual life, marked by prayer, mass and daily communion, a strong Marian devotion, the practices of piety typical of the time, and a style of Christianity with a strong social awareness and compassion. Although her faith was rock solid, it was never ostentatious and she was never tempted to proselytize, so much so that she was respected even in her atheistic and anticlerical working environment, where her religious sentiments were certainly not shared.

Although Luigi and Luigia worked at the same job according to the stories and descriptions of the two that have come down to us, this did not necessarily imply that they shared the same political views or religious beliefs.

The editorial staff of a political newspaper like the one run by Cesare Battisti, which was well connected with the historical, political and geographical context of the area of Trent in the early twentieth century, was a cross-section of activists, intellectuals, projects, ideas and passions. It contained news about the debates that animated the life of the Italian and Austrian socialist parties, expressing the political views of the border territories of the Austro-Hungarian Empire (in particular the provinces overlooking the Adriatic) and the echoes of the struggles and ideologies of the various European socialist factions. This was a period marked by division between revolutionary movements aimed at the overthrow of capitalist systems, and reformist ones that considered it necessary to engage in action gradually, in the struggles to increase political and social rights through electoral and parliamentary agreements, in close contact with trade unions and within the framework of the institutions of the nation states.

There was much interest in Trent in the themes of self-determination of peoples and of autonomy, as opposed to western nationalism and imperialism. But there was also room for the pacifist and internationalist thinking of the reformist constituents, as well patriotic or irredentist support for the war.

In 1909, for some months, Luigi Lubich shared lodgings with a certain Benito Mussolini, at the time a socialist with radical and revolutionary views, already known as a journalist and polemicist, political agitator, and trade unionist. He had been called to Trent to write for *Il Popolo* and *L'Avvenire del Lavoratore* and to instigate political militancy in the area of Trent. The heated controversy sparked by his articles and rallies, often marked by a strong anticlerical tone, resulted in his being denounced, condemned, censured and, at the end of September, expelled from the territories of the Empire. He then returned to Italy.

Luigi shared the great ideals of socialism, aspiring to build a society based on justice and equality. Although engaged in purely practical work, composing and checking the text of many articles and liaising with editors and correspondents, he certainly came into contact with many elements of this political and cultural climate. His enlistment in the Austrian army at the outbreak of the war on August 1, 1914 and his departure for the Eastern Front suggest that his views differed from those of his director. Battisti, on the 11th of the same month, left Austrian territory and moved to Italy, engaging in an intense campaign for action against Austria and for annexation of the area of Trent. The following year he enlisted in the Royal Italian Army, until his tragic end in July 1916, with his capture on the Pasubio, his trial and execution. Luigi Lubich was wounded in battle on the Galician front at the end of 1914, spending a long time in hospital. When Italy went to war in May 1915, Luigia, for reasons still unknown, was not evacuated to the northern territories of the Empire, as was most of the population of Trent. She was not even interned, as happened to many political activists and those suspected of pro-Italian feelings, in concentration camps such as Katzenau.

After they got married, during wartime when Luigi was on leave, their first son, Gino, was born on January 21, 1918. His father met him some time later when he was granted extra leave. Two years later Silvia was born, and in the following years Liliana (1922) and Carla (1925). After the war, when Battisti's printing house was closed for good, Luigi began a business exporting wines from southern Italy to Northern Europe. This activity, in the first years, guaranteed the family a modest level of comfort. The unity and harmony of the family were strong, despite the differences in character and convictions of the two parents.

Luigia brought up the children in the faith with great respect and sensitivity, focusing above all on example. This complimented Luigi's life, which was based on respect for the law, honesty, humanitarian ideals, and on the solidarity characteristic of his political beliefs. Apparently, he showed no interest in spiritual or religious matters. However, one day, due to an innocent invitation from little Gino and Silvia, he approached the sacraments and discreetly began to go to church. This incident shows the special relationship between Gino and Silvia, which could be described with many other anecdotes. Despite the very different paths that their respective personal itineraries would take in the following years (Gino became a medical student, a communist activist, a partisan committed to the Resistance, and a journalist for the communist newspaper *L'Unità*), their bond was reinforced in the mid-1950s in the context of the Focolare Movement.

According to the few facts and testimonies available to us, Silvia had a peaceful and happy childhood, with a sense of inner freedom and deep respect for the opinions of others, moral uprightness, and trust in providence. Her particular aptitude for reflection and sense of the absolute is reflected in her lack of interest in dolls ("because they were fake') and in fairy tales ("because I wanted the truth').

The sensitivity that from adolescence Silvia showed towards social questions was certainly favored by her homelike religious and supportive surroundings, and by the civil and ecclesial educational context in which she grew up.

FORMATION BETWEEN THE TWO WARS

A LITTLE CHILD TO THE CHILD MARY

In addition to the influence and teachings from her family, Silvia's initial religious formation took place in the house of "the Sisters of Charity of Sts. Bartolomea Capitanio and Vincenza Gerosa," commonly called the "Sisters of the Child Mary." Founded in Lovere (Bergamo) in 1832, they arrived in Trent a few years later. Their charism was "based on charity, according to the examples left by the most lovable Redeemer." They cared for the youth and the sick with an active involvement in the life of the local Church.

From the end of the nineteenth century they worked at the kindergarten named after Fr. Giovanni Battista Zanella and we know that little Silvia went there. After the war they opened a women's oratory in Via Borsieri, where every Sunday the girls spent their afternoons attending catechism classes, praying together, and having Benediction, but they also played and did drama. Within a few years that place became the most important center for the religious formation of young women in Trent.

There Silvia was prepared for her First Communion and Confirmation. She became particularly fond of Sister Carolina Cappella, from whom Chiara Lubich recalled having received a sort of initiation into her own experience of faith.

This sister used to accompany the children to the Church of the Blessed Sacrament, which was built and consecrated in 1926 in memory of the first diocesan Eucharistic Congress and the Eucharistic doctrine defined and summarized in the decrees of the Council of Trent. Having been taught adoration of the body of Christ in the monstrance and the recitation of the prayer to Jesus to let his light and warmth penetrate her soul, little Silvia began to "see the white host as black and the darkness that surrounded it looked white."

Sister Carolina, sensing Silvia's deep spiritual attitude, taught her to live a Christian life by example and simplicity in loving Jesus, basing her teaching on goodness, prayer, and small sacrifices which she faced with joy. With the same simplicity and spontaneity, she taught Silvia to love Our Lady, mother of divine grace. And the following incident was closely linked with grace.

She was hospitalized at the age of ten for peritonitis and the doctors had given her little hope of survival. Luigia and Sister Carolina entrusted the child's fate to the child Mary. The operation was successful and, after a few days suspended between life and death, Silvia recovered. This experience made a deep impression on her, so much so that she was reminded several times of how her "understanding of the presence of pain in life and the possibility of bearing it out of love" began then.

At school in 1926

In October 1926 Silvia began to attend the Giuseppe Verdi primary school, housed in the building which in the early 1960s became the Faculty of Sociology of the University of Trent.

Trent had a long-standing tradition of schools open for all children, dating back to the reforms promoted by the Empress Maria Teresa of Austria in 1774. What was different about the Teresian initiative was making the schools compulsory and free for all citizens of the Empire (boys and girls), thus establishing the right and the duty to study. The management of the schools was entrusted to the municipalities, thus recognizing the territorial principle. The state, which was both absolutist and enlightened, retained the function of coordination and cultural direction, defining the common disciplines and teaching methods. Reading, writing, arithmetic, catechism, and learning by memory were the fundamental principles of the Teresian schools. Every pupil of every nationality was guaranteed the right to the protection and development of his or her own language and identity.

After the Great War, with the annexation by the kingdom of Italy the gradual process of Italianization of schools began in the former Tyrolean territories and they were radicalized with the rise of Fascism. On October 2, 1922, the violent occupation of the German primary school *Elisabeth Schule* in Bolzano by a Fascist team from Trent and Ferrara was considered the dress rehearsal for the march on Rome.

Later, the school became a prime location for the forced Italianization of the region. With the application of the reform law by Giovanni Gentile, Italian was introduced as the only language of instruction (after that, in South Tyrol, German was taught only in the so-called catacomb schools). This process continued with the establishment of the province of Bolzano (in 1926) the exclusive use of Italian in public life (with offices that investigated the origin of place names, official communications, surnames etc.). German-language schools were closed and there was a significant immigration of Italian workers and businesses.

In this context, in October 1926 Silvia Lubich began her schooling. She was in the A grade, made up of 55 girls, under the guidance of her teacher Anna de Pretis. Little Silvia's lively intelligence and dedication to study always gave her brilliant results, except for her time in the IV grade during which she was affected by the health problems already mentioned. However, the following year when she took her Licentiate exams, it was clear that she had recovered as she achieved excellent grades which opened the possibility for her to embark on a demanding course of study. Instead Silvia was enrolled in the Narciso and Pilade Bronzetti school, which provided professional training to enter the world of work more directly. This choice was dictated by the difficult economic conditions of the Lubich family after years of relative prosperity, because after the war Luigi's business failed.

This situation was probably caused by the general economic crisis of the second half of the 1920s (which led to the great depression of 1929), but it was certainly also due to Luigi's failure to join the Fascist Party, which was contrary to his deepfelt ideals. Because of these principles, he refused the advice of many to turn to Mussolini to resolve his situation. The Lubich family found itself facing substantial hardship. They often went hungry and finally had to move to a new house. Luigi and Luigia faced this situation with patience and dignity, even though they were worried about their children's future, and Chiara recounts how they encouraged them, even with cheerfulness and often laughing at themselves.

Silvia's excellent grades, apart from the one in "fascist culture," meant that she was exempt from school fees and this helped the family situation. In 1934, she passed the Licentiate exam with a grade of 94/110 (she came third in the entire institute), gaining the possibility of a scholarship for a course in higher education. To contribute to the budget at home, Silvia gave private lessons, and the prospect of being able to start work once she had obtained her commercial license rather than continuing her studies was certainly a matter discussed in the family. Although aware of the sacrifices that this choice would entail, the Lubich family decided to support their daughter's abilities (and desire) by having her enrolled in a course of higher education.

AT HIGH SCHOOL

However, being accepted for the course was not a foregone conclusion, as Silvia had to pass a strict entrance exam to verify her knowledge of certain subjects (e.g. Latin) and of some subjects that were not part of her previous basic education. Preparing for this entailed an intense year of study, which she did independently at the Sacred Heart Institute. She passed the exam, albeit with a re-sit in September in Latin and German and, in October 1935, Silvia was able to attend the final three years of her education at the *istituto magistrale* (teacher training college) Antonio Rosmini, in Grade B, with 40 female students. This was an outstanding college attended mainly by girls and organized according to the dictates of the "Gentile reform"[34] with its nationalist character (albeit tempered by the traditional restraint and aversion to extremism in Trent society). It was also very much affected by the wave of propaganda that the Fascist regime had set in motion and by the events that had defined international politics in those years preceding the great tragedy of the Second World War.

In the same years, together with her growth in faith, Silvia developed a constant yearning for truth. Hence her passion for philosophy, for the great thinkers of modern times like Kant, who on the one hand she found attractive and on the other hand did not satisfy her unrest, especially when they explained the question of truth in moral law seen in its practical applications as simply an expression of reason and of the will. She had similar problems with Hegel's "speculative method."

Silvia's need was not limited to the purely intellectual dimension:

---

34. The "Gentile Reform" of 1923 was a reform of the Italian educational system through a series of royal legislative decrees by the neo-idealist philosopher Giovanni Gentile, minister of education in Benito Mussolini's first cabinet.

Researching ancient and modern philosophers in search of the truth was what fully satisfied my mind and heart. But, being educated in a Christian way and perhaps driven by an impulse of the Spirit, I soon realized that I was taken above all by the profound desire to get to know God.

The maxim "As if there were no God" *(Etsi Deus non daretur)*[35] of the great thinkers of the age of enlightenment and idealism proved itself wrong precisely in its confrontation with history, showing how far human cruelty can go and the reality of evil in the great tragedies of the first half of the twentieth century.

Of note is the episode, often recounted, of Silvia's disagreement with Girolamo Gaspari, professor of philosophy. When he criticized certain truths of faith and certain positions of the Church, Silvia repeatedly intervened, even though she did not have the theoretical tools to justify her argument, stating: "Professor, that is not true!" This was quite an act of courage if one thinks of the authoritarian approach of teaching of the time and the danger, for Silvia, of jeopardizing her scholarship, without which she would no longer have had any guarantee of continuing her studies. However, the teacher showed himself to be an enlightened and tolerant man, not judging the student's complaints as impertinent or disrespectful and acknowledging, throughout her studies, her exceptional performance. Silvia was moved by her love for God-truth and what she did was solely for the good of her neighbor, who, at that moment was her teacher. Her desire, of which she was only partly aware, remained that of

---

35. "As if there were no God" was a formula originating in the fourteenth century as a "thought experiment" in disputes about the nature of the natural moral law. In later centuries it became a catch-cry of a secular worldview that saw man to be independent of God and that moral laws are simply the fruit of reason and/or the will, and have nothing to do with any metaphysical reality of good or evil. In other words, they need to be looked at as if God (nor the Devil) exist.

knowing God and loving him, as a truth greater than any other, even if codified in great philosophical systems. During a chance meeting a few years later Professor Gaspari confided to Chiara that he had "begun to pray to that God in whom you believe."

Despite the ongoing financial difficulties in her family, forcing her to give many private lessons, Silvia's intelligence and hard work were such that, with an annual scholarship, she completed the entire course of study. In 1938 she graduated with high grades.

The years Silvia spent at high school were fundamental for her intellectual and spiritual growth, allowing her personality to mature. They had an impact that would mark all her work in the years that followed: a faith never removed from history and grounded in the connection between thought and reason; a concept of truth always embodied and animated by a deep conviction of the unity of knowledge, which in turn is based on the unity of truth; the goodness and beauty of creation as proof of the existence and essence of God; prayer and meditation on Sacred Scripture as the primary source of one's actions and of understanding the natural and metaphysical world.

Probably some inspiration from the Spirit and a few passages from the writings of Antonio Rosmini contributed to Silvia's growth in maturity. He was the philosopher whose work at that time was still subject to the scrutiny of the ecclesiastical authorities and to whom the lay Italian authorities dedicated the teacher training college of Trent in 1923 by.

The years of Silvia's studies coincided with a complex period in the relations between the Italian State and the Church, which had repercussions on the area of Trent. During the post-war reconstruction of the institutional system in the new context of the "kingdom of Italy" and in the following years dominated by Fascism, the question of education systems was one of the focuses of the debate, especially with regard to the autonomy of schools and the teaching of religion, which, in the pre-war period had been entrusted to the clergy. The Catholic movement was mobilized in this area especially through the Federation of Associations of Fathers of Families and the Trent Catholic Teachers Association. These two entities, supported by the various lay and economic-social organizations, conveyed the firm will of the Church to commit itself to the education of youth, investing energy and resources in a debate with the state systems and the politics of the day that lasted for twenty years and which will be mentioned again in the following pages.

To give an example of how high the tension was regarding schools and teachers, reading the passage below will help to explain the situation (even with a little irony...). On, June 22, 1935 an informer from the area of Trent sent a report like this– now kept in the Central State Archives—to the headquarters of the Fascist Party in Rome:

> In the area of Trent, the teachers are all or almost all in the hands of the priests, who are the absolute leaders. The youth organizations exist, it's true, but they work only in appearance. The only ones that work in effect are the Catholic youth organizations. The Balilla, the Little Italian ones, meet only on days when they cannot do without them, that is, on national feast days; they make an appearance in ceremonies and then leave. This is not the case for priests, who are together all day with the little ones or in the school, or on well-organized trips, or during recreation. They then find allies in the teachers, who during the lessons talk about the Church to the pupils, but little or nothing about their country; the little ones all know who Don Bosco is, St. Louis etc., but very few have heard of Cesare Battisti, Damiano Chiesa, Nazario Sauro etc. For good behavior or for service to the school, holy cards of saints are being distributed to the schoolchildren as prizes, but never images of our heroes

or photographs of "il Duce"[36] *.... In some schools the nuns still work as teachers, who make the little ones go crazy with too much religion, to the detriment of the school curriculum and learning about their own country.*

---

36. The Italian Fascist Party leader Benito Mussolini was commonly referred to as Il Duce (The Leader).

FROM CATHOLIC ACTION TO THE THIRD ORDER[37]

Trent: Church and fascism

At school, Silvia took an increasingly active part in youth associations within the various groups of Catholic Action. During her secondary school education, she certainly participated in the activities of the women's student section, whose diocesan assistant was the Franciscan Fr. Marco Vanzetta, and later joined the Student Youth, led by Fr. Alfonso Cesconi.

The activities included weekly formation at the headquarters in Via Borsieri, charitable and recreational activities, spiritual retreats and meetings with other diocesan activities such as "the social weeks," which tried to promote a Christian presence in the world of youth.

The activities of Catholic Action around Trent in the second half of the 1920s and throughout the following decade are inseparably linked to the more general history of the Church and to politics. Bishop Celestino Endrici was never accommodating towards the political agenda and the aggressive style of Fascism. Many diocesan priests were openly against the regime. They concentrated on the formation of the laity and their social commitment. They were the inspiration for many cooperative

---

37. "Third Order," whether Franciscan or from other religious families, are lay people, men and women, who seek to live the spirituality of their order in their ordinary everyday lives.

and trade union initiatives and conscious advocates of the democratic method in public life and they supported the People's Party (*Partito Populare*) led by De Gasperi.

A particularly significant testimony to this situation can be found in a letter that the prefect of Trent, Marcello Vaccari wrote to Mussolini on January 9, 1927:

> We have to be convinced that bishop Celestino Endrici is of dubious political faith, he is attached to his role as bishop, to the old institutions ... It is therefore necessary to point out that, if on the one hand the government is aware of the high social and spiritual function of the priest, it can no longer tolerate that in the church – and under the guise of faith – grudges, slander, poison and defamation are being expressed and perpetuated at the expense of authority and Fascism.

Within the Catholic world of the Province of Trent, even if the Catholic world around Trent was less receptive than elsewhere to the ideology conveyed by Fascist propaganda, a part of the public were "of half consent or of consent with reservation towards the regime." After the closure of the Catholic newspaper *Il Nuovo Trentino* following a Fascist raid that destroyed its printing press, the bishop decided to start a diocesan press service. On December 23, 1925 the first issue of the weekly *Vita Trentina* was published, with the aim of "guiding people towards truth and justice, making them vigilant in the face of error in the confusion of ideas that cloud the world." It advocated an resolute line of defense of Christian principles, of the right of opinion and of firm opposition to any dictatorship. On February 11, 1929, the pacts between the Italian State and the Holy See were made in the Lateran, establishing the Vatican City State and definitively closing the "Roman question"[38]. It was a political and diplomatic act that formally

---

38. The "Roman Question" was the dispute between the papacy and the Italian Government regarding the temporal power of the popes as rulers of a civil

resolved the historic dispute which had started in 1870 with the events of the *Risorgimento*[39] and the occupation of Rome.

The Church of Trent and its bishop greeted the signing of the pacts without any apparent reservation, underlining the fact that the historical differences had been resolved in a positive way and that they were confident in a future with greater freedom. The general appreciation for the agreement was also due to the positive economic results it would secure for the dioceses of Trent and Bressanone. They obtained the commitment of the Italian government to contribute to the living expenses of the clergy for a quota no less than that previously guaranteed by the Austrian government and the assurance that the German language would be permitted for religious instruction and pastoral work among the people of South Tyrol.

The Catholic press expressed great optimism in the renewed atmosphere brought about by the reconciliation. It made proposals for greater responsibilities for Catholics in the social sphere. The main method for achieving this program would be Catholic Action, whose recognition the pope had demanded in the text (art. 43) of the pact. The elections for the twenty-eighth legislature of the kingdom of Italy were organized and strictly controlled by the prefectural authorities and monopolized by Fascist propaganda. The ballot was limited to a yes or no vote for a single list of candidates chosen by the Grand Council of Fascism. In line with the Lateran Pact, the regime demanded a strong support from the Church. This was guaranteed, apparently without conditions. With an average turnout in Italy of 89% of those entitled to vote,

---

territory in the context of Italian re-unification. It ended with the Lateran Pacts between King Victor Emmanuel III of Italy and Pope Pius XI in 1929.

39. The political and social movement in the nineteenth entury that consolidated different states of the Italian peninsula into the single state of the kingdom of Italy in 1861. This included the conquest of the papal states.

around Trent only 73% of those on the electoral roll turned out to vote. The votes against reached 6.5% in Trent, compared to the national average of 1.6 %.

Pope Pius XI had hoped that reconciliation would make the Italian State's attitude more open to the demands and values of the Catholic world, but he was soon disappointed by the behavior of the government and il Duce. The uneasy imbalance, that existed between the desire for total control on the part of the regime and the strategy of Christianizing all elements of civil society on the part of the Church, resulted sometimes in open conflict. In the spring of 1931, on the occasion of an initiative by Catholic Action to create workers' secretariats, the regime organized a ruthless press campaign that led to the dissolution of all youth associations not belonging to the *Opera Nazionale Balilla* or the National Fascist Party. On June 29, Pius XI, with the encyclical "We do not need" (*Non abbiamo bisogno*), responded to the Fascist attacks on Catholic Action, challenging the State's claim to have a monopoly on the education of youth and denouncing a whole range of characteristics of Fascism that were contrary to the principles of the Christian faith. The following September 2, after a series of difficult negotiations, an agreement was signed between the Italian State and the Holy See whereby the autonomy of Catholic Action was recognized but limiting its activity to the religious sphere and emphasizing its diocesan character and its dependence on the ecclesial hierarchy.

National events had an immediate impact on Trent's ecclesial environment, which was always at the forefront in promoting Catholic Action and the education of young people. On May 30, 1931, following Mussolini's instructions, the Prefect of Trent ordered the dissolution of all non-fascist youth associations: 139 men's and 221 women's Catholic associations were suppressed. Also, it was decreed that the Juventus Association of the students of Trent, and 86 parish oratories and theatres be closed.

Three days later the newspaper *Il Brennero* was published under the title "To Fascism the education of the youth!" One of the most serious episodes of the crisis, on June 4, was a raid by Fascist mobs on the headquarters of *Vita Trentina*. On the same day, the oratories of the cathedral in Trent and the parishes of San Marco and Santa Maria in Rovereto were invaded and placards of the *Opera Nazionale Balilla* were displayed. Endrici's reaction was immediate, with an invitation to the clergy and faithful to persevere in the work of education and the apostolate and with a pastoral letter condemning the evil fruits of an education not inspired by Christian principles. The conflict between the Church of Trent and the regime continued in the following months. After the agreement between the Holy See and the government the following September, the situation, at least apparently, calmed down. Catholic Action could continue to operate, but was limited to the religious sphere, excluding all organized social and trades union commitments, and even sports. Those who had been members of the People's Party in the past were banned from all positions in the association. In apparent compliance with this ban, Endrici appointed as president of the diocesan committee of Catholic Action someone with clear anti-fascist feelings: Guido de Unterrichter.

The ecclesial assistant of the diocesan council of Catholic Action, Bishop Oreste Rauzi, who had replaced Bishop Guido de Gentili in 1927, was moved to the major seminary, because he was too hostile towards the regime and had received death threats.

Propagandist

In March 1935, Silvia Lubich introduced herself to the assistant of the women's youth section of Catholic Action, Fr. Alfonso

Cesconi, with clear ideas that were as concise as they were ambitious: "I want to become a saint!"

Struck by such clarity and determination (evidently, he had been told about her) and by her level of maturity and grasp of the spiritual dimension, he put her into the course for "propagandists." This was the most motivated group of girls who showed themselves capable of promoting the association and becoming its leaders. They had an aptitude for the apostolate of encouraging young people to search for God and to love the Church, especially through example in prayer, in charity, in recognizing every action as being moved by God's love, and in the constant yearning for perfection.

The school of propagandists was based on a well-established method and on texts such as "The Soul of Every Apostolate" by Dom Jean-Baptiste Chautard and "Apostles in the World" by Fr. Matthew Crawley. The courses focused on the history and organization of Catholic Action, the catechism (at the time it was that of Pius X), moral teachings, the social teaching of the Church and alternative currents of thought (in particular Marxism). They also included Christian apologetics (with debates on historical-religious issues). It was a three-year course, at the end of which the students received a solemn mandate that allowed them to announce openly the Christian message.

The cells of propagandists and, more generally, the organization of the women's youth section were started in the Ambrosian diocese by Armida Barelli, with the support of Cardinal Andrea Ferrari, and had been made official in the statutes of Catholic Action in 1923. They represented, for the whole of Catholic Action, a unified mass movement that took root throughout the country. It responded better than any other organization to many of the needs expressed by the Church of the time on various fronts: the coordinated participation of the laity in the life and mission of the Church without distinction of status and class; the spread of a sense of ownership in regards of giving witness to the faith; the setting up and execution of formation programs for the Christianization of society as set out by Pope Pius XI after the war. All this contrasted starkly with the great ideological ideas and political proposals that sanctioned the triumph of the state over the human person.

Its organizational structure (with its three main men's and three women's branches), guaranteed a possibility to mobilize and to establish the kingdom of God on earth with great effect. This contributed to the Church being seen as anti-nationalist and not in tune with the atmosphere of compromise induced by the politics of the Concordat in those years. In keeping with tradition and the historical development of the Italian Catholic movement, Catholic Action was pursuing a kind of autonomy regarding its intellectual approach, in contrast to the official doctrines and institutions of the regime. It was carrying ahead a long-term vision and a Christian understanding of society and culture. That collective path was the fruit of a "Christian formation of the individual life" as set out by Pius XI and taken up by Catholic Action to manage the formation of the laity against the prevalence of the surrounding culture. To this end, they used the most suitable means at their disposal starting from the youth groups.

Several members of Catholic Action in the Trent area were in contact with the wider academic world both in Italy and Europe. This helped them to reflect more on the growth of their cultural and spiritual identity during the years of Fascism. They did not feel at ease with the expression of the eighteenth-century unknown author of the "Letter to Diognetus," who saw the condition of the Christian in relation to the world as being a "foreigner at home."

They rejected this description, desiring to become part of the world again, and relate to contemporary ideas by proposing ideals for a new form of Christianity, capable of expressing an all-inclusive form of humanism and setting up projects for the rebuilding of society inspired by the values of freedom and democracy. They were aware of the so-called "crisis of civilization," which suffered from the contrast between modernism and anti-modernism within the Catholic world. They saw it in the light of the German Christian-social tradition and of the theological-political analyses of Jacques Maritain, Charles Journet, Étienne Gilson, and Emmanuel Mounier. These people looked at the world without nostalgia and without any *a priori* rejection of modernity. They followed closely the developments of the ideas of the wider Catholic political world that was working out an anti-totalitarian "third way" based on the values and principles of Christianity.

There was a well-established link with the Morcelliana publishing house, founded in Brescia in 1925 by a group of young Catholic intellectuals: Fausto Minelli, Alessandro Capretti, Giulio Bevilacqua, Mario Bendiscioli and Giovanni Battista Montini (the future Pope Paul VI). They tried to promote a Christian culture in dialogue with the latest lively ideas coming from Europe in opposition to the totalitarian world surrounding them. They started on an editorial project, in line with the Italian Catholic Federation of University Students (FUCI), that was led by Montini himself and animated by passionate academics such as Igino Righetti, Guido Gonella and Sergio Paronetto. This was a project aimed at overcoming the divisions caused by the condemnation of modernism. They tried to promote and appreciate everything in it that was compatible with Catholic teaching. It was based on the need, felt by many in the Church in Italy and further afield, for a cultural renewal capable of accommodating religion and modernity, of expressing the truths of faith in a new way, of a radical reform in spirituality and liturgy.

The Trent diocesan weekly and the Catholic Action's periodicals drew on the most up-to-date European Catholic publications, drawing attention to the theological and pastoral ideas from Germany and France, as well as to the theories expressed in the works of Jacques Maritain and Emmanuel Mounier, Fr. Léonce de Grandmaison, the Christian *Weltanschauung* of Peter Lippert, Karl Adam and Romano Guardini. It also referred to the biblical and liturgical movement that was spreading in Europe in those years, heralding the season of ecclesial renewal that would culminate three decades later with the celebration of the Second Vatican Council. This openness was even more striking when seen in the context of the ecclesial situation and the cultural climate of the area of Trent at that time. It was a period marked by the obvious weariness of Celestino Endrici (who from 1934 onwards was suffering from the effects of a stroke) in the governance of the diocese, whose pastoral methods now seemed to be hampered by traditional formulas, with spirituality and Christian culture reduced to pragmatism and conformism. It was not just the bishop but also, in part, the local Church that was exhausted by so many conflicts, fought in that heavy going and difficult first part of the twentieth century. They had had to cope with anti-modernism, the national question, the Great War, reconstruction, anti-Fascism, the crisis of civilization... It all had taken its toll.

The weekly *Vita Trentina* included comments on the events and problems of international politics as they appeared in the Vatican press written by Alcide De Gasperi, Igino Giordani, and Guido Gonella. They shed light on that tormented period of European history which built up to the crisis that eventually resulted in the tragedy of the Second World War. The editorial staff and student circles of Catholic Action read "L'Avvenire d'Italia," the in-depth analysis of "L'Illustrazione Vaticana" and "La Civiltà Cattolica," the FUCI magazines "Studium" and "Azione Fucina," the French Catholic periodicals (in particular "Esprit," "Vie catholique" and "La Croix," the magazine of the French Jesuits "Études" and that of the Dominicans "Vie Intellectuelle') and also German periodicals (in particular "Hochland" and the Viennese "Reichspost"). The racial laws passed in 1938, and discrimination against Jews, were openly condemned in the bishop's weekly magazine. The bishop had followed the rise of Nazism in Germany from the beginning, sensed its disastrous consequences for the future of the world, and openly condemned its anti-Christian nature and violent methods.

Europe was going through one of the darkest moments of its history, which would prove a real turning point for the history of the world. In March 1938, Benito Mussolini and Adolf Hitler met in Rome. A few days later Austria was annexed to the Third Reich. In September, the Fascist parliament approved the persecution of the Jews. In the same days, the Munich Pact between Mussolini, Hitler, the English Prime Minister Neville Chamberlain, and the French Prime Minister Édouard Daladier, allowed the Nazi armies to occupy the Sudetenland. A year later, the attack on Poland would start the Second World War.

Another traumatic event for the population of the Trent region was the so-called "options" law. As a result of the alliance with Germany, the rules of October 21, 1939 were implemented which provided for the voluntary transfer of German-speaking inhabitants from South Tyrol (but also from the area of Trent) to Germany. An extremely high percentage took advantage of the opportunity. After the end of the war, the problems caused by their return would put a strain on the peaceful coexistence between the Italian and German-speaking population.

Silvia received her mandate as propagandist in 1938, when the women's section of Catholic Action counted over 19,000 members, gathered in 356 locations. Presiding over the ceremony was the auxiliary bishop Enrico Montalbetti who, during his three years in Trent, most likely had a decisive influence on Silvia's spiritual growth. Montalbetti, in spite of numerous resistances and misunderstandings within the Curia of Trent, exerted a considerable fascination and influence on the laity, for the way he presented his charisma as a Christian educator, as a brilliant and profound communicator, and as an insightful and effective announcer of the Gospel. He always showed a preference for the young and to teachers and their formation.

In September 1939 Silvia became a member of the commission of the section for minors, and the following month also deputy head of catechetical action. This then made her a member of the diocesan governing body of the women's youth section. In November 1940 she was appointed vice-delegate of the girls' youth.

From October 3 to 8, 1939, a meeting for the young leaders of Catholic Action took place in Loreto. In the shrine of that town in the Marche region, they venerate the little house that according to an ancient tradition belonged to the Holy Family of Nazareth, transported there from the Holy Land by a host of angels. While on her way, Silvia immediately perceived the call to something that she could not express. It provoked in her a most particular state of mind, on the one hand totally absorbed and on the other a certain restlessness. Having arrived at her destination, as soon as she had a free moment from the meeting, Silvia went to the Marian shrine, heading immediately to the dome where the Holy House is situated. Standing in front of the image of the Madonna and Child with their blackened faces and wrapped in a mantle, she was overcome by emotion and the sensation of sharing in the mystery expressed by that place. It was like a guardian of divine treasure emanating from the Word made flesh, but in the simplicity of family life:

> I knelt beside the wall blackened by the lamps. Something new and divine surrounded me, almost crushed me. I contemplated the virgin life of the three. So, Mary will have lived here – I think – Joseph will have crossed the room from there to there. The Child Jesus in their midst will have known this place for years. The walls will have resounded with his infant voice...

The fascination and attraction that that place had on her drove her to return several times, and every time she felt the same emotions and sensations very similar to those of a call, much stronger than those she had experienced until then in her spiritual journey.

The conclusion of the course included a mass at the shrine, in which the girls of Catholic Action participated with their heads covered by a white veil. Seeing the church in that way dotted with many white veils she felt a particular sensation: "It seemed to me that behind me, there would be a host of virgins following me." She didn't know yet how, but her path seemed to be marked...

After returning from Loreto, when a priest asked her how she imagined her future, Silvia expressed her intention not to get married, not to become a nun, not to remain a virgin in the world – the three typical vocations and conditions that the Catholic culture of the time attributed to women. Following that journey and experience, Silvia sensed that for her there was a fourth way in the Church, which, however, still did not seem to her to be clearly defined. She only knew that it had to do with the little house of Loreto, with the family and the hearth (focolare) of Nazareth, symbol and heart of a communitarian spirituality, which would give meaning and form to the word "unity."

Teacher in the Mountains and in the City

The end of the preparation course and the mandate from Catholic Action coincided with the end of her education. Continuing her studies was certainly what Silvia had in mind, although she realized the difficulties that this would entail for her family (her brother Gino was already attending medical school in Pavia, thanks to a scholarship at the Borromeo College).

Aiming to enroll at the Catholic University of the Sacred Heart in Milan, she counted on one of the grants made available by that university, at the Marianum women's college, but Silvia was number thirty-four out of thirty-three places available. Her distress was so great that not even her mother Luigia seemed to be able to console her. Suddenly, however, her suffering abated when she felt a mysterious voice in the depths of her soul saying: "I will be your teacher...."

Once her course of studies was completed and the prospect of attending university was lost, the path of primary school teaching seemed the most natural way to go, also in order to ensure the family of the financial support they still needed. The first position offered to her by the Department of Education was the primary school of Castello di Ossana, a town in the north-western part of the province of Trent, in the Val di Sole. The Tonale pass towered over it and it was surrounded by the great mountain ranges of the Brenta, the Presanella and the Ortles-Cevedale. The beauty of the area, now a renowned tourist destination, was indisputable, but then it was quite different from today. Ossana is about 70 kilometers away from Trent, which could be reached, very slowly, using the tramway that connected the capital to the town of Malè. The remaining 15 kilometers of dirt track had to be covered by any means of transport that could be found on the spot, often one's own legs. The social situation was common to all the mountain valleys: two hundred people living off fieldwork and livestock farming; a general economic condition based on survival, lived with dignity but without great prospects. The alternative was emigration, seasonal or permanent, in search of work.

Silvia found herself managing a class of forty-three pupils, where the theories learned at college could be applied and combined with her natural aptitude for teaching. Her principal method above all was not to leave anyone behind, which meant to follow with special attention the children who had difficulties, and not to continue with the lesson until everyone had demonstrated that they had understood.

In settings like this, the teacher, together with the parish priest and a few others, was usually an authority and a point of reference for the whole community. Silvia immediately established an excellent understanding with the local priest Fr. Francesco Marcolla, who entrusted her with the organization and leadership of Catholic Action for women. Her most attentive and faithful pupil was Elena Molignoni, who, when Silvia left Castello di Ossana at the end of the school year, was entrusted with the group of Catholic Action aspirants with the words: "If you are a saint, your children will be good." Her teacher entrusted her with a further task: to receive and sort the letters she promised to send weekly to her "disciples" of Val di Sole to continue their relationship and to continue her work of apostolate. This showed Silvia's attention to relationships and communication, which, in the years and decades that followed, would unfold in ways unimaginably greater than that first, simple exchange of letters.

The following year Silvia obtained an assignment of only two months, as a substitute teacher, in Varollo di Livo, in Val di Non. For the school year 1940-1941, marked by Italy's entry into the war, she was assigned a high position, still temporary, at the primary schools of the Opera Serafica of Cognola, on the hill of Trent. This institute, founded in 1912 and run by the Capuchin Fathers, housed a school for the basic training of orphans and underprivileged children, preparing them for work. This was a demanding job that involved long working hours, living in, and a very modest salary. As a result of her early work experience and constant contact with the pupils, her dedication to teaching, her gentle authority, and her pedagogical skills were immediately put to good use and noticed by everyone.

Inspired by the Gospel passage "Truly I tell you, just as you did it to one of the least of these who are members of my family, you did it to me" (Mt. 25:40), Silvia explained her enthusiasm for that job by saying that she saw Jesus in each of those children. The relationship with them was like that of Jesus the teacher who reveals to mankind the love of the Father.

Tertiary

The activity at the college on the hill of Trent put Silvia in contact with another lay activity: the Franciscan Third Order, linked to the Capuchin Friars Minor.

Trent has always been rich in religious families, especially the mendicant orders (the Franciscans were already present in the 1220s, during the lifetime of the founder), while the contemplative orders almost never "took root." The Benedictines were there for only a brief period between the 12th and 13th centuries and were later replaced by Dominicans. Martha and Mary, prayer and service, strong missionary commitment and intense charitable activity have always characterized the religious presence in the province of Trent. The activity of lay congregations (the so-called tertiaries) linked to the orders was equally flourishing, promoting in the people a spirituality based on the Franciscan model, the refinement of Christian perfection, the constant exercise of charity and piety, and the devotion to worship. These approaches were often quite different from those proposed by Catholic Action.

One of the episodes mentioned several times by Chiara Lubich and reported in the writings about her, and which is considered fundamental for her spiritual development and her subsequent choices, happened at the house of the Capuchins of Cognola. One of the friars asked her to offer an hour of her own day for the apostolate. Ready to do so, though somehow taken by surprise the young tertiary girl's response was: "Why only one hour? I would like to offer the whole day!"

The friar was astonished and blessed her, uttering a sentence that would remain engraved in Silvia's mind: "Remember that God loves you immensely." It was an image of God, defined in his closeness and boundless love, that at that time was not part of the theological language nor of the vocabulary of manuals and formation courses. It did not even enter the imagination of the faithful. Chiara always described that sentence as an illumination, and she called it a "thunderbolt."

Fr. Casimiro Bonetti was only a young Capuchin friar when he was called by the provincial to lead the Franciscan Third Order and to preach in Cognola, in the hill above Trent. He was originally from Perarolo, in Cadore. Because of his father's anti-fascist ideas, the family had had to wander around Italy in search for work and tranquility until they arrived in Rovereto, where they found a house near the railway station. Here their two sons Alvise and Rodolfo soon met the nearby Capuchin convent of St. Catherine, where they were looked after and educated. They decided to become followers of St. Francis, with the name of friar Casimiro and friar Gian Maria. In an interview with the "Avvenire" in 2010 Fr. Casimiro recalls:

> *I had just finished my studies* [he was ordained a priest in 1939]. *The Provincial Superior* [Fr. Bruno da Verla] *had entrusted the Franciscan Third Order to me. So I went around preaching ... that day I spoke in the orphanage in Cognola to three very young teachers. I spoke of the ideal of St. Francis, of his "fire of love." At the end I asked them what they thought about it and only one, Silvia Lubich, answered me with words that I have never forgotten: "Father, I have never heard such things. I too want this fire of love; I want to bring it into the world." I looked at her and saw her burning with the same fire.*

In the autumn of 1942 Silvia entered the Capuchin Franciscan Third Order. Inspired by the radical evangelical choice of St. Clare of Assisi, whom she admired immensely, she took the name of Clare [Chiara], with the desire to imitate her spiritual journey. On Easter night, 1211, a girl from Assisi was the first woman to join Francis' group at the Portiuncula. This was a shocking act, causing a total break from her family, the community, and the codes of conduct of her time. What the girl from Trent had experienced would, in time, prove to be similar in many ways...

The director, Fr. Casimiro, soon appointed her as novice mistress. Her charisma and example attracted many young women, to whom she gradually gave a special kind of spiritual direction, which could be summarized in one word: unity. This, too, was a term that sounded incomprehensible. It did not exist in the religious language of the time. The tension towards Christian perfection in these tertiaries was now to be directed towards the fulfilment of Jesus' prayer to the Father: "that they may all [believers] be one," modelling their life on that of the first Christian communities as described in the Acts of the Apostles and recognizing the central place of the Word of God as the universal rule of life.

Chiara's apostolate immediately attracted the attention of many young people who were fascinated by the prospect of living Christianity in a new way and with such a radical choice of life. They took every opportunity to meet up, to talk and to reflect on the Gospel. One of the places where they met most often was St. Mark's church, in the old Augustinian convent in the city center. From October 1942 "Saturday meetings" were held in the room dedicated to the Capuchin missionary Cardinal Guglielmo Massaia. After Fr. Casimiro's meditation, Chiara recounted her new "discoveries" from reading the Gospel texts and transmitted her enthusiasm to all those present. The names and faces of these first friends often recurred in the stories of the birth and growth of a community experience that, in the following years, would develop in such a way and on such a scale that none of them could have remotely imagined.

Chiara's life continued with the same commitment, teaching at the *Opera Seraphica* throughout the school year of 1942-1943. Driven by her passion for study (especially philosophy), in the academic year 1943-1944 she enrolled at the Ca' Foscari University of Venice, at the department of foreign languages and literature within the Faculty of Economics and Commerce, with the number 23305L. She did this even though it was not possible for her to attend the lectures because of the difficulties that the state of war imposed on everyone.

Part II

THE FINGER OF GOD

LIGHTING THE HOME FIRES
(FOCOLARES)

BOMBS ON THE CITY

The summer of 1943 marked a deep break in history, not only for Italy, but for the twentieth century. It was during those days that the first Anglo-American military contingents landed in Sicily, and that heavy bombings by the Allies took place on Italian cities. All this, added to the tragic experiences of three years of war already suffered by the whole country, was leading to an ever-growing discontent and a desire for return to peace and freedom. They were the days when Mussolini lost his majority to the Grand Council of Fascism and was arrested by order of the king. After that, the government was presided over by Pietro Badoglio and there was a vague hope of an imminent end to the war. Trent, at the end of July 1943, would have happily greeted the fall of the regime, and the promoters of the anti-fascist forces met together to establish a series of initiatives and projects thinking of a future of freedom and democracy. They had plans for devolution and institutional autonomy and for the reconstruction of the civic and economic social fabric.

These hopes were short-lived because of the ever-growing occupation of territory by the Nazi troops. A few weeks later, after the announcement of the armistice on September 8, the area around Trent was to be annexed (together with the provinces of Bolzano and Belluno) to the Third Reich and included in *the Alpenforland*, the zone of military operations in the foothills of the Alps. The administration of the region was entrusted to the

Nazi provincial governor of Tyrol and Voralberg, Franz Hofer. He appointed as the prefect of Trent the lawyer Adolfo de Bertolini, a person renowned for his honesty, balance, and administrative experience. De Bertolini had not compromised with Fascism and would protect the local population from the worst disasters of the war, putting up with personal discomfort and risks while making choices that made life uncertain. Citizens who were fit for military service were enlisted into three sectors of the German army, which de Bertolini managed to keep deployed close to Trent: the anti-aircraft artillery (Flak); the Trent Security Corps (military police force); and Todt, the military organization which specialized in the reconstruction of what had been destroyed by the bombs and the building of further defense structures.

During the same period the resistance movement began to get organized, as well as the first cells of CLN (Comitato Liberazione Nazionale), the national committee of liberation, in which Gino Lubich, Chiara's brother, was actively engaged. The armed resistance, which was active above all along the borders, was also working through other forms of civil and moral opposition, above all at the level of welfare assistance. It was especially the Catholic world that showed this kind of commitment through several forms of support for wandering Italian soldiers, for fighting partisans, for escaping Jews and through anti-war propaganda.

At that time, the first heavy allied bombings began over the city of Trent and along the Brenner railway line, which provided the link and enabled provisions between Germany and the Italian front. Thursday, September 2 was the first attack. At 11:45 the air raid sirens began to sound. Few people seemed to be worried since the alarm had already sounded several times without anything happening. This time however the sirens were justified. In just three minutes 19 American bombers, which had taken off from Tunisia, dropped tons of bombs over Trent. The target of the operation was the railway yard, but this was only grazed by the explosions. Almost all the bombs fell on the working-class district of the Portèla. They destroyed many houses, including the Casa Malati building (opposite the house where Chiara was born). They damaged the church of St. Mary Major, the medieval Vanga Tower and the Romanesque abbey of San Lorenzo. They totally wiped out piazza Dante. Almost 200 people died.

From that date until May 3, 1945, eighty air attacks were recorded at the administrative center of Trent, 1792 buildings damaged, and a total of more than 400 victims. From September 1943 until the end of the war, the air raid sirens sounded on 246 days, sometimes more than once a day. 10,000 tons of bombs were dropped on the railway line between Verona and Innsbruck, and 20,000 bombs on the Adige Valley alone, making Trent one of the most heavily bombed areas in the whole of Italy. The number of displaced people peaked at 22,959 on September 30, 1945.

December 7, 1943
"Give yourself completely to me"

In that period of great suffering, Chiara's vocation was becoming clearer: she was now twenty-three and she wanted to dedicate the whole of her life to God. One day her mother Luigia asked her younger children Liliana and Carla to go and get some milk, a couple of kilometers from home at a place called Madonna Bianca. Chiara realized that her little sisters wanted to get out of that task because it was very cold, so she offered to take their place. When she was passing under the Valsugana railway bridge, she heard a voice calling her with the words "Give yourself completely to me."

Struck by that inner call, Chiara wrote a letter to Fr. Casimiro, asking for permission to give herself completely to God. After a profound conversation in which he tried to identify and clarify the rationale of this young tertiary and after consulting with his fellow monks, he gave his consent, without the normal trial period. He made just one "condition," the promise not to leave Trent, so she could continue accompanying the group of girls that had been born within the Third Order (formed basically because of Chiara's commitment and witness).

Tuesday, December 7, 1943. The appointment for the private ceremony during which Chiara was to consecrate her life to God forever, was set for early that morning. Chiara's own account, where she describes her journey towards that moment, is significant:

> A storm was raging, so I had to force my way ahead pushing my umbrella in front of me. This too was not without meaning. I felt it expressed the fact that the step I was about to take would be met with obstacles. That storm and the headwinds seemed to symbolize that someone was against me. When I reached the college a completely different scenario: a huge door opened automatically. Sense of relief and of welcome almost as if it was the open-armed embrace of that God who was waiting for me.
>
> The chapel was simply decorated. At the back there was a big statue of Mary Immaculate.... Just before receiving communion, in a flash, I realized what I was about to do; my consecration to God was like crossing a bridge; the bridge collapsed behind me. I would never be able to go back into the world. I was married – I had married God. And it was that God who later revealed himself to me as abandoned. I remember that moment when I realized what I was about to do, it was quick, momentary, but a tear fell on my missal. I think I raced quickly back home. I just stopped, maybe near the bishop's house, to buy three red carnations for the crucifix that was waiting for me in my bedroom, as the sign of our common celebration.

In the days that followed Chiara reflected deeply about where the search for Christian perfection was leading her, without excluding the idea of abandoning the world altogether and entering a contemplative religious order. The conviction of her spiritual director that she had a clear aptitude for an active life and a growing internal maturity, led her to understand that total correspondence with the spirit of the Gospel can be reached in any state of life, condition, or vocation, whether religious or lay, married or consecrated to God. She understood that the real way to perfection was to do God's will, to look for, to discover, and to follow the plan of God for her. Chiara kept her act of consecration secret for a long time, even from her family. The fullness and the sacredness of that act, which took place in a hidden way and in poverty, sounded in Chiara's soul louder than the atrocity of the war that stayed in the background, almost like the "frame" of a picture.

December 7, 1943 has always been considered as the date of birth of the activities through which Chiara was to become a protagonist in the story of the Church in the twentieth century: the Focolare Movement. But certainly, on that day, Chiara had no idea of this. She had no intention of founding anything; simply that she was "marrying God." And this was everything for her.

The First Companions

With ever greater frequency and destructive power the onslaught of the powerful United States B-24 Liberator and British Lancaster bombers continued over Trent. The night skies were also lit up by the machine gun fire of Spitfires and Mustangs, the flashes of anti-aircraft guns, and searchlights. The city was torn by material and moral wounds that it had never witnessed. However, at the same time, a group of young people had drawn close to Chiara. Each one in different moments and for different reasons made it clear that they wanted to follow her way. Their names: Natalia Dallapiccola, Doriana Zamboni, Giosi Guella, Duccia Calderari, Graziella De Luca, Gisella and Ginetta Calliari, Valeria and Angelella Ronchetti, Bruna Tomasi, Marilen Holzhauser, Aletta Salizzoni, Silvana Veronesi, and many, many others. They became the first "pope"[40], as Chiara liked to call them (meaning "children" in the dialect of Trent). They came from different social backgrounds. The reality of the war made them question the meaning of life. They didn't find the answer in a rational process or in complicated ideas but found it by living the ideals of fraternity and unity proposed by the Gospel. These proposals at first sight might not seem to show great originality... but what is new lies in the way they are put into practice and lived, truly "literally" and in a radical way. And this was done in a specific historical context where they demonstrated their convictions through their example. In a conversation, Chiara and Natalia Dallapiccola used this comparison: "Just as blood carries the medicine into the whole body, even if it entered in just one point, so the Holy Spirit, through us, will take this new medicine into the whole of the mystical body."

Despite the bombings, Chiara had decided to stay in the city, so as to support those who shared in her work of apostolate and assistance to the poor and the evacuees, as well as to comply with the promise she had made at the moment of her vow. Many of her companions decided to do the same and they met together every day to help the poor and to continue reading the Gospel together, often in the darkness of the air raid shelters, with the desire to put its words into practice. They opened it randomly to see and understand what it wanted to tell them. The words of Jesus were

---

40. Pronounced *po-pay*, [pó-pe], feminine plural. The feminine singular is "popa," masculine singular, "popo," and masculine plural, "popi."

fully understood in all their depth, and they became a program for their daily life.

These words of Chiara sum up better than any narrative these moments and the depths of understanding this way of living was giving them:

> But who do we find around us at the first signs of life of our movement? The poor, those in need. I was still living at home in Via Gocciadoro. I don't remember exactly who encouraged my companions and me to launch ourselves with so much zeal towards the poor people in our city. Maybe it was the words of Jesus: "Just as you did it to one of the least of these who are members of my family, you did it to me" (Mt. 25: 40). I cannot forget the hallway in my house, it was fairly long, and it was full of everything that could be of use to them: crates of jam, tins of powdered milk, bags of flour, clothes, medicine, wood... it all came from who knows where! No doubt from God's providence.

Jesus Forsaken

During that same period and within the same context an intuition emerges that will mark Chiara's spiritual journey and will make her identify the goal of her life: the abandonment of Jesus on the cross and the participation in the fulfillment of unity asked of the Father by Jesus. In every situation of pain, of division, of deep wounds, one can recognize the face of Jesus forsaken and discover that his will, shown by his consigning his spirit into the hands of the Father, is to recompose every rift or wound.

> Happiness, discoveries, graces, conquests. Certainly this is the Gospel. But right from the start there was the understanding that everything contained also a different aspect, that the tree has

its roots... *"Unless a grain of wheat falls into the earth and dies, it remains just a single grain; but if it dies, it bears much fruit"* (Jn 12: 24). *Jesus crucified is the personification of this. Thanks to something that happened during the early months of 1944 we had a new understanding of him. Through circumstances, we heard that the greatest pain suffered by Jesus, and therefore his greatest act of love was when on the cross he experienced the abandonment of the Father: "My God, my God, why have you forsaken me?"* (Mt. 27: 46).

This was the profound mystery of the abandonment of Jesus by his heavenly Father; the sensation of the height of aridity and desolation; the sign of the greatest betrayal and total annihilation; the break-up of the intimate harmony between two persons of the Trinity...

In the history of Western thought, from the very first Aristotelian reflections and definitions, as well as in many other cultural contexts, people are defined as subjects depending on their ability to interact and dialogue, on their natural and necessary predisposition for relationships. But God too is relationship. He enters the life of a person with a word which is a question, a call that asks for an answer. And if the person moves away from these dynamics, if they withdraw, they close in on themselves and betray themselves. Jesus too in the Gospel has questions. And in the darkest and most dramatic moment of his life, all he has is a question: "My God, my God, why have you forsaken me?" He too finds himself in an unexplainable reality that he cannot comprehend by himself. But his strength lies in his relationship with the Father, a relationship in which there is room for every question, for every fragment of life; nothing is excluded, and so everything is saved. Chiara writes:

> *We were deeply touched by this. And our youth, our enthusiasm but above all the grace of God, pushed us to choose him alone, in his abandonment, as the way to achieve our ideal of love.*

> *And from that moment, it seemed to us that we were discovering his face everywhere. He who had experienced in himself the separation of people from God and from one another, and had felt the Father far from him, was recognized by us not only in all our personal sufferings which were never missing, and in those of our neighbors who were often alone, abandoned, forgotten. But we also recognized him in all the divisions, injuries, rifts, mutual indifferences, whether big or small, in family situations, among generations, between rich and poor, in the same Church at times and later between the various Churches, and later on between religions and between those who believe and those who don't have a religious belief... And he was the one to teach us how to face them, how to live them, how to work together to overcome them when, after the abandonment, he put his spirit in the hands of the Father: "Father into your hands I commend my spirit" (Lk. 23: 46). In this way he gave humanity the possibility to recompose itself and its relationship with God, showing the way. He revealed himself to be the key to unity.*

The difficulty lies in following Jesus on his way to Calvary. Only there can we know him fully. Conversion and following him in an authentic way mean destroying our worldly idols, which prevent us from recognizing him and from following the way of the poor, suffering with the marginalized, or giving up our social reputation. In the dark cellars of Trent, under the bombs – at the same time as the horrors of the extermination camps and the point of the greatest distance of humanity from God in history – they recognized this image of the abandonment of Jesus and they began to reflect on it through a spiritual intuition and a charism that had been born in that context. This cry coming from the cross threw light on the understanding that was already present in the prayer of Israel (Ps. 22), which cried out against the abandonment by God, but at the same time trusted in his promise and in the covenant, letting the relationship and the reasons for hope prevail.

That intuition of Chiara, although also present in the reflections of the great mystics and theologians of the twentieth century like Hans Urs von Balthasar, Sergei Bulgakov, Karl Barth, and Dietrich Bonhoeffer, found an outlet in the magisterium of the Church only at the end of the century and of the millennium, through the words of John Paul II in his encyclical *Salvifici doloris* (as well as in the apostolic letter *Novo millennio ineunte*):

> *One can say that these words on abandonment are born at the level of that inseparable union of the Son with the Father, and are born because the Father "laid on him the iniquity of us all" (Is. 53: 6). They also foreshadow the words of St. Paul: "For our sake he made him to be sin who knew no sin" (2 Cor. 5: 21). Together with this horrible weight, encompassing the "entire" evil of the turning away from God which is contained in sin, Christ, through the divine depth of his filial union with the Father, perceives in a humanly inexpressible way this suffering which is the separation, the rejection by the Father, the estrangement from God. But precisely through this suffering he accomplishes the Redemption, and can say as he breathes his last: "It is finished'"(Jn 19: 30).*[41]

We had to reach the end of the "short century,"[42] with all its conquests and all its horrors, in order to recognize fully that the climax of human suffering was reached in the passion of Christ, and to link this to a completely new dimension, bound to love. This is a love that creates good, even drawing it out from evil, obtaining it through suffering just as the supreme good of the redemption of the world was drawn from the cross of Christ. The cross of Christ has become a source, from which spring forth rivers of living water.

---

41. *Salvifici doloris* 18
42. As coined by Eric Hobsbawm

Stars and Tears

On May 13, 1944, following the umpteenth alarm, one of the heaviest bombardments devastated a large part of the city of Trent. There were 124 dead, almost 200 wounded. Every hour, the British and American fighters were flying low as they fired on everything that moved and then climbed straight up to disappear into the sky. They were looking for columns of German troops, but the bullets didn't recognize the uniforms and the flags, so people began moving only at night. Those who could, took refuge in the villages in the nearby mountains, in Civezzano, Pergine, Pinetano...

The Lubich house was also damaged. Luigi decided to take the family into Gocciadoro Park and the following day to head off towards Valsugana where many of their fellow citizens had taken refuge. Chiara recalls those hours spent in the open as "the night of stars and tears." The idea that distressed her most was to abandon her family. An extract from Virgil's pastoral poem, gave her light and strength:

> *From that night, lying on the ground with the others, I remember just two words: stars and tears. Stars, because as the hours passed, I saw them all move across the sky over my head; tears, because I was crying, knowing that I wouldn't be able to leave Trent with my family whom I loved so much. I could already see in my companions the movement that was being born; I couldn't abandon them. And it seemed that the Holy Spirit, to help me understand his will, was suggesting to me words I had studied at school: Omnia vincit amor,[43] love conquers everything. Could love for God overcome even this? Did I have to let my family leave alone, I who was the only one who supported them economically?*

---

43. Virgil (70 BC – 19 BC), *Eclogue* X, line 69

The following morning, she told her parents what she had decided. Luigi understood and agreed immediately. Luigia's reaction was quite different. She needed more time to process and understand that decision and that detachment (and maybe she never really did). Her father, a socialist who had many doubts about "what is of God," recognized his daughter's intentions and encouraged her; her mother, a devout believer, initially opposed that choice and couldn't really understand. Maybe this too was a sign of "unity in diversity"?

> *I did it with my father's blessing, and while they were going towards the mountains, I set off towards the bombed city. At a certain point I remember, in Corso 3 Novembre,[44] a lady who was really desperate came up to me, and taking me by the shoulders she cried out "Four of my family have died." I consoled her as best I could and I understood, with an understanding that can never be cancelled out, that from that moment on, in the place of my pain for having left my family, now I would have to carry in my heart the pain of suffering humanity. I went to look for my companions in Via San Martino among the houses and the streets, all reduced to debris. Thank God, they were all safe.*

Straight after this Chiara went towards the hospital to look for her brother Gino. He was studying medicine and was working under the direction of Dr Mario Pasi, the leader of the communist partisans of Trent. Looking at the houses reduced to ruins and the battered bodies of the victims, he whispered to her "You see? Everything is vanity of vanities."

At the end of June, Gino, together with many of his fighting companions, was captured by the Nazis and interned in the Bolzano concentration camp. It was a place of violence and absence of any kind of humanity, dominated by the S.S. torturers

---

44. A street about 500 meters from the St Vigilius Cathedral.

from Ukraine, Misha Seifert and Otto Sein, and by the German concentration camp guard Hildegard Lächert. The partisans from Trent were tried on August 2 by the German military tribunal. The military judge Werner von Fischer asked for the death penalty for all of them. Two of them were shot; the others – including Gino – were condemned to hard prison labor. Chiara had no news of her brother and fell into a deep state of hopelessness, which only disappeared when she heard he was still alive.

THE LITTLE HOUSE

Piazza Cappuccini

After her parents and her sisters had left Trent, Chiara found temporary accommodation with one of the tertiaries. Later she moved to the convent of the Our Lady of Sion sisters. In the autumn of 1944, she was offered a two-room apartment, opposite the monastery church, at no. 2 Piazza Cappuccini. Soon after, Giosi Guella moved there too. The state of the house and the decoration were poor and basic. On the wall of the dining room was a huge portrait showing the lacerated face of the dying Jesus; a reminder that they would remember the need and the commitment to share in the many material and spiritual crosses of the time of war and of every time. The other companions who lived in different parts of the city joined them whenever possible. That place began to be called "the little house":

> We were offered a little apartment in Piazza Cappuccini. *The first focolare?* We didn't know it but that was what it was. Through the war and its consequences, the things and people that had been the hopes and ideals for us young people, were disappearing... study... a family... your own house. The lesson that God was offering us was clear: everything passes, everything is vanity of vanities. At the same time the Holy Spirit was putting a question into my heart, for all of us: is there an ideal that no bomb can destroy, to which we can give the whole of ourselves? Yes, was the answer, there is. It is God. God, who is there in the midst of the war that was the fruit of hatred, God appeared to us

more than ever for what he is: love. God-Love. And we decided to make of him the ideal of our life.

The assertion of God as the only ideal that does not crumble was reinforced in the life of Chiara Lubich and her first companions. The dialogue and the relationship with God became deeper and deeper, above all through a few extracts from Scripture that were destined to become the key points of the spirituality of unity.

The birth of the Ideal

A hundred meters from the little house was "the dugout," an air-raid shelter hollowed out of a stone quarry. Chiara and her companions rushed there several times a day whenever the anti-aircraft sirens sounded. There they continued to read the Gospel by candlelight, with the echo of the explosions in the background, sometimes close by, sometimes far away. They were all words to live out with those who were near them:

> *We opened it and those words, although well known, because of the new charism were lit up as if a light had been turned on beneath them. Our hearts were set on fire and we were prompted to put them into practice immediately. I read for everyone: "Love your neighbor as yourself" (Mt. 19: 19). Your neighbor. Where was my neighbor? There, close to us, in all the people affected by the war, wounded, without clothes, homeless, hungry and thirsty. And immediately we dedicated ourselves to them.*

A new word of the Gospel gave them another principle which was to become a cornerstone of their spirituality of "sharing everything':

> *But the shelter where we were wasn't very safe. We were always being faced with death. Another question gripped me: is*

there a word of the Gospel that is particularly pleasing to God? If we were to die, we would want to have lived that one, at least in our last moments. And the Gospel reveals it: "this is my commandment: love one another as I have loved you. No one has a greater love than this: to lay down one's life for one's friends (Jn 15: 12-13). We looked straight at one another and we declared: I am ready to give my life for you, I for you, I for you… All for each one. It's a solemn pact. But if in the meantime we are not asked to die, let's live this pact by sharing everything we have among us: our few material goods, our spiritual goods, our sufferings, our joys, our trials.*

Another shelter, in a dark cellar in the historic center of Trent, was the backdrop for the latest illumination, derived from reading the Gospel: "Father, may they all be one." They realized that they were born to fulfil precisely "that page":

The war continued. One day we came together to shelter from the bombs in a dark cellar in Via Travai, with a lighted candle and the Gospel in our hands. We opened it and read: "Father … that they may all be one" (Jn 17: 21). It is the prayer of Jesus before he died. Because of the gift we have spoken of, we always had the impression that we could understand a little of those words which were difficult and challenging, and in our hearts the conviction sprung up that it was for this page that we were born, almost as a magna carta of our movement; for unity, and that means to contribute to the unity of men and women with God and with one another. In that same prayer, Jesus continued: "…may they also be in us, so that the world may believe that you have sent me." And this is what happened around us who were so united through our mutual love. People who had lost their faith started to believe again. Those with little faith started to believe more. There was a multiplication of people who changed their way of living, of conversions to God. People found the strength to follow his call that they had felt in their hearts, or to remain faithful to choices already made. After a few months, about 500 people in Trent, but also in Povo, in Martignano and other nearby places, people of every age, men and women, of every vocation, of the most varied social backgrounds, shared our ideal and formed there, in the midst of the world, a community that was similar to that of the early Christians.

Chiara and her companions negotiated their way every day through the poorest and most run-down areas of the city, carrying heavy suitcases packed with everything they had managed to put together from the goodness of people:

> I remember that because everyone was working or studying, straight after lunch each one of us set off with two heavy suitcases to visit the three poorest areas of the city: the Laste, the Portela, the Androne. It meant climbing up rickety staircases, worn away by time and mice. They were old and dangerous, in almost complete darkness, with a feeling of despair that hurt our young hearts. And maybe we entered a dark room where there was a poor man or woman in bed, with nothing. But… it was Jesus! We cleaned the room, we washed, we consoled, we made promises in the name of the all-powerful God. Once, one of us, Dori, cleaning everything, caught an infection on her face that became a huge wound. But from that moment she rejoiced; she had done everything for him, for Jesus.

Sharing their (poor) meals with the poor of Trent in the little house was another regular appointment during the day. It was linked to a more ambitious program, which defined a present and forecast a future that was strongly directed to social commitment:

> When a poor person came to our house, we chose the most beautiful tablecloth, the best plates and cutlery. When we were out on the road, each of us had a notebook and we were full of joy when we met a poor person. We approached them with great love,

and we asked for their name and address so as to be able to be of service to them always, even in the future. Yes, because for us, if the initial idea was certainly to help individual poor people, the whole thing started from a very precise program: we wanted to work together to solve the social problem of our city.

The Word of Life

Their "living exegesis" in search for the "words of eternal life" continued in their experience of divine providence. God's transcendence manifests itself in his providence, in facts and in people, as a confirmation of his relevance in everyday life and in history:

We read again: "Give, and it will be given to you" (Lk. 6: 38). We give, we keep giving and every time it comes back. We had just one apple in the house that day. We gave it to a poor man who came asking. And in the course of the morning a dozen apples arrived, maybe from one of our relatives. We gave them away too and in the evening a suitcase full of apples arrived. And it was always like that.

"Whatever you ask for in prayer with faith, you will receive" (Mt. 21: 22). We asked in prayer and we received. One day, and this is one of the first episodes that we often share, a poor man asked me for a pair of shoes size 42. Knowing that Jesus identifies himself with the poor, I went into the church of St. Clare, near the hospital of the same name, and I directed this prayer to Jesus: "Give me a pair of shoes size 42[45] for you in that poor man." When I came out of the church, a lady, Duccia Calderari

---

45. Shoe size 42 (EU) is equivalent to size 8.5 (British) or 9 (USA).

> *(a nurse and a colleague of Gino Lubich in the hospital and in the resistance) offered me a parcel. I opened it: inside a pair of shoes, size 42.*
>
> *Our hearts became alight with joy. Jesus had promised and now he keeps his promise. So, he isn't just a reality of the past, but of the present. And the Gospel is true. These verifications gave wings to the journey we had just begun. We shared with others what was happening so that when they met us, they didn't feel they were meeting a group of girls but the living Jesus.*

A spirituality was developing that seemed to be leading those young girls to keep their distance from the world, but at the same time it was increasing their awareness of the social and historical dimensions of the faith and therefore of the apostolate. They saw the poor as individual brothers and sisters, but also as a category of people. A typical objection to divine providence has always been the scenes of misery and death, of a world full of injustice, dominated by the triumph of evil and the inhuman and desperate signs of a society without God. The poor were the victims of the bombing of Trent, the people who were being deported along the railway line of the Brenner Pass, en route to the Nazi concentration camps, and who, like the pious oppressed Jew in the Old Testament, were praying and crying out: "Where is God?"

The answer to this cry and to the invocations for divine providence came from the signs of mercy, from sharing the misery and weakness of brothers and sisters. It came from the charity that opens the eyes of faith and moves hearts towards God, from the hope and the trust that God is taking care of us, from the perspective of a future that lets us resist and struggle, and frees up our energies so as to build a better world.

Chiara, who was passionate about philosophy and theology and was enrolled at the University of Venice, understood that for the development of the newly born movement there was another precise request from God: that of "putting her books in the attic." This is how she tells us about that:

> *I was hungry for the truth, I had lived in an absurd way, looking for it through the study of philosophy, when I could find it in Jesus, the incarnate truth. And I left my studies to follow Jesus .... After that choice that God asked of me, I experienced light in great abundance.*

Having put God in the first place, he became the teacher who made Chiara and her companions discover more and more all that God had created, including the intelligence of men and women, as a manifestation of the love of God. The intellectual experience – which would be resumed and cultivated in the later development of the Movement – in this way became simply one of the expressions and effects of love for God and for neighbor. So, thought developed that was rooted in life, which in turn nourished it.

This group of young people was re-evangelized by their "existential" approach to Scripture, their individual, communitarian and reciprocal experience of the apostolate, and the practice of charity, by their vision of the transience of every worldly experience, and their immersion in it, which was all intensified by the destruction caused by the war. It remodeled their relationship with God and their neighbor. It gave form and content to their "Ideal" which was going to be the polestar of their experience and existence for the future:

> *There was an ideal, only one, that would never fail, not even with our death. It was God. And it was to God that we attached ourselves with all the strength of our souls. We didn't cling to him because we had nothing left, but because a Force in us made us happy to have found him in our life as our only Everything, the only Eternal one, the only one worthy to be loved because he doesn't pass away, the only one therefore who would satisfy the*

needs and desires of our heart. Already for several years we had been receiving communion every day and we believed, because we belonged to various Catholic organizations, that we were good Christians. Only when God took everything from us, so as to give us Him alone, did we understand for the first time God's first commandment: "Love me with all your heart, with all your mind." We understood, because only then did we really feel that we had to love him in this way, with the whole of our mind, our heart and our strength so as not to be misled.

Meetings

Quite soon the little house became a reference point for many people, and not just for those from Trent. A place to share a simple meal with joy and dignity with the poor, a place of meeting and fraternal dialogue with whoever knocked at the door looking for material and spiritual comfort, or with any other kind of question. The mutual love that they tried to put into practice within those walls was the concrete translation of "For where two or three are gathered in my name, I am there among them" and it became the light to illuminate every sentence they read in the Gospel. That God, present among them, could not be questioned or destroyed, not even by death. This awareness filled them with the desire to communicate such a "treasure" to as many people as possible. Around this key element, an ever-growing community was springing up spontaneously, made up of men and women of every age, state, vocation, based on the model of the first Christian communities at the time of the apostles.

One of the many meetings that took place in the little house, destined to mark indelibly Chiara's story and that of the newly born Movement was the one with Marco Tecilla. This young electrician, who worked on the Trent-Malé railway, was frequently called upon to do some maintenance work because of the condition of the house, and so had the possibility to observe and enter bit by bit into contact with the style of life and the ideals of these girls of Piazza Cappuccini. A conversation with Chiara became decisive for his choice of life. He was won over by the enthusiasm and the conviction with which she spoke of God and about the need to be true Christians and not put away our make-up at the end of Sunday, as people do in the theatre when they come off the stage:

> *People who are actors learn their part and when it's the moment to go on stage they put on their make-up, they immerse themselves in a specific character and they play their role. When the play is over, they remove their make-up and go back to being as they were before. This is also what many Christians do: every Sunday they put on what we might call the Christian make-up, they go to mass and then, once home they remove their Christian make-up. . . . If Jesus were to come in this twentieth century, he would be Jesus twenty-four hours a day: Jesus who works, who prays, who eats, who rests …. but, always Jesus.*

That conversation made a deep impression on the young Marco: "I left the house with my soul in Paradise and I felt that, beyond the heavenly sky, God was present. My Christianity had been turned upside down."

A short time later, Marco was the first man to become a focolarino.[46]

"Now the whole group of those who believed were of one heart and soul, and no one claimed private ownership of any possessions, but everything they owned was held in common"

---

46. Focolarino (male single), focolarini (male plural), focolarina (female single) and focolarine (female plural) are consecrated men and women with vows or promises and who belong to focolare communities.

(Acts 4: 32). This led the first focolarine to live like the first Christians, to put everything in common and not to consider anything as their personal possession. This witness of fraternity attracted many of those who met the community and became an element of curiosity for many others. There were some, observing things from a political perspective, who either felt suspicion or attempted to explain everything in the light of their own ideological system. One day two young militant communists came to the door of Piazza Cappuccini. They wanted to know if what Chiara's group was achieving in the local context could be come about in the wider world, which was the mission to which these two young men wanted to dedicate all their energy. To their question as to the secret of Chiara's achievement, she pointed to the crucifix: "We are small, poor and few... but God is on our side."

That certainty summed up in Chiara's answer, apparently quite simple and the fruit of some kind of blind trust, hid an awareness and an inner predisposition that were much more complex. The desire for the Lord, the need to stay with him, are never completely satisfied and above all it is always destined in some way to open up to the other. There is no true meeting with the Lord that doesn't make even more room for the neighbor. After welcoming them back from their mission, Jesus takes his apostles to a lonely place (Mk 6: 31). He explains to them the meaning of the parables (Mk 4: 34). He takes them to Mount Tabor (Mk 9: 2). He doesn't ask them difficult questions in front of everyone (Mk 9: 28, 13: 3). The personal and intimate relationship with Jesus is made up of listening and sharing, of the revelation that the Lord makes of himself to his disciples. But that lonely place that was so isolated could be reached easily. The people knew exactly where to find them. And it was there that Jesus and his disciples were simply called to become aware of the situation, to feel the hunger of the people, to make their search for life their own. They were called to find rest, not so much in peaceful solitude, but in an inconvenient welcome of the other. This experience is called "compassion" (Mk 6: 34). The struggle that the disciples are called to live in the desert can be found in this passage in this readiness to make space for a Lord who doesn't belong to them, sharing his same passion for humanity.

We do not know how much the two communists understood or shared her answer. What is certain is that Chiara interpreted that meeting as a social challenge.

Enzo Bianchi[47] reminds us of how John Chrysostom used to warn against what's *mine* and what's *yours*. "These cold words have introduced into the world an infinite number of wars… There was a time when the poor didn't envy the rich because there weren't any poor since everything was held in common."

Food, a tangible symbol of what is essential for living, is such when it is shared. Completely abandoning the concept of almsgiving and elevating the concept of charity to the maximum degree of authenticity, Chiara asked each person to "give every month whatever they could afford, without harming themselves and their proper needs. . . .Everyone brought their surplus, above all in money and each one took on a commitment to give a specific monthly amount. The donor and the promised amount remained a secret."

Giosi Guella and Marco Tecilla had the task of recording all the needs in a notebook, how much had been received and how to manage the funds. Already in the first month thirty needy families received a dignified lodging and support. Full communion with God was desired for the others as much as one's own. In this way, the image of Jesus who is present in the bread, became real, but he is recognized when there is the breaking of the bread…

---

47. Enzo Bianchi founded the ecumenical monastic Bose Community in Italy in 1965.

CHIARA AND THE FATHER BISHOP

Protocol

The complexity of customs and the norms of protocol at the basis of institutional relationships, the language developed over centuries from a vast patrimony of signs, symbols, and gestures defined the way of speaking to a bishop with the title *Most Reverend* and addressing him as *Your Excellency*.

According to the practice that developed during the twentieth century (especially after the Second Vatican Council), the expression with which one speaks to the bishops of different Christian denominations is often simply: Father.

In the thick file of documents regarding the many years of the close relationship with the Archbishop of Trent, Carlo de Ferrari, (put together in minute detail and published by Lucia Abignente in the book *Here is the finger of God*[48]), it may seem peculiar, especially to those of us who now are used to less formal titles, to see that Chiara Lubich uses both addresses, calling him "Most Reverend Excellency, our Father."

---

48. Shortly to be published by New City, UK.

The first doubts ...

Straight after the war, the presence of the new-born movement in Trent had stirred up interest, curiosity, and some concern in the local ecclesial authorities. There was the group of the Franciscan Third Order who met together in the church of San Marco and the community who lived together in Piazza Cappuccini. There were also the groups of girls who every day walked through the streets and the alleys in the center and in the outskirts of the city, carrying huge suitcases packed with every kind of food for the poor people who lived in the most destitute areas... Their presence was easily noticed in a small city, where social life was based on "the quiet life," accustomed to centuries of ecclesial government, and where news circulates with discretion, but also with great speed. And the news that was spreading from the shops to the sitting rooms, from the oratories to the sacristies, gave rise to questions that often showed a misunderstanding of what was happening.

Already in February 1945, while the war was still raging there was a memo on the archbishop's desk, scrupulously prepared by some of the leaders of Catholic Action in Trent, expressing their concerns because of the presence and the activities of these young people. They were concerned about groups of lay people speaking about and reflecting independently on the Gospel. They were puzzled by young women who lived together and put their goods in common, independently of Catholic Action. They used the word "love" a lot, at a time when this was mainly linked to secular vocabulary and worldly environments, rather than to theological terminology and pastoral practice, where what prevailed was the word *charity*, often used in the sense of "almsgiving." They had a mysticism that was detached from the spirituality and practices of traditional devotion. All this was sufficient to bring up the questions and the suspicions that were spreading around the town in two words that in those days were considered the most serious and dangerous deviations within a society that was organized in a Christian (or rather a Roman Catholic) way: Protestants and communists.

The immediate result of all these voices and prejudices was that Chiara and her companions wanted to meet their bishop as soon as possible, so as to emphasize first and foremost their desire to be in communion with and at the service of the local and universal Church. They also wanted to ask for his opinion and his advice regarding their ideas, their style of life, and their plans to organize themselves as a movement.

Here were all the conditions for a first meeting. We don't know the precise date, except that it was during 1946.

Bishop Carlo

After the death of Celestino Endrici, Carlo de Ferrari was appointed Archbishop of Trent on April 12, 1944. He entered the diocese on June 26, the solemn feast day of St. Vigilius, the patron saint of Trent.

He was born in Prato allo Stelvio, near the border with Switzerland. His father's family was originally from Val di Sole near Trent. His mother, Pauline Prantner, was from South Tyrol. When he was thirteen, Carlo entered the congregation of the Stigmatines.[49] In 1906 he made his solemn religious profession and was ordained a priest in 1909. He then was entrusted with

---

49. The Congregation of the Sacred Stigmata (or Stigmatines for short) are a Catholic Clerical Religious Congregation founded in 1816 by Fr. Gaspar Bertoni in Verona, Italy.

various roles in the houses, the schools and the colleges of the congregation, showing a special talent for the work of educating young people. After getting a degree in Canon Law in 1923 he became a consultant of the Sacred Congregation of the Council (now renamed as the Congregation for the Clergy) and lived in Rome from 1919 to 1932. He then spent a period in Udine as the director of the Bertoni College and in January 1936 he was consecrated bishop by Pope Pius Xl in the diocese of Carpi, where, with its solid socialist and anticlerical tradition, Fascism had barely scratched the surface. It had a culture with its own repercussions in the ecclesial world, with some completely new pastoral experiences. They were the years when, in the parish of St. Giacomo Roncole di Mirandola, the community founded by Fr. Zino Saltini was taking its first steps. It was trying to live according to a style inspired by the Acts of the Apostles, and after the war it took the name of Nomadelfia.[50] The bishop, despite criticisms from those with political power as well as those in ecclesial circles, understood it and defended its charism and intuition, giving it his blessing.

A decisive element for his nomination to guide the archdiocese of Trent was most likely the appreciation that the Fascist regime had for him. He was considered a man of order (on some occasions he had approved the heavy-handedness of the police of the regime). He was patriotic and loyal. In Rome he oversaw the spiritual formation of the Balilla,[51] with a strong pastoral sensitivity and a marked cordiality. This was quite different from the intransigence and independence that was shown during the twenty years of Celestino Endrici and most of his clergy. In Trent,

---

50. Nomadelfia (based on Greek meaning "where fraternity is law") is a Catholic community of families and lay unmarried people who adopt a lifestyle of brotherhood inspired by the first Christian community.
51. The Balilla was a Fascist paramilitary youth movement in the time of Benito Mussolini.

many people would have liked a bishop who was the expression of the local Church. The name of the auxiliary bishop and diocesan administrator, Oreste Rauzi, was being mentioned. He was considered a worthy successor to the bishop who had died and would have continued in the same pastoral direction. The nomination of de Ferrari provoked a lot of unease in the clergy and in the local Catholic world, including some objections that were more or less explicit.

His first years as bishop were determined by the events of the war and by a lot of activities organized by the Church in support of the people. At the level of diocesan leadership, de Ferrari did not alter the organizational set-up, nor did he bring about changes (as was obviously desired by the representatives of the Fascist regime) compared with the era of Endrici. As far as organizing the laity was concerned, he relied on the plans and the structures that were already in place, especially Catholic Action. Certainly, his behavior wasn't generically right wing and "conservative" as one historian has tried to emphasize by presenting only a partial picture of the person of de Ferrari. In his first letter to the diocese, in June 1941, one gets a glimpse of a new pastoral approach. "We need to courageously revamp certain systems which don't stand up to modern day dynamics; we need to bring fresh air into our sacristies and presbyteries... I would dare to say, hoping it wouldn't be misunderstood, that a little bit of the twentieth century could enter also among the resources of the apostolate."

Soon after this, the diocese that was entrusted to him saw one of the first manifestations of the "Springtime of the Spirit" in the life of the Church of the twentieth century. The protagonists were the young people around Chiara Lubich, who were ready to live the Gospel in all its purity in faithfulness to the Church and to their bishop.

The diocesan territory included the zone known today as "Trentino," with Italian as its language and culture and which extended north into the territory of the present-day province of Bolzano, with a population that is German-speaking and which was organized into ten deaneries. This organization, strongly characterized by its ethnic and linguistic elements, constituted an extremely delicate factor for the internal equilibrium and for the organization of the pastoral activities especially during the Nazi period. De Ferrari showed little support for the politics of occupation. He tried to work with the prefect of Trent, de Bertolini, for the good and the safety of the civil population, and on various occasions he didn't fail to make it obvious that he disagreed with some of the decisions of the provincial governor Franz Hofer.

After the end of the conflict he promoted and supported the pacification process for the good of the people, the effort for reconstruction and the activity of the anti-fascist forces, most of which was an expression of the Catholic world. He tried to establish a future of freedom and democracy, with a traditional eye on decentralization and autonomy for the area of Trent and for the reconstitution of civic and economic life. He dedicated himself to the reanimation of the pastoral care and the spiritual life within the territory, guaranteeing his presence in the parishes that were furthest away. He organized the repair of the churches that had been damaged and the construction of new places of worship, schools and oratories, all the while supporting the vocations of priests and lay people, missionary activities, and the work of the religious orders.

As said in a recent essay by Luigi Bressan, the retired Archbishop of Trent: "One of the great merits of Carlo de Ferrari was that of ensuring that a climate of diligent relaxation should prevail, in which the spiritual richness of the various charisms could flower."

The period after the war

The years in which these events took place corresponded to the period in which Trent was going through profound changes in the aftermath of the Second World War. There was the effort to rebuild everything that had been destroyed, and the first steps were being taken towards setting up autonomous regional structures, while maintaining strong links with the models of social and religious organization which had characterized previous decades. The benefits of establishing an autonomous administrative set-up were still not being felt everywhere and, above all in the mountain valleys, there was a predominance of underdeveloped economic conditions and a high level of emigration. The political debate was polarized on how to implement the agreement between the Italian prime minister De Gasperi[52] and the Austrian minister Gruber, which had been signed on September 5, 1946 at the Peace Conference in Paris, and on the interpretation of the norms proposed to define the form of self-government of Alto Adige, regarding the safeguarding of the rights and desires of the German-speaking minority.

The position of the Church in Trent, with a diocesan territory that covered most of Alto Adige, and with the pastoral care of ten German-speaking deaneries, was particularly delicate. The bishop had the moral responsibility to guarantee the safeguarding of the minorities and the inter-ethnic peace. However, he was confronted on a daily basis with political tensions which risked spilling over into the pastoral dimension, so much so that from

---

52. De Gasperi (1881-1954) was an Italian statesman who founded Italy's post-WW2 Christian Democracy party and served as Prime Minister of Italy from 1945 to 1953. As a leading anti-fascist in the 1920's, he was arrested and imprisoned by Mussolini. Following his release, he worked in the Vatican library until the fall of Fascism in 1943.

several sides came the proposal to redefine the boundaries of the dioceses of Trent and that of Bressanone to make them coincide with their respective provinces.

In his timely book called *Viaggio in Italia* (Journey through Italy) Guido Piovene gave a description of the area of Trent during those years. He portrayed it, maybe a bit one-sidedly, in its economic aspects and in the key moments of both its recent and remote history. For the social and political aspects, this writer from Vicenza emphasized the power of the Catholic movement, guided by a clergy that was "influential, innovative in politics (republican in the elections), rigid concerning principles of faith and moral conduct, educating an army of lay people to become active in public life and political action." At the headquarters of Catholic Action he had a long conversation with Bishop Alfonso Cesconi (the same one who had followed Chiara Lubich in her role as propagandist of Catholic Action) with whom he spoke about the social reforms of the local Church, about the concern of the clergy with regard to the education of the laity and about the cooperative movement, which was the main model on which the economy of the province was based. From his observations and from his meeting with the priest, the writer drew this conclusion about the province:

> *It's a kingdom of small properties, of poor autonomous local councils, often centralized in the priest. The way of life is archaic with few desires; almost no ambition for distractions that could be called modern. Their vision is limited to their work in the fields, mass on Sundays and simple entertainment to the music of the accordion. In them there is a mixture of devout obedience and a stubborn attachment to economic independence; each one king in their own poor homes. Therefore, here you have the best conditions for small ownership, which in fact works well here, anchored as it is in discipline to rural banking associations, cooperatives and social meeting places.*

This observation, while not giving the whole picture, still gives us a substantially truthful image of the region of Trent, with a Catholic world constituting the main social component and expressing the prevailing political structure, with Catholic Action that – as Severino Vareschi[53] wrote – was "a movement and an institution, the summit and the base, the knot that linked the ecclesial and the social, ideology and politics, propaganda and devotion and, last but not least, provided for the gathering of the economic resources."

The model for the Church, developed theologically and codified at a canonical level in that period, was described in Pius XII's encyclical *Mystici Corporis*, published on June 29, 1943. This document brought together all the themes of ecclesiology present in the tradition of the Church and the various ideas developed during the previous century. In it, Pope Pacelli described the spiritual and visible relationships that unite men and women to the Incarnate Word, offering a dogmatic and theological synthesis that two decades later, would be the main platform for the Council debate and for the constitution *Lumen gentium*. Drawing from the primary sources of Scripture, represented by the letters of St. Paul, and of theology, represented by the *Summa* of St. Thomas, it confirmed the teaching that all Christians are closely united to Christ like the members of a single body. The concept and image of the Church as the mystical body of Christ became well established. In it, Christ is the infinite source of grace and the symbol of unity, like the vine that feeds all its branches. The document caused great excitement in ecclesiological research, revisiting topics such as tradition and apostolic succession, and hitherto neglected topics such as the relationship between Church and sacrifice, Church and Trinity, the biblical images of the Church (such as that of the "people of God'), the laity and

---

53. An Italian priest-historian.

the royal priesthood of the faithful, the ecclesiology of other Christian denominations, the relationship between Church and history and between Church and Mary.

Theological reflections were developing on the role of the laity in the Church, no longer limited to the function of executors in society of the will of the hierarchy, but carrying their own specific vocations and contributing to an ecclesiology which, until then, had relegated them to positions of spiritual subordination and merely (and often mediocre) executive tasks. The suggestions coming from French thought (in particular Jacques Maritain's "Integral Humanism," published in 1936) contributed to define the action of the laity in the spiritual sphere, identified as members of the mystical body, projected towards the goal of eternal life, responsible for their own actions that engage the credibility of the Church. In addition, Christian lay persons, as citizens and acting according to Christian values, are as such fully responsible for the life of the earthly city and of the world. They also participate in and are responsible for areas where the spiritual and temporal spheres converge, such as the vision and construction of the family or the principles and practices of education, where they can also commit themselves on behalf of the Church.

These elaborations on the features and the role of the laity and the autonomy of the earthly realities, as well as the teachings of *Mystici Corporis* (which changed the perspective of the roles within the Church, valuing the different charisms and the participation of the baptized in the mystical body, inserting them on an equal level in the mission indicated by Christ), constituted the breeding ground on which, in those post-war years, many seeds would be sown, generating a spiritual ferment which, shortly afterwards, would flourish in various ways.

The First Meeting and the Finger of God

This was the context in which the meeting between Archbishop de Ferrari and Chiara Lubich took place. Chiara described that moment, which was to mark her future and that of the Movement that was born from her intuition, in the following terms:

> *A word of the Gospel struck us in a special way: "Whoever listens to you (the apostles) listens to me" (Lk. 10: 16). We wanted to put it into practice straight away. We went to introduce ourselves to our archbishop, Carlo de Ferrari. He is a successor of the apostles. He listened, smiled, and said, "Here is the finger of God," and this approval, and his blessing accompanied us ever after, until his death. This first approval from the ecclesial authority had a double effect: it assured us that the light that we followed and continued to follow was authentic, authentically Christian, and it made us accelerate our race ahead.*

That first informal and fatherly approval expresses the deepest and truest aspect of the person of de Ferrari, as does the importance of the trust that he showed in the new-born movement. This trust kept growing despite continuing hostility. The spreading of the movement increased suspicion and opposition from Catholic Action and with a good number of the clergy as well. Some families were alarmed by the fear of losing their daughters to "those focolares" where they would have lived in poverty, offering almost everything "to Jesus in the poor." But even when many demonstrated their hostility to the Movement and were deaf to its message, but quick to criticize, the bishop always defended those young people and saw that their way of life was in harmony with his vision of the Church. That first meeting, just like the story that followed, was a clear sign of communion between the hierarchy and a charism, which was to prove authentically and mysteriously fruitful. With their shared desire that the development of the Movement should be well grafted one word the tree of the Church, the archbishop and Chiara showed in a practical way what ecclesial communion is about. They both demonstrated that they knew how to live the sentence of the Gospel "Those who abide in me and I in them bear much fruit" (Jn 15: 5).

As Lucia Abignente explained, the relationship of Chiara with her bishop from the beginning was based on "respect, obedience, but also simplicity, trust, the blind trust of a daughter... The father protects, safeguards, educates and corrects, forgives and plays down if he sees repentance; he consoles and jokes when he sees that is what's needed. When one is sure of fatherly love, it is natural to express oneself fearlessly, in a sincere and authentic way and... with boldness *(parresia)*. You do not consider whether you are just a child, a young person or an adult: you speak as a daughter and this is what counts."

ORGANIZING UNITY

Focolare and Catholic Action

Looking at the ecclesial dimension of the Focolare Movement and the circumstances of its birth, we can compare it to the great lay movement in Italy at the time: Catholic Action.

The focolare idea of "living" the Gospel and, in particular, the last prayer of Jesus "that they may all be one...," was revolutionary for its time. It was a reading of the Gospel without the use of commentaries even before Chiara had had any contact with the Evangelical or Reformed Churches. This was in contrast with the more prudent approach of Catholic Action, whose contact with Scripture was usually mediated by the presence and interpretation of a priest. Catholic Action also made constant reference to the Ten Commandments (with particular attention to the Sixth and Ninth...), the Catechism of Pius X, and the constitutions of the Council of Trent. Equally problematic was the Movement's vision of the Church, which it saw as communion rather than hierarchy (while fully respecting the latter), not always in line with the ecclesiology of the Council of Trent and Vatican I.

The Catholic Church in Italy was still very much concerned with Church-State relations, so a lay charism, feminine in origin, and not part of Catholic Action or any of the Third Orders, aroused a certain amount of suspicion. The Movement also practiced the communion of goods, "give and it will be given to you," and encouraged the laity to take an active role in the community without being under the direct control of the hierarchy. The model was one of "weekday holiness," which sprang from everyday life lived in simplicity and poverty. Rather than following the classic examples of sanctity, Chiara and her followers saw themselves as Christians whose function was to be "yeast in the dough."

It was a vision of Christianity based very much on St. Paul's description of the Church in his letter to the Corinthians: like a body, with each part of that body having a special function or, as in the Letter to Diognetus,[54] Christians are like "strangers in their own land." Living in this way, lay people began to make a difference in society. In later years, this way of living the Gospel led to the growth of a dialogue with Christians of other traditions and then with members of other faiths. It was all based on the desire to build genuine relationships with everyone.

We have to imagine how all this was taking place in a "Tridentine Church" (the adjective is both geographical and historical-ecclesial) of the 1940s. Ever since 1475, when the local Jewish community had been accused of the "ritual murder" of a child found dead near the ghetto, Jews had been persecuted. Up until 1960 there was an annual procession in Trent with the instruments of the (alleged) martyrdom of little boy Simon (declared blessed by popular piety) by the "perfidious Jews." This basic anti-protestant ecclesial culture dated from the time of the Council of Trent, but had seen a resurgence in the first decade of the 20th century, at the beginning of the episcopate of Celestino Endrici, with the anti-modernist battle and the political struggle against the Pan-German forces of the *Tiroler Volksbund*.[55]

Compared to other organizations of the period, the nascent Focolare Movement's structure was light and fairly "fluid." This

---

54. Letter to Diognetus is an early Christian apologetic work probably dating from the 2nd or 3rd century AD.
55. The *Tiroler Volksbund* was a Pan-German association founded in 1905 and dedicated to the idea that Tyrol should remain united. It promoted an anti-Italian program of Germanization in the region.

enabled it to be a "leaven" within the Christian community and in civil society.

The confusion at the doctrinal and organizational level, of which the first focolarine were accused, more or less openly, should rather be understood as "con-fusion" – "fusing together." This does not mean that it was chaotic, rather that it was building a whole network of people linked by the presence of Jesus in the midst. Again, it was completely different from the structures of Catholic Action, which clearly opposed first Fascism, and then Communism, and all the forces in society opposed to Christianity. Catholic Action's model was strongly inclusive: all the faithful should belong to the association.

Let's not forget that Catholic Action, especially through the organization of the Civic Committees[56] created by Luigi Gedda, was the main instrument of control and intervention of the Church in the political world. It saw the unity of the Catholic world around the Christian Democrat Party and was inspired by the principle, coined and applied by St. Robert Bellarmine, of the *potestas indirecta ecclesiae in temporalibus* (the indirect power of the Church in temporary matters). Catholic Action presented itself as a monolith, but it was not monolithic. There were plenty of tensions and anxieties within it, which sometimes imploded and filtered through to the outside.

Criticisms of Gedda's vision came particularly from the youth and the more culturally committed branches of CA (Catholic Action), which referred to the person and leadership of Giuseppe Lazzati. There were strong protests in 1952 and 1954 with the resignation of the presidents of the Italian Youth of Catholic Action

---

56. With the blessing of Pope Pius XII, Gedda established "Civic Committees" in some 18,000 parishes to support the Christian Democrat Party during the 1948 election and after.

(the GIAC[57]) Carlo Carretto and Mario Rossi. This last episode had some traumatic repercussions also at the local level. On April 28, the diocesan council, whose leadership was strongly linked to De Gasperi's vision of politics, had approved a document that was extremely critical of the positions taken by President Gedda. It accused him of "skepticism towards the democratic regime" and of sympathy for the right wing, anti-communist political forces. The response from Rome was immediate and drastic: President Flaminio Piccoli and the ecclesial assistant Alfonso Cesconi were removed from office and expelled from the association. The crisis was tackled by Bishop de Ferrari with the prudence and wisdom that distinguished him and with Manzoni's[58] tried and tested technique of "soothing and keeping silent"... Everything was resolved peacefully, so much so that during the following years the two leaders remained in place in Trent.

In comparison with the Focolare Movement, it makes one reflect on how the Church of those years (institutional and doctrinal) was often[59] not conceived in a positive way as the body of Christ, but as the fruit of opposition to "adversaries," with many "antibodies"...

At various levels there was a real need for renewal and reform: in the models of Christian life, in pastoral care, in the approach to theological reflection and in the function of the Magisterium, which aimed essentially at denouncing doctrinal errors and defending Christian truth.

---

57. GIAC (Gioventù Italiana dell'Azione Cattolica – Italian Youth of Catholic Action) was a national Catholic youth organisation built around local parish groups. It was established under the authority of Pope Pius IX in 1867.
58. Alessandro Manzoni (1785–1873) was an Italian poet, novelist, and philosopher. He is famous for the novel *The Betrothed* (*I promessi sposi*), generally ranked among the masterpieces of world literature.
59. The result of opposition of "adversaries" (of many antibodies), rather than something intentionally thought out in a positive way as the body of Christ.

Towards the First Statute

The fervor with which Chiara and her companions wanted to announce the ideal of Jesus forsaken and of unity led them, immediately after the war, to expand further in the city of Trent, and later in nearby Rovereto and in the neighboring valleys.

Without the nightmare of the bombing and having returned to a relatively normal life, the cornerstones of their spirituality were subjected to new tests, but also to important confirmations. Scripture continued to be the foundation: "We felt we had to be the Word, that we had only meaning by being the Word." The absolute centrality of the word of God in their lives confirmed the absence, equally absolute, of other plans and intentions: "We wanted to be Christians and that was all. The challenge to live the Gospel stimulated us to a coherence of life not yet experienced in such a radical way."

The only reference to a "formalization" of their commitment in the period immediately after the war can be seen in the Regulations of the Congregation of the Franciscan Third Order of the Capuchins of Trent of 1946. It speaks of "young tertiary women divided into groups, called "units," because every tertiary woman in her group not only had to strive for Christian perfection, but also to fulfill Jesus' prayer to his Father "that all believers may be one." The description of the aims of these groups said: "the units are modelled on the life of the first Christians so that the units together form the 'Franciscan community," which should be a perfect example of the first Christian community as described in the Acts of the Apostles."

In the early days of 1947, a specific encounter would mark the beginning of the expansion of Chiara's ideal well beyond the borders of Trent.

In those days Chiara read booklets written by the Conventual Franciscan Leon Veuthey, a scholar of asceticism and mysticism, in which the term "unity" was given prominence. These booklets carried the imprimatur of the Bishop of Assisi, the Benedictine Joseph Placido Nicolini, who came from Trent.

Struck by the contents of those writings, in which she heard an echo of some of the key words of her own mission, Chiara decided to go to Rome to meet the author.

At that time Fr. Veuthey, together with some confrères and a laywoman, Pauline Morani, had given life to the Crusade of Charity, set up to be "the soul of all religious and social associations aimed at the good and happiness of humanity." It was to be a place where everybody could unite "preserving their special purpose, in the common effort for the search for truth in charity, in order to achieve perfect unity."

The personal resonance and the heartfelt sharing of spirit between Chiara and the work of the Swiss Franciscan was immediate. Their frequent meetings and discussions and immediate collaboration changed the name of the "Crusade of Charity" into the "Crusade of Unity." One of their initiatives was the "Monthly Word": a passage from Scripture with a commentary saying how it could be lived. It was distributed as widely as possible to all men and women of good will, primarily lay people, to anyone who showed an interest in living their faith in this way.

This became known as the Word of Life and it continues to be at the basis of the life of the Focolare today.

The collaboration with Fr. Veuthey also considered the prospect of a fusion between the movement in Trent gathered around Chiara Lubich and the Crusade, which had its driving force in Assisi.

Archbishop de Ferrari, in all probability in agreement with Br. Placido Nicolini in the birthplace of St. Francis, encouraged collaboration, but urged Chiara and her followers to better define the identity and aims of their experience, summarizing them in a statute to be examined by the diocese. This document, made up of 27 articles, obtained episcopal approval ad annum (i.e. in need of confirmation), registered by the chancellery on May 1 with the title of "Statute of the Focolare of Charity (Apostles of Unity)."

Their purpose as described in art. 2: "the promotion in the world of charity, the center of the Gospel which finds its most perfect expression in unity." The prime movers in this mission were the small communities, composed of three to seven women, dedicated to the evangelical ideal of unity with God and with their brothers and sisters, and to its diffusion.

The association was recognized officially by the Church, as a "Secular Institute," as set out in the apostolic constitution *Provida Mater Ecclesia*, issued in that very year by Pope Pius XII.

With this, albeit provisional, canonical recognition, the term "focolare" was born more or less spontaneously. It identified the small community that had arisen in Piazza Cappuccini, Trent, and progressively entered the common lexicon to identify its spirit and organizational methods. Now, in some way, it was institutionalized.

The term, "Secular Institute" was never supported by Chiara Lubich. It was probably the fruit of various ideas and contributions, first of all from Fr. Veuthey, in order to give it a place in the theological world and from the Bishop of Trent in order to insert it in a juridical and pastoral context. However, these ideas and contributions aimed at summing up the meaning of an experience that sprang from the warmth and the light given off by God's love for humanity, and prompted it to spread and radiate its energy in the world through charity. It represented the apostolic ardor shown by Chiara and her companions from the beginning of their adventure, to take the Trinity as a dynamic model, as a constant source of love to spread like a fire in the world.

The spirit of the focolare had officially entered into the Church; it was both human and mystical...

Forty-eight

The forty-eighth year of the last few centuries has gone down as particularly significant for humanity, marked with various crises and traumatic events.

In the Middle Ages, the Black Plague pandemic reached its climax in 1348, halving the European population and triggering the crisis of traditional conceptions of humanity and the universe. The sense of fear and death shook the certainties of faith and humanity's relationship with God. The Diet of Augsburg of 1548 was a fundamental stage in the definitive division of Europe between the Catholic and Protestant worlds, providing legal and institutional confirmation to the schism within Christianity three decades earlier. In 1648 the Peace of Westphalia put an end to the Thirty Years' War, with the ultimate fragmentation of the Holy Roman Empire and the application of the political principles of the modern sovereign nation state. In 1748 Montesquieu published *De l'esprit des lois* (The Spirit of the Laws), a synthesis of the legal theories underlying modern law and institutions, which defined the fundamental rules to which people and societies are subjected, denying any form of absolute power. 1848 is universally recognized as the "springtime of the peoples," the cause of the revolutionary uprisings that shook Europe with the intention of overthrowing the absolute governments born of the Restoration[60] and replacing them with liberal regimes, bearers

---

60. The restoration of the dynasties in Europe after the fall of Napoleon.

of the values born with the French Revolution. Their impact on European societies and cultures was so profound as to generate, at least in Italian, the expression "do a forty-eight" as a symbol of sudden disruption and subversion of any order.

On December 10, 1948, the Universal Declaration of Human Rights promoted by the United Nations Organization was signed in Paris. It was the new Magna Carta of planetary coexistence, of human freedoms and rights, of ethical foundations of the new international law. In India Mahatma Gandhi, a protagonist in the struggle for decolonization and the affirmation of justice and peace, was assassinated. Following complex international mediation and a controversial UN resolution, the State of Israel was born.

In Germany, occupied by the Allied forces, the "Berlin blockade" by the Soviet Union began, an antechamber of the Cold War that for forty years would see the USA, the USSR, and the nations within their respective spheres of influence, facing each other politically, diplomatically and ideologically. In the same year, the United States of America implemented the Marshall Plan with economic aid to the countries of Western Europe, still prostrated by the aftereffects of the war, while strengthening its political influence over the whole area. The congress of the European Movement, meeting in The Hague, promoted the birth of a "European assembly" and some political initiatives were put forward aimed at founding the first supranational institutions. On May 5 of the following year the Treaty of London would establish the Council of Europe, based in Strasbourg and with the aim of fostering an ever closer union among its members and protecting and promoting the ideals and principles on which the rule of law and democracy are based.

In Italy, the democratic forces that took part in the anti-fascist struggle worked together to provide the new-born republic with a constitution, which came into force on January 1, 1948. The principles of freedom and democracy, the secularity of the State and religious freedom, human and social rights and the duties of the citizen, were defined by the experience of people who had suffered under the dictatorship and had already paid the price for the defense of the values they included in the Constitutional Charter[61]. The soul of the constitution was that of tormented seekers, often divided by completely different ideological beliefs and political positions, who looked for common denominators in the name of democracy and the common good. On April 18, the political elections resulted in a win for the centrist coalition led by Alcide De Gasperi, protagonist of the post-war reconstruction and of the reforms that led Italy to full recognition in the context of Western democracies. The Church of Pius XII, who only in 1944 had recognized democracy as the preferred form of government, and the fear of Communism, were De Gasperi's great allies in this process.

And Chiara Lubich? For her as well as for the nascent Movement, 1948 was a particularly busy year with complex and, at times, painful events, which can only be interpreted through the understanding of the cross as a necessary way to fully understand the resurrection.

In the first few months of the year, Trent's civil society was fully occupied with the political elections set for April 18 within an atmosphere of political polarization. All the components of the Catholic world were involved and mobilized, the ecclesial hierarchy and all the "associated" realities concentrated their appeals and organizational efforts on achieving the maximum consensus around the Christian Democrat Party and to counter with all means the forces and propaganda of the social-communist coalition, whose possible victory was considered to be disastrous for any hope of building a Christian society. The situation and the general "climate" led to a heated debate and extraordinarily strong tensions in Italian society. The appeals for support and the

---

61. Constitution of the Italian Republic (1947).

threats of excommunications induced by the directives of Pius XII were certainly far removed from the sensitivity and charism of the young teacher in Trent and her followers. However, their commitment was not lacking, alongside all the forces of Trent's Catholicism, first and foremost Catholic Action, to help their candidates to win.

A SPECIAL GUEST

At the beginning of April of that year, the community in Piazza Cappuccini was, unwittingly, involved in an extremely complex and thorny affair, linked to one of the most dramatic and bloody passages in the history of the German occupation of Rome during the war, and to the political and judicial drama that followed after the liberation and the end of the conflict.

Two women got out of a car in front of the "little house." The elder of the two spoke to Chiara, saying she came in the name of the Bishop of Assisi, Placido Nicolini. The purpose of the visit was the request to host the other woman, an extremely attractive girl in her twenties, with long, jet black hair. The request concealed an extremely delicate situation, organized by the lady, Elena Hoehn Alvino. The young woman was Celeste Di Porto, a young Jew from the ghetto of Rome, accused of having been an informer and Fascist collaborator and of having had several members of her community arrested in 1944. For this she—nicknamed the "black panther"—was tried and condemned after the war. Following the amnesty, she was released. Elena Hoehn, herself of German origin, wife of the Neapolitan businessman Luigi Alvino and very much part of Roman high society, had met Di Porto at the time of her detention, had become her confidante, had supported her materially and followed her conversion to Catholicism.

The request for hospitality in Trent was the result of a suggestion by Nicolini, who knew Chiara through Fr. Veuthey. They wanted somewhere safe and secluded, to protect the girl from any possible attempts of revenge against her. The operation, willingly accepted by the focolarine in order to comply with the desire to live the Gospel in charity and organized with all the discretion that the case suggested, was, however, unsuccessful, due to the guest's lack of reserve and prudence. A few too many, albeit always accompanied, walks in the city center, her attractiveness, not properly concealed by inconspicuous clothing and hairstyles, a few loud jokes that betrayed an accent that was not exactly local, led to the young woman being recognized. Posters even appeared in the city with explicit references to her person. In that climate, exacerbated by the political confrontation, her stay at the focolare was no longer possible, and the girl moved away from Trent, finding hospitality elsewhere.

However, the bond between the focolarine and Hoehn and her husband, who would soon become Chiara's mentors in the capital, remained strong. And so Elena was nicknamed "Frate Jacopa," inspired by Jacopa de' Settesoli, the noble Roman follower of St. Francis and the first Franciscan tertiary, who helped the poor man of Assisi during his stay in Rome.

Charges and defenses

On May 1 that year, Archbishop de Ferrari confirmed the statutes of the Focolare of Charity for the following three years. In those very days, however, "formal accusations" were presented to the prelate against those responsible for the Movement. The accuser was a "former distinguished member from among the first apostles of the Focolare Movement" and now a little antagonistic to Lubich, followed by two others. Chiara and Fr. Casimiro were accused of "spiritual despotism and terrorism"; for one the charge was "presumption" and for the other "abuse of confession," and both were accused of lacking clarity in the administration of property. Added to this were the constant misunderstandings with Catholic Action and the anxiety of some families about their daughters' choice to leave home to live in community.

As these accusations surfaced after the elections and after the Church and the Catholic movement had been reaffirmed in their position and authority, the accusations could be construed as having been brought about by a "plot" coordinated by various factions and not just by a single person, and might even have been related to the issues with Catholic Action. Moreover, these accusations were brought not just to the archbishop but to Pope Pius XII as well, , with the strategy that the problem would have been solved, albeit negatively, by invoking the principle "Roma locuta, causa finita" (once Rome has spoken, the issue is closed).

The suffering of that period was lived spiritually in the light of the passion of Jesus forsaken, the perfect expression of God's merciful love, and summarized in the choice of the Word of Life for that month of July, taken from the passage in the letter to the Hebrews (9: 22) which reads "without the shedding of blood there is no forgiveness of sins...."

Where two or three are gathered...

In Chiara's diary of this period, these problematic and painful pages are superimposed on others that describe her renewed commitment and enthusiasm for spreading the Ideal also outside the confines of the city of Trent.

At that time a small community had formed in Rovereto, twenty kilometers south of Trent, entrusted to Valeria Ronchetti, one of Chiara's first companions. Violetta Sartori describes the make-up of the group which included:

> the head of the telephone company, a maths teacher, a shoemaker, a watchmaker, a dad and a mum, boys and girls. There were so many of us and we really loved one another. Every time we met as a community, we tried to make a new commitment to live the Gospel, to change our lives and to care for the needy around us.

The group met in the house where Antonio Rosmini was born, and one of the Rosminian priests, Clemente Rebora, safeguarded the group with authoritative, caring, and discreet spiritual assistance. He welcomed them and shared their ideal "that all may be one," and the vision of a world united in love.

Rosmini's ideas fit in very well with the spirituality of the nascent Focolare Movement: a burning love for the Church, a passion for spreading the Gospel and the wisdom that emanates from it.

After a short period of rest in Ortisei, South Tyrol, as guests of some friends, the apostolic zeal of Chiara and the focolarine began again with vigor, aiming to spread beyond the diocesan and regional borders. Their message spread with surprising speed in Veneto, Lombardy, Piedmont and, after an adventurous voyage in the hold of a ship a few months later, the girls even reached Sardinia.

In the autumn Marco Tecilla and Livio Fauri, both tertiary Franciscans, opened the first men's focolare. Reading the passage of Matthew (19: 29) "And everyone who has left houses or brothers or sisters or father or mother or children or fields, for my name's sake, will receive a hundredfold, and will inherit eternal life," they decided to leave everything and dedicate themselves, body and soul, to spreading the Ideal, going to live in a room made available by the Agostini family in 13 Via Antonio da Trento. They had brought only two mattresses, a stove they had made themselves and a wardrobe donated by Chiara. When they went to the house of the archbishop to ask permission to establish a focolare, they were seriously questioned about their motives and referred to the Apostolic Constitution *Provida Mater Ecclesia*, according to which, a community should consist of at least three members. They answered calmly that if their choice was not judged to be in accordance with God's plan, they would return to their homes. The audience closed with this sentence from the archbishop: "Go ahead; in the meantime, I will be the third one!"

Prospects of unity

The plethora of personal contacts and letters, writings, ideas and suggestions that animated Chiara's life and activities during this period brought her into contact with the Austrian Franciscan Fr. Beda Hernegger, who, in 1934 in Ljubljana, together with the prelate Johannes Kalán and with the approval of Pius XI, founded the *Regnum Christi* Movement. Fr. Hernegger was also the author of a successful book *Katholische Solidarität! Ein Ruf zur Einheit und Gemeinschaft* (Catholic Solidarity: a call to unity and the Christian community), published in Vienna in 1948 and immediately translated into Italian.

This movement, which already had thousands of adherents among religious and lay people, sought to oppose the process of de-Christianization and the spiritual malaise that was gripping the contemporary world. Its aim was to stir the conscience of the Catholic world about the need to promote Christian universalism and collaborative unity among the communities. The first meeting with Fr. Beda took place in Trent, with a positive response from the archbishop. He suggested a "fusion" of the two works, in order to better promote and spread the ideal of unity in Italy and in the world, also in virtue of the already vast ramification of *Regnum Christi*, in particular through the three Franciscan congregations and their respective Third Orders. The two movements had much in common and there was a strong desire to join forces. It now seemed right to shift the center of gravity of the Focolare Movement's activity from Trent to the heart of Western Christianity, that is, the city of Rome.

The time had come for the discernment expressed by the evangelist Luke (12: 56-57) and to act accordingly: one had to judge the *kairos* (the right moment of opportunity). Unity is shown through fidelity to God's commandment: "Choose life so that you and your descendants may live, loving the Lord your God, obeying him, and holding fast to him" (Deut. 30: 19-20).

IN THE ETERNAL CITY

Friend Foco

On September 12, 1948, Chiara, accompanied by Livio Fauri, went to Rome (passing through Assisi) to meet Fr. Veuthey, Fr. Herregger and Fr. Casimiro who were engaged in spiritual exercises in Bagnoregio. These representatives of the three Franciscan religious families who, in the course of history, had not always lived the spirit of their founder in harmony and communion, met with Chiara to set out a common strategy on the path towards unity.

On September 17, through the mediation of a young friend from Tivoli, Argia Papini, Chiara and the three friars were received in Montecitorio by the Christian Democrat MP Igino Giordani. The official reason for the meeting was the request for help in finding an apartment in Rome.

The conversation turned out to be of a different kind, destined to become a fundamental moment in the history and destiny of the Movement. The meeting lasted about a quarter of an hour, from which Giordani said that he came out transformed. He was struck primarily by the pure evangelical passion that emanated from the words of this young woman from Trent. He was also taken by the coherence and concreteness of her ideas, anchored in the message of Christ.

Giordani, then fifty-four years old, was married and a father of four children. He was a lay Christian committed to politics in those years of renewed participation in the reconstruction of "the common home." He had already been a protagonist in the intense and contrasting experience of Fr. Sturzi's[62] popularism in the early 1920s. He had endured the fatigue and suffering of opposition to Fascism and moral and cultural resistance to the regime. He was now experiencing the enthusiasm and the tension linked to the return to democracy and post-war reconstruction.

He was a multifaceted intellectual, scholar of patristics and ecclesial history, essayist, journalist, and official at the Vatican Library, where he founded the prestigious school of library science. Since 1929 he had been a columnist of *L'Osservatore Romano* and editor of *Fides*, the monthly magazine of the Pontifical Work for the Preservation of the Faith, which he took over in 1932.

Giordani was a forerunner of the ecumenical movement, opening the dialogue with what he already then called "separated brethren," with the invitation to seek "what unites rather than what divides." His writings were always characterized by a broad cultural breadth, by perspectives and sources that were never restricted or provincial, always open to the international panorama and debate. The Fathers of the Church constituted his preferred field of study, with essays and critical translations of the works of Justin, Tertullian, Clement of Rome, Cyprian, John Chrysostom, and the Greek apologists at the time of the first Councils.

The Vatican library and newspapers were culturally cosmopolitan and stimulating, especially when compared to the cloak of obtuse and violent nationalism that oppressed Fascist Italy. They offered him access to extremely varied and authoritative sources of information, as well as cultivating a series of contacts and friendships with important people including Fr.

---

62. Fr. Luigi Sturzo was an Italian Roman Catholic priest and prominent politician. He was known as a "clerical socialist" and is considered one of the fathers of the Christian democratic platform. He was also the founder of the Luigi Sturzo Institute in 1951.

Agostino Gemelli, Romolo Murri, Giuseppe De Luca, Piero Bargellini, Giovanni Papini, Alberto Moravia and Ezra Pound.[63] His acquaintance with leading figures in the Vatican diplomatic arena and the Catholic political world (at the time in secret), were equally distinguished. He knew Cardinal Eugenio Pacelli, Bishop Giovanni Battista Montini, Alcide De Gasperi, Giorgio La Pira, Guido Gonella, Giuseppe Spataro and many others. In the second half of the thirties he wrote some important books: *The Social Message of Jesus, The Social Message of Christianity, The Protestant Crisis and Unity of the Church*. In 1942 he published *Le encicliche sociali dei papi da Pio IX a Pio XII* (The Social Encyclicals of the Popes from Pius IX to Pius XII).

In occupied Rome, Giordani worked on the preparation for and constitution of a party of Christian inspiration and, after the liberation of June 1944, he became editor of the new Catholic Action newspaper *Il Quotidiano*, with the aim of guiding Italian Catholics to a political culture that had freedom and democracy as its founding principles.

In 1946 he was elected to the Constituent Assembly of the Christian Democrat Party, participating in the work of that great collective test of political maturity and democratic culture that led to the drafting of the Constitutional Charter. He was re-elected to parliament in April 1948. As Stefano Trinchese put it, in the course of his political and parliamentary activity in those years, Giordani "in the era of opposing blocs and Catholic anti-Communism represented within the broad spectrum of the Catholic party, the evangelical soul, open to dialogue and contradiction, neither conformist nor aligned, certainly a minority." He distinguished himself in the debate on peace issues where he showed dissatisfaction with the treatment of Italy in the postwar treaties and expressed the fear that the Atlantic Pact would

---

63. These were eminent poets, writers, film critics, newspaper and journal editors.

become an instrument of war. His political matrix was deeply rooted in Sturzian popularism. However, it did not prevent him from trying to follow and synthesize the most advanced currents of European Catholicism, before all else the French one. His concept of politics was strongly internalized. He could not give a definition of democracy without a qualifying adjective. And that adjective would be one defined by Christian Humanism and contrary to any principle that referred to Machiavelli's ideas. His was a Christianity that saw politics as "victorious vulnerability," because – Giordani wrote in 1949 – "a sea of hope and an ocean of charity are needed to drown the selfishness of the world," as well as the courage of a Catherine of Siena, who wrote to the powerful of the world to remind them that cities were not their property.

The meeting with Chiara in September 1948 deeply affected Giordani. He wrote: "I felt something new, an unusual timbre in that voice... Holiness within everyone's reach." He was so impressed that he was diverted more and more from his dedication to politics. He had always felt the importance of the role and appreciation of the Catholic laity which, not without a good dose of irony, he called "the proletariat of the Church." In his writings and by his example he had always pointed the laity towards the goals of faith and to a courageous witness, taking on a new spiritual dignity, and developed the idea, as described by Tommaso Sorgi, his main biographer, of a "secular-church," which in some way anticipated and promoted some of the issues faced by the Second Vatican Council.

Chiara often gave a "new" name to her friends. This was intended as a way of recognizing and indicating the "true self" of each one. She often recognized in a person certain abilities and attitudes yet unknown to the legitimate owner. The enthusiasm and the immediate adhesion of Igino Giordani to the Ideal and the presence of the Holy Spirit in his life, earned him the nickname of "Foco" (fire).

This is how Chiara relates her meeting with Giordani in 1948, in a 1981 interview with Jean-Claude Darrigaud:

> Giordani had been waiting all his life for some kind of road to open up for him regarding that desire that was eating away at his soul, of total consecration to God despite his married state. He had tried so hard, but he certainly did not think that meeting a Movement that had just been born in Italy after the war meant anything to him. On the contrary, he was very wary of some people who at that time seemed to have some solutions for the rebirth of Italy, and he had waited two years before accepting the meeting with me....
>
> ...Giordani welcomed us, but, as he said, more because he saw in the new interlocutors possible voters than for anything else. I don't remember what he said as soon as he saw us. I, forgetting completely why we had made that visit, found myself briefly explaining the little story of our Movement, which made a great impression on him, as he himself narrates in an autobiographical page.
>
> As we were leaving, he accompanied us. He approached me, asking me to write down what I had said. It was a way for him to keep in touch. Later I realized who I'd met. He wrote to me: "Thoughts like his, so rich in doctrine of wisdom and fire, I didn't believe they existed on earth." God had prepared him all his life to encounter the charism of unity. And what came then were personal or group meetings that matured an unexpected development of the Movement.

At the threshold of St. Peter's

Chiara fully understood and shared the spiritual harmony expressed by Giordani. She responded to his invitation to draw up a summary of the contents of their conversation at Montecitorio. This was then published in the October issue of the magazine of religious culture *Fides*, published in the Vatican, with the title "The Christian Community." This started the long journey of the expansion of the spirituality of unity and the development of the Movement in the Eternal City. It was a journey that also wished to gain full recognition by the Holy See. It was not easy to graft the Movement into the old strain of the Catholic movement as a whole, recently restructured by Bishop Montini around a renewed Catholic Action. There were hypotheses and vague prospects of merging with Fr. Veuthey's *Crusade of Unity* and with Fr. Hernegger's *Regnum Christi* movement. The initial attitude of Cardinal Marchetti Selvaggiani[64] was not to create new movements, but to limit them to "preaching and above all living the Gospel." The prudent patience of de Ferrari, who took it upon himself to watch over the Focolare Movement, had separated it from the Franciscan Third Order.

Chiara, accompanied by Giosi Guella, Ada Schweitzer and Graziella De Luca were initially housed with Luigi Alvino and his wife Elena Hoehn, who made available to the focolarine an apartment in Via Giovanni Battista de Rossi. Thus, the first Roman focolare, was opened. The following year it moved to the Garbatella district.

The important social and business relationships of the Alvino family in the Rome of that time and the enthusiastic support of Giordani in many political and ecclesial environments enabled Chiara to move in circles of the capital that would otherwise have been precluded to a young woman from the provinces. Unfamiliar

---

64. At that time, head of the Vatican's Supreme Sacred Congregation of the Holy Office whose role was to spread sound Catholic doctrine and defend those points of Christian tradition which seem in danger because of new and unacceptable doctrines.

with the opulence and seats of power in Rome, she was eager only to announce and spread the message of unity, the Gospel lived as a solution to every individual and social problem. For her it was a completely new adventure to be received in the salons of the "black nobility"[65], by aristocratic families who counted popes and cardinals in their genealogies. Among these, she gained the respect of the Marquise Elisabetta Pacelli Rossignani, sister of Pope Pius XII. Many of these people were still not completely resigned to the outcome of the reunification of Italy. They struggled to accept the end of the temporal power of the popes and the status of capital of the Kingdom (first) and of the Republic (later) conferred on the city of Rome. They were frightened that Communism might take over Italy. Listening to Chiara's speeches, some were struck, sometimes positively, sometimes less so, by references to Scripture to direct one's life to God and to the service of the other, living in poverty. Some followed, others meditated, others reported...

Outside these restricted and exclusive circles, the opportunities for meetings multiplied rapidly in religious institutes and colleges pontifical universities, parishes, lay associations, and chance meetings in the street or in bars.

Chiara writes:

> Faith and love, which God lived in us, brought us in contact with all those who he made us meet every day and this love drew them spontaneously and freely to the same ideal. We never thought of doing apostolate. We did not like this word. Someone had abused it, defaced it. We only wanted to love in order to love God. And we soon realized that this was the true apostolate

---

65. The black nobility were Roman aristocratic families which remained faithful to the Papacy after the unification of Italy and the subsequent conquest of the Papal States (including the city of Rome) by the Kingdom of Italy. Many members of the Black Nobility held high offices in the ranks of the papal administration.

> *There were seven, fifteen, one hundred, five hundred, one thousand, three thousand and more people of every vocation, of every condition. Every day they multiplied around Jesus among us. Our humanity, put on the cross by the life of unity, attracted everyone....*
>
> *There is the* porro unum necessarium[66] *(the one thing necessary) of the soul in its relationship with God. There is also the* porro unum necessarium *of the soul in its relationship with its neighbors and this is loving them as oneself until they are consumed in one down here, waiting for the perfect consummation of souls in the One, Jesus, in heaven. This is the Christian community.*

Focolarino and (future) priest

Among the many meetings of this period, of special importance for Chiara and the history of the Movement was the one with the young Pasquale Foresi. He was born in 1929 in Livorno into a devout Christian family. His father Palmiro had founded the Christian Democrats in Pistoia during the wartime clandestine period. In 1946 he was elected and participated in the work of the Constituent Assembly and continued as a member of Parliament during the first and second post-war governments.

Pasquale, educated in a Catholic environment, felt from a young age the need to combine the Gospel and life. After the surrender of the Fascist government on September 8, 1943 and the subsequent Nazi invasion he took part in the Resistance, working in various partisan divisions in Tuscany, Lazio, Abruzzo and

---

66. See Lk. 10: 42.

– following the stages of liberation – in Northern Italy. No one in his family knew anything about his activities and his destiny until after April 25, 1945.

After the war, he felt a vocation to the priesthood and attended the seminary in Pistoia and then the Collegio Capranica in Rome for a few years, until he had a crisis of faith.

Intellectually brilliant and with a restless spirit, Pasquale was in constant search of something more. He wanted a "more" that took shape in the encounter with the "apostles" of the Movement, Antonio Petrilli and Graziella De Luca, through his father's friendship with Igino Giordani. Immediately afterwards he also wanted to meet Chiara. He describes his feelings in his own words:

> *Opening my missal and reading the passage of the precious pearl, for which the rich merchant sells everything he owns, I understood that it was worth selling everything, selling intellectualism, criticisms, the goods of this earth, a career, also selling one's reputation, since at that time some people looked at this movement with suspicion and distrust. Everything was worth selling, in order to buy this precious pearl that we had found: Christ living in a community of people. . . .*
>
> *I noted, in the people of the Movement, an absolute faith in the Church and at the same time a radical evangelical life. So, I understood that this was my place and soon the idea of the priesthood reappeared.*

Pasquale recognized in the first steps taken by Chiara Lubich and her companions "an evangelical spring that had risen up in the Church." Thus began a relationship that would last almost sixty years, which would lead him to finish his studies and become a priest (in 1954, incardinated in the diocese of Trent) and to make a fundamental contribution to the development of the Movement. He became responsible for organizing theological and cultural initiatives and establishing and maintaining some important relationships within and outside the Church. Like Igino Giordani, he is considered a co-founder of the Movement. He too was soon given a "focolarino new name." He became "Chiaretto," to underline the function of confrère attributed to him by Lubich.

As Maria Voce[67] writes: "In the case of the founders of great spiritual movements it has been noted that God often places, alongside the original depositaries of the charism, people who perform a very important function in relation to its historical configuration." Pasquale Foresi always embodied this very important role "helping to translate into concrete terms the insights and motions that the Holy Spirit was gradually stirring up in her... creating fundamental dimensions of the charism of unity in the field of thought and culture, of its juridical system, of its formational structures, its editorial activity, and much more..."

The intensity with which she had lived that first period in the Eternal City, and the tiredness generated by all the difficulties that arose, never made Chiara and her people lose the most authentic and genuine basis and purpose of their spirituality. The Word of Life addressed to the community of Rome in June 1949 read: "We can be one only at the condition of each one being another Jesus: another living expression of the Word of God."

---

67. Maria Voce took over the presidency of the Focolare Movement after the death of Chiara Lubich.

PARADISE '49

ON EARTH AS IT IS IN HEAVEN: MYSTICISM AND PROPHECY

In June 1949, returning from a period of very intense, tiring and sometimes painful activity, Chiara, Giosi Guella, Graziella De Luca, and Livio Fauri left for a period of rest in the mountains. They went to the region of Trent, in the remote and pleasant Dolomite valley of Primiero. The focolarina Lia Brunet, originally from that place, put a small chalet at the disposal of the young people, in the village of Tonadico.

In that very special place, in full harmony with uncontaminated nature, a horizon dominated by the intense green of the forests and pastures, by the bright grey of the limestone of the *Pale di San Martino*, by the crystalline blue of the sky, it seemed that God opened to her – and, through her, to the small body of the nascent movement – the full understanding of the charism of unity and the work that would be born from it.

Chiara described this experience as an "entrance into heaven, into the bosom of the Father." Through grace, she was able to contemplate the secrets of heaven and the vision of all uncreated and created reality.

Chiara gave this experience the name Paradise '49. She would write later about those months:

> *If 1943 was the year the Movement started, 1949 marked a leap forward. Unthinkable circumstances, but foreseen by*

Providence, caused the first group of members of the Movement to withdraw from the "world" in the mountains, to rest. We had to withdraw from people, but we could not distance ourselves from that way of life, which was the reason for our existence. A small, rustic mountain lodge housed us in poverty.

We were alone: alone among ourselves with our great ideal lived moment by moment, with Jesus in the Eucharist, the bond of unity, from which we drew every day; alone in rest, prayer, and meditation. And there began a period of special graces. We had the impression that the Lord opened to the eyes of the soul the kingdom of God, which was among us, the Trinity who dwells in a cell of the mystical body: "Holy Father, keep in your name those you have given me, that they may be one, like us." We seemed to understand that the movement being born would be nothing less than a mystical presence of Mary in the Church. Of course, we would not have come down from that mountain, that little Tabor of our soul, had God's will been different. And it was only the love for Jesus crucified and forsaken, who lives in humanity immersed in darkness, that gave us the courage.

In that place and at that moment in history, God introduced a "charism" into the world. It was a gift conveyed through the Holy Spirit, to help humanity understand in a new and original way the mystery of God and trinitarian love. Chiara was called to welcome these gifts for all of humanity, and for the rest of her life she would be called to transmit them in their absolute genuineness.

The Pact of unity

The small community, gathered in the Primiero valley, began to increase in number. Among the first to flock there was Igino Giordani, who was to become co-protagonist of that experience.

The Focolare Movement remembers July 16, 1949 as the day on which Chiara and Foco made a "pact of unity," which was the basis of Chiara's mystical experience and all that would happen afterwards. Her narrative describes the climate and features of that moment, a prelude to the spiritual events she was to experience shortly afterwards and for the duration of that summer:

We were living these experiences when Foco came to the mountains.

Throughout his life Foco, who had a deep love for St. Catherine, had sought a virgin he could follow. And now he had the impression of having found her among us. One day, therefore, he suggested something: to make a vow of obedience to me, believing that in doing so he would be obeying God. He added that like this we could become saints as did St. Francis de Sales and St. Jane de Chantal.

I did not understand at that moment either the reason for obedience or this two-person unity. The Movement did not yet exist and there was not much talk among us of vows. And I did not understand a two-person unity because I felt called to live "that they may all be one."

At the same time, however, it seemed to me that Foco was moved by a grace that ought not be lost.

And so I said something like this to him: "It may really be that what you feel comes from God. So we ought to consider it. I, though, don't feel this two-person unity because all should be one."

And I added: "You know my life: I am nothing. I want to live, indeed, like Jesus Forsaken, who annihilated himself completely. You too are nothing because you live in the same way.

"So then, we will go to church tomorrow and I will say to Jesus-Eucharist who will come into my heart, as into an empty chalice: 'On the nothingness of me may you seal a pact of unity

with Jesus-Eucharist in Foco's heart. And, Jesus, bring about between us the bond which is known to you.'" Then I added: "And you, Foco, do the same."

Giordani became Chiara's interlocutor and her support. He was the first "interpreter" of what she contemplated. In one of their dialogues Chiara recounted the illuminations she had just had and Foco made a presentation and a "translation" of it. Foco's hermeneutics allowed Chiara to see and understand things with greater clarity and lucidity. The "sapiential" understanding of what his young friend contemplated certainly came from his vast knowledge of the sources of Christianity and of the history of the Church. It came from his awareness of the need to apply reason and free will to understand what was revealed by God. It came from his vision of reality within a cosmic and providential perspective of the human person vis-a-vis itself, the heavenly Father, time, and eternity. But it was also the fruit of grace working in that particular place and time, where and when the soul shares in the divine nature and receives a spirit as adopted children with the right to inherit eternal life (Rom. 8: 15-17).

Both of them, in different ways, were enlightened by grace which elevates human faculties to beyond the natural order and makes the intellect capable of intuiting the divine essence and of understanding revelation, what Dante described as "the light that conditions him to see" (Dante Alighieri, Paradiso 14, 48).

This original dynamic was the keystone for the implementation of unity. Their pact, (progressively extended to the other companions) which allowed the contemplation of the absolute, took on an ecclesial dimension. They were experiencing the Church as the living body of Christ in history. Thanks to that pact of unity, the first focolarine also became participants in those mystical events, and Chiara called this group "Soul." It was a new experience of collective spirituality that would become the basis for the foundation of a new work in the Church.

Chiara's soul gradually became aware of God's plan, which called her to begin this work. Now she could say, writing to her bishop: "I see all that will be."

Many years later, recalling that experience of "nothingness" in mutual love summarized in the pact of 1949, she wrote:

> *The Father begets the Son out of love: coming completely out of himself, so to speak, he, in a certain way, becomes "non-being" out of love; but that is precisely how he is the Father. The Son, in his turn, as an echo of the Father, returns out of love for the Father, he too, in a certain way, becomes "non-being" out of love, and that is precisely how he is the Son; the Holy Spirit, who is the mutual love between Father and Son, their bond of unity, also becomes "non-being" out of love. He becomes that non-being, that "void of love," in which Father and Son meet and are one: but that is precisely how he is, Holy Spirit. If we consider the Son in the Father, then we must think of the Son as nothing (a nothingness of Love) in order to think of God-One. And if we consider the Father in the Son, we must think of the Father as nothing (a nothingness of Love) in order to think of God-One. There are three Persons of the most Holy Trinity, and yet they are One because Love is and is not at the same time.*

"Insane, who hopes our reason may explore, which hold three persons in one substance knit" (Dante Alighieri, Purgatorio 3, 34-36). The trinitarian mystery, the most complex dogma and the one least comprehensible to human reason, assumed new consistency and evidence in the light of that experience. Just as the biblical episode (Gen. 18: 1-3) of Abraham, who with his wife Sara welcomed three guests at the oaks of Mamre and provided for their feeding, was interpreted by St. Augustine in a trinitarian sense ("tres vidit, unum adoravit"), so the pact of 1949 and the spirituality of unity took on a trinitarian dimension, a paradigm of a new mysticism and a new sociality. Being in Jesus puts everyone in a trinitarian relationship with the others, in the trinitarian life of love.

Perspective '49

At the end of that summer Chiara left Primiero and the paradise she had experienced there with a clear vision of God's plan and the awareness that it had inspired her to begin a new work within the Church. Before returning to Rome, she asked for a special blessing from Archbishop de Ferrari, writing: "I see all that will be... Jesus brought this movement to birth, and in his Church he will preserve it from all human infiltration, confirm it, and extend it wherever the Church is." The vision was specific: its boundaries were those of the world and its face that of all of humanity. Both elements needed unity with God.

In the following months, and much more so in the years that followed, when she returned to Rome, Chiara consulted many authors and masters of Christian mysticism, as if she wanted to measure her experience with the tradition of the Church, seeking to discern what was present in the illuminations she had received and "bring out of her treasure what is new and what is old" (see Mt. 13: 52). To the knowledge of the mystical experiences of Francis and Clare of Assisi she would add the comparison of the encounters and intimacy with God of Catherine of Siena, Angela of Foligno, Teresa of Avila, John of the Cross, Therese of Lisieux and others.

Having kept the lived Gospel as her only reference for a long time, Chiara now felt the need for this relationship with the saints of "nothingness and everything." They were capable of expressing this relationship of the creature with God better than any treatise on theology, without the "nothingness" ending up as annihilation or depersonalization, but leaving the whole space to God. The object and intermediary of this relationship was Jesus, in his person, in his love, in his redeeming passion, who united all the mysteries of faith: unity in the Trinity, creation and salvation, Mary and the Church, the universal call to holiness, charity as the only love of God and neighbor. Chiara was now part of this tradition of the theology of the cross, which had been present in Christianity, especially since the late Middle Ages, with its emphasis and orientation on two fundamental elements: Jesus forsaken and unity. The solution of human contradictions was recognized in the mysterious depth of abandonment, of being in nothingness. In the "why have you forsaken me?" Jesus addressed to the Father, all the deepest questions of humanity were condensed, and at the same time they became perfection of love and response. The mystery of redemption passed through Jesus' mystical body, capable of taking on the sins of its own members, that is, of all men and women, so that they might receive his grace. Sin turned out to be a lack of unity with God and with neighbor, healed by Jesus forsaken, capable of giving us his unity of love with the Father in the Holy Spirit. The presence of Jesus in the midst among those who live in unity ("For where two or three are gathered in my name, I am there among them." [Mt. 18: 20]) also became an element of attraction for all those not united because of sin.

One of the most dense but representative spiritual writings of the experience lived during that summer and of what it would mean for the future, is dated September 20, 1949:

> *I have only one Spouse on earth: Jesus Forsaken; I have no other God but him. In him is the whole of Paradise with the Trinity and the whole of the earth with Humanity.*
>
> *Therefore what is his is mine, and nothing else.*
>
> *And his is universal Suffering, and therefore mine.*
>
> *I will go through the world seeking him in every instant of my life.*
>
> *What hurts me is mine.*
>
> *Mine the suffering that grazes me in the present. Mine the suffering of the souls beside me (that is my Jesus). Mine all that is not peace, joy, beautiful, lovable, serene… in a word: what is not Paradise. Because I too have my Paradise, but it is that in my*

Spouse's heart. I know no other. So it will be for the years I have left: athirst for suffering, for anguish, for despair, for sadness, for separation, for exile, for forsakenness, for torment, for... all that is him, and he is Sin, Hell.

In this way I will dry up the waters of tribulation in many hearts nearby and, through communion with my almighty Spouse, far away.

I will pass like Fire that consumes all that must fall and leaves standing only the Truth.

But it is necessary to be like him: to be him in the present moment of life.

Her friend Eli Folonari, commenting this passage many years later, testified how Chiara's main anxiety had been to show Jesus forsaken that his suffering had not been in vain:

Yes, it has brought about the redemption of humanity, but Chiara wanted to show him that it is possible to live already today, in every situation as redeemed, as fulfilled Christians. And this means to let the orphan find the Father again, the abandoned woman a support, the distressed friend a true friend, the lonely person a safe companion, the doubtful the truth... and one could go on endlessly.

The above-mentioned relationship, during this period, with the writings and the thought of the "saints of the ineffable" led Chiara to write a great deal. Some of the writings were published in a relatively short time (some will be referred to in the following pages); others remained unpublished for many years and have been the object of study only in the last years of the author's life. In the first group there was a short passage entitled *The Church*, written in 1950. Fabio Ciardi describes this text as:

a hymn to the Church captured in its charismatic dimension, a dimension that the ecclesiology manuals of the time ignore, limiting themselves to dealing with the Magisterium and the sacraments. In this passage Chiara sees the Church as a succession of charisms, almost a "Christ unfolded through the centuries," a living, incarnate Gospel, which is brought into existence above all through the flourishing of religious orders.

Chiara describes the Church as "a magnificent garden in which all the Words of God flourish... As water is crystalized into tiny stars of every shape when it falls upon the earth as snow, so in Jesus Love ... .took on various forms and these are the Orders and the Religious Families.. . ." and that each one is a "ray of the order that is God, a light of the light that is Jesus." That image of the winter snowfall was a prelude to the springtime of the Church which was germinating in many ecclesial circles and in numerous spirits and intellects capable of reading the *Zeitgeist* and the signs of the times, and which was to unfold a decade later with the Second Vatican Council, "made of grace" which would mark a point of no return for the Church and the world.

The experience of Paradise "49 contains and summarizes the foundations of the spirituality of the Movement, constantly meditatively reconsidered and reinterpreted by the founder, by many members of the Movement and many lay scholars. It is a point of reference and a sort of polar star to decipher God's plan for her work, to understand its meanings, its ends, and developments.

The contents of that mystical experience lived by Chiara in the Dolomites represent the hermeneutical key to everything that would happen afterwards, both in terms of the elaboration and diffusion of a spirituality with strong new features, and in terms of concreteness, from the organization of the Movement to initiatives in the ecclesial, social, cultural, ecumenical, and interreligious fields.

The analysis and interpretation, with varying degrees of depth, of the contents of that founding moment would occupy Chiara herself, the focolarini, and many minds, both spiritually and intellectually for many years. A spiritual and intellectual effort for the theological understanding, also in a historical perspective, of the charism of unity that would live a particularly intense period after more than forty years since that summer of 1949. In 1990, in fulfilment of Chiara's wish, the Abba School, a group of experts from the most diverse geographical, cultural, confessional, and religious backgrounds, began to meet. The task of this team was to analyze the mystical experience of 1949 in the light of their respective disciplinary and scientific fields, theological research, and the various branches of secular thought. In later years this activity and approach was also taken up by the Sophia University Institute in the little town of Loppiano. Of these we will speak in the following chapters.

Part III

A DIFFICULT JOURNEY

ENCOUNTERS AND CHALLENGES

Unity in the Era of Divisions

From Stettin in the Baltic to Trieste in the Adriatic an "iron curtain" has descended across the Continent. Behind that line lie all the capitals of the ancient states of Central and Eastern Europe. Warsaw, Berlin, Prague, Vienna, Budapest, Belgrade, Bucharest and Sofia, all these famous cities and the populations around them lie in what I must call the Soviet sphere, and all are subject in one form or another, not only to Soviet influence but to a very high and, in some cases, increasing measure of control from Moscow.

This quote is from Winston Churchill's famous speech given March 5, 1946 at the Westminster College, Fulton, Missouri, in the presence of the president of the United States of America Harry Truman. Two days later the Italian translation of the entire speech appeared on the first page of *L'Osservatore Romano*. The phrase *iron curtain* very quickly became part of history and a symbol of the Cold War that for more than forty years would divide Europe and a large part of the world into two opposing political and military blocs, one under the influence of the United States and the other under the control of the Soviet Union. On one side the western democracies, and on the other the countries ruled by communist ideology and socialism.

In April 1949, twelve western countries, including Italy, formed the Atlantic Pact, which was the precursor of the NATO military alliance. Their main rival, the Soviet Union, responded quickly with a similar initiative: the Warsaw Pact, which was aimed at defending itself and extending its own influence beyond the geopolitical boundaries established at the peace conference in 1945. The Korean War (1950-1953) which followed, and the exacerbation of tensions in international relations in the Far East intensified the Cold War and the climate of tension around the world.

That political situation affected human life on various levels, reaching deep into its most intimate existential and spiritual spheres. During that period any speech that referred to unity would have been considered absurd. However, at that historic juncture which was dominated and threatened by the nuclear risk that constituted an "apocalyptic ridge" (an image that Thomas Merton and Giorgio La Pira conjured up), humanity had to choose between global destruction and a millennial peace, between the disappearance of the human family and the flourishing of a civilization dedicated to universal brotherhood. Isaiah's parable that "they shall beat their swords into ploughshares, and their spears into pruning hooks; nation shall not lift up sword against nation, neither shall they learn war any more" (Is. 2: 4), represented the hope of a planetary convergence to build a world of peace, which the prophet placed "in the last days" (Is. 2: 2).

"Isaiah's road" had to be cleared of the heavy and cumbersome "stumbling stones" (Rom. 9: 32) with which humankind had littered it throughout its history. To tread that path, humanity had to learn to knock down walls and instead build bridges.

During those years and within those complex scenarios, there were nevertheless exemplary achievements. Above all, there was the project of a united Europe. On the ashes of the Second World War, and thanks to the dedication to peace of enlightened statesmen like Robert Schuman[68], Konrad Andenauer[69] and Alcide De

---

68. Robert Schuman, a member of the Christian Democrat Party, was Prime Minister of France in 1947 and French foreign minister between 1948 and 1952. He is regarded as one of the founding fathers of the European Union.
69. Konrad Adenauer was the first Chancellor of the Federal Republic of Germany

Gasperi, the idea flourished of going beyond the old conflicts, that had characterized the history of the previous centuries on the old continent, making way for the process of European integration. May 9, 1950[70] became the symbol of this new hope.

CHALLENGES AND ENCOUNTERS

Just when Chiara was coming out of her experience of total intimacy with the Father and detachment from earthly matters, she faced a strong confrontation with the world. When Chiara returned to Rome, she found herself for the first time, at the request of her bishop, having to review the expansion, the organizational characteristics, and the dimensions that the Movement had reached by then. The reason for the bishop's request was an instruction by the Holy Office[71] to the archbishop to place the Movement of Unity under the supervision of a "prudent and experienced" diocesan priest, and to detach it completely from the Franciscan Third Order.

A letter of October 21, 1949, represented the first "census" of the Movement, which listed nineteen focolarini, 3,520 adherents,

---

(West Germany) from 1949 to 1963.
70. The Schuman Declaration of May 9, 1950. The creation of a European Coal and Steel Community, whose founding members were France, West Germany, Italy, the Netherlands, Belgium and Luxembourg, was the first of a series of supranational European institutions that would ultimately become today's European Union.
71. The Holy Office between 1908 and 1965 was officially known as the Supreme Sacred Congregation of the Holy Office. It is the oldest of the nine congregations of the Vatican's Roman Curia. Its primary objective was to spread sound Catholic doctrine and defend those points of Christian tradition which seemed in danger because of new and unacceptable doctrines.

2,461 of whom were in the area of Trent (rather 2,462, given the declaration that the archbishop made the year before to Marco Tecilla…), 308 in Rome, 721 in the rest of Italy, and thirty abroad.

Chiara sent those first statistics to de Ferrari, while admitting to having always neglected the organizational part and never having paid much attention to data and numbers. She promised to pay more attention to them in the future, and confessed that she was not sure of the "exact number of souls enlightened and warmed up by the fire of the love for Jesus amongst us," but only of those already present in paradise.

The bishop believed that Bishop Modesto Revolti, who had been the archdeacon of the cathedral of Trent since 1935, had the prudence and the experience that the Vatican department had asked for. Because of his personality and the office he held, Revolti had a good knowledge of the people of Trent, and of the virtues as well as of the hardships of a large part of the population. He was the repository of many personal and shared secrets. When it came to social relationships, he was able to identify what was Caesar's and what was God's. He had sound judgement and could make independent decisions with the required prudence.

The priest scrupulously examined the situation of the various groups that were present in and around Trent, their lifestyle, the characteristics of their spirituality, their goodwill and the good that they had produced. He also noted their naïveté and the imprudent actions that they had undertaken as part of their apostolate. He noted that the presence of a priest would have been desirable particularly in meetings during which the Word was being interpreted and commented on. This presence would also have been useful in keeping an eye on the "spiritual tone and the financial management" of the Movement. He also recommended that the bishop's and parish priest's prior approvals be sought and obtained for any initiative that was to take place in their territories. These thoughts were summarized in the "brief report on the Movement of Unity" which he provided to de Ferrari the following February.

Meanwhile, aware of the difficult path to juridical recognition of the Movement by the Church, de Ferrari had consulted and involved Fr. Giovanni Battista Tomasi (1866-1954), a fellow Stigmatine and a consultant to the Holy Congregation for the Religious.

The long experience of Fr. Tomasi was needed essentially to define the right canonical setting for the Movement, which until then was identified as a "secular institute" approved by the diocesan bishop according to the provision of the apostolic constitution *Provida Mater Ecclesia*. Approval by the Holy See would be something else, as it would rely on the competence and discernment of the Congregation for the Religious when it came to examine any new organization.

The first encounter between Chiara and Fr. Tomasi took place in Rome at the beginning of October 1949 after he checked informally – in agreement with the bishop of Trent – whether the Vatican department would be willing to consider and evaluate the practices of the focolares.

The meeting took place at the general headquarters of the Stigmatine order, in the shadow of the picturesque church of St. Agatha of the Goths, in the Monti area of Rome. Following the exposition of the history and of the spirit of the Movement by Chiara, who had returned just a few days before from the period of light that she had lived in the Dolomites, there was a thorough analysis of the document on secular institutes. They also compared the compatibility of the characteristics and of the first statutes of the Association of the Apostles of Unity with the contents of the apostolic constitution and other canonical regulations.

Writing to de Ferrari, Fr. Tomasi defined Chiara's project as a "brilliant vision perfectly adapted to our times." He sensed its universal perspective and its potential for diffusion beyond national boundaries, thus confirming his initial positive impression and the intention to proceed to an institutional recognition, while expecting to encounter several challenges, particularly from diocesan bishops and from Catholic Action.

In a letter dated August 4 of that year, he wrote to Chiara: "Nothing happens unless it is either wanted or permitted by God, and everything contributes to our greatest good and to the greater good of our ideal, the divine character of which will become more evident as it wins the most difficult and apparently most destructive struggles."

Facing the Holy Office

These last words of Fr. Tomasi sounded like an omen in relation of what was being planned regarding the evaluation of the Movement by the Vatican authorities. While the Sacred Congregation of Religious was engaged in assessing the organizational and juridical questions, in the meantime the Supreme Sacred Congregation of the Holy Office was carrying out an evaluation on the doctrinal and disciplinary levels. It was drawing on information and reports that it had received and that were gathered, more or less confidentially, throughout those years. An explicit doubt or a negative opinion by that Congregation would have compromised any possibility of recognition. Archbishop de Ferrari, on his part, rightly avoided any official intervention, but never lessened his involvement nor spared his counsel on the steps to be taken. He contacted, in confidence, Fr. Arcadio Maria Larraona at the Congregation of Religious and was having ongoing discussions with Fr. Tomasi and with Chiara herself. This considered and discreet approach was not driven by a noncommittal attitude to protect his reputation. He was aware that Rome could have interpreted any explicit action by him in favor of the cause of the Movement as an attempt to force the hand of the responsible authorities, thus running the risk of compromising the whole project. The situation of "suspension" could last for a long time. The doubts and fears regarding the outcome and future of the enterprise were many, but the exercise of the virtue of patience, as called for by the gospel's parable of the king and the servants (see Mt. 18: 26-29), of the cardinal virtue of prudence and of the theological virtue of hope, would have vindicated the Archbishop of Trent's behavior. Backing him was the common sense, experience, diligence, and enthusiasm of his old Stigmatine brother, Fr. Tomasi Their aim was to make the Focolare a "secular institute" according to the Church's norms. The major difficulty consisted in bringing together both the nucleus of those who were consecrated (a limited number, but they represented its center and spiritual identity) and the multitude of adherent members, who were committed in various ways to conduct a life in the pursuit of perfection and who were deeply involved with the spreading of the ideas.

The coexistence of two kinds of members, the issue of living in community, and the question of the structure made things difficult. The form of organization needed appeared to be complex and couldn't call on pre-existing models. Tomasi had already written on March 31, 1950, to his bishop friend, that to make a sound judgement on the Movement, the Church authorities would 'need much experience and therefore time." The possible way forward would be through several stages. The creation of a secular diocesan institute seemed premature, so Tomasi advised that the Focolare be recognized as a "pious association" placed under the supervision of the bishop, awaiting the maturation of the conditions that would fully justify a canonical recognition at a higher level.

The progress, albeit slow, to address the juridical and organizational questions had to include an encounter with the supreme "tribunal of doctrine," whose approval would be a determining factor for proclaiming the full orthodoxy of the contents and the eligibility for the canonical recognition of the Movement. At the end of October, de Ferrari compiled a report on the issue for Bishop Alfredo Ottaviani, officer and future cardinal prefect of the Holy Office, who was following "the case" of the focolares. Alongside the bishop's document there were positive opinions put forward by Fr. Modesto Revolti, the assistant delegate for the community of Trent, and Fr. Carlo Pagani, the superior of the Rosminians, who was in charge of following the path of the large group of adherents to the Movement which met in the house of the great thinker from Rovereto. Having abandoned their initial perplexities, both diocesan assistants unreservedly praised the spirituality and the behavior of the members of the association. They highlighted the coherence of their lives with what the Word of God indicated, the practice of charity, their frequenting the sacraments and their participation in the liturgy with conviction. They also noted their love for the Church and docile obedience and adherence to the directions of the bishop and of the superiors that he had put in charge.

Between those last months of 1950 and 1951, Chiara underwent a thorough examination by the Holy Office and a series of interrogations and interviews. We know almost nothing of the content of this experience. The official records of the investigations are not yet accessible in the archives of the department, which in 1908 had inherited the functions of the Holy Inquisition and after the Second Vatican Council, became the Congregation for the Doctrine of the Faith. The references are rather indirect, partial, and fragmented. Chiara, as is the canonical norm, had to remain silent about it, and in order not to burden her companions by describing the hardship of that trial, she did not tell the community anything. Sometimes no one even knew where she went. They understood it when she returned home worn out and often crying. The only available sources are the recollections of those who accompanied Chiara during these delicate times, in particular Graziella De Luca, and the letters that she exchanged with her bishop. No doubt, the contents and the features of the spiritual proposition of the Focolare were dissected and analyzed with all the intellectual instruments that the theological and canonical knowledge of the time had at their disposal. One of the problematic issues was the concept, central to Chiara's thought, of "Jesus in the midst" of believers, outside the sacraments. This raised a potential threat to the sacramental life of the faithful and possible danger for the hierarchical order of the Church, if not at a juridical level, then at least in the perception anchored in the conscience of the Catholic world at the time.

The direct discussions that Chiara had with the experts of the ecclesiastic tribunal, who by the nature of their role had to play the "devil's advocate," and whose task it was to delve into the doctrinal questions, were accompanied by a series of opinions and additional and entirely favorable reports, from the Archbishop of Trent and Fr. Tomasi. Fr. Gabriele Maria Roschini, of the Order of the Servants of Mary, a renowned expert in Mariology and consultant to the tribunal also took part. Fr. Roschini's report was audited by Cardinal Giuseppe Pizzardo, secretary of the Congregation of the Holy Office, who then sent a report directly to Pope Pius XII. The persisting feeling of "desolation" that distressed Chiara during the first months of this difficult course, changed with time into a state of moderate optimism, strengthened by the constant and comforting diffusion of the ideal of unity in the city of the popes and beyond.

There were many "steps backward" and calls for obedience and discipline. An infinite series of "Hosannas and Crucify," as Chiara called it, lived in the spirit of *sentire cum Ecclesia* (thinking with the Church) and approached with trust from the perspective of Jesus forsaken.

In the spring of 1951, Fr. Roschini was formally instructed to cease all contact with the Focolare. Similar measures were imposed on priests and religious who had approached the Movement of unity. Igino Giordani was discreetly advised by Cardinal Ottaviani to disassociate himself from the Movement. He declined the invitation and suggested instead that an expert Visitor[72] be nominated who could make a judgement and provide a definitive direction for its future. That nomination had already been arranged by the Vatican authorities. The person chosen was Fr. Enrico Corrà, a religious, originally from Trent, from the Order of the Friars Minor Conventual and already a consultant to the Holy Office.

Halfway through 1951 the attention of the friends and foes of Chiara was turned to the interpretation of and opinions about her role within the Movement. De Ferrari was trying to caution her in relation to the "very soft form of tyranny" that she was charged with as a leader of the Focolare, above all organizationally, in particular how she allocated duties and destinations to the various members. Fr. Tomasi was less worried about this. However, they both gave her fatherly advice to keep a low profile in this respect, and to limit that alleged "tyranny" to the presentation and interpretation of the Gospel texts, which until then had not attracted any theological concern.

An unambiguous and urgent recommendation that arose during those months from the ecclesiastical tribunal was the need for Chiara to stop leading the Movement. At the beginning

---

72. The role of Visitor was an official (in this case) appointed by the Holy Office, both to inquire into charges of improper behavior, misconduct, or doctrinal error brought against the Movement and to discern the authenticity of the spiritual life and experience of its adherents.

of 1952, this advice was formalized through an official decree (albeit non-public) that relieved Chiara from her office and kept Fr. Corrà as the Apostolic Visitor, with the additional mandate of notifying the relevant bishops to prevent the opening of new focolares in their diocesan territories and to be vigilant and to report on the activity of those that existed.

That state of "suspension," *sine die e donec aliter provideatur* (without a date and until further provision is made), impacted heavily on Chiara's soul and psyche (with physical repercussions). It was the start of her dark night ...

THE DARK NIGHT OF THE SOUL

There is plenty of literature describing an experience of abandonment and of the "dark nights" (an expression of St. John of the Cross) by those who have lived through a tangible communion with God, from the fourteenth century to our days, from the German and Dutch mystics of the late Middle Ages to Mother Teresa of Calcutta.

A common trait is the extended sense of emptiness and spiritual aridity, anxiety and disorientation, helplessness, and distress which they perceive as the absence of God and forsakenness by him. This sense shrouds all of life's aspects like a mantle of darkness ranging from the intellectual to the emotional, leaving behind only a sense of profound grief. This dramatic depression of the spirit, often coupled with that of the body, is felt when facing the harsh reality of existence in all its hardship and complexity and without the support of a breath of love that would comfort and console. But this state of depression, as in the case of any process of psychological development and human growth, becomes essential to acquire a new relationship, a new vision, and a fuller understanding of what is real and what is divine.

The "dark night" of the mystics is a painful yet necessary transition that ensures purification, refinement, and the deepening of the relationship with God. Afterwards, and thanks to such an experience, God is no longer a partial and separated object, but can be grasped and perceived more completely in his total and integrated dimensions. The psalmist of the Old Testament knew of the disorientation that the silence of the creator led to: "To you, O Lord, I call; my rock, do not refuse to hear me, for if you are silent to me, I shall be like those who go down to the Pit." (Ps. 28: 1). The experience of Jesus forsaken on the cross, with the dreadful feeling of remoteness form the Father, is the sign that he wants to enter fully into human nature. His cry: "My God, my God, why have you forsaken me?" illustrates his wish to intersect with the human story to help humanity understand the meaning of suffering.

The tradition of spirituality and mystical theology, which sees in John of the Cross and Teresa of Avila, both proclaimed Doctors of the Church, its most authoritative interpreters, recognizes the dark night of the soul as a stage of passive purification. It is summed up in the concept of the "purgative stage" which is necessary to prepare and lead to the two following stages: "illuminative" and "unitive," the perfect union of love with God. This is a teaching that involves one's incremental liberation from every link to worldly things, so as to come to an encounter with the absolute in purity and freedom. The Spanish mystic draws a comparison with someone who looks at the sun without a filter and, due to the excessive brightness, has the impression of seeing a black stain. This comparison calls to mind the following passage in the gospel: "Therefore consider whether the light in you is not darkness. If then your whole body is full of light, with no part of it in darkness, it will be as full of light as when a lamp gives you light with its rays." (Lk. 11: 35-36). What is new and original in the spiritual experience of Chiara Lubich, which she herself recognized, consists in the fact that the pattern that guided her was different than the paths of the great mystics. Her particular itinerary seems to overturn even that point of view, by putting the illuminations and the intimacy with God, which occurred in its fullest form in the summer of 1949 with the so-called "Paradise," ahead of the stage of the sufferings of the dark nights, the first of which took place in 1952 and was followed by a long series, until the last years of her life.

Eli Folonari, Chiara'a friend and secretary, was particularly close to her during that extremely painful period. She left a vivid written account about it. Fr. Tomasi turned out to be the point of reference that may help us understand what, to the young lady, seemed like having been abandoned by God and by the Church, to which she had dedicated her life:

> One day, Fr. Tomasi gave Chiara a big book of St. John of the Cross: The Ascent of Mount Carmel. Chiara opened it immediately and was always very drawn to reading those pages. In them, the saint was describing the "dark night of the soul." Greatly relieved, Chiara called us and read us some sentences and told us that they mirrored exactly the state of her soul. St. John of the Cross was describing the so called "dark night"' as such a strong light that enlightens the soul to such an extent that it sees clearly its own shortcomings and its imperfections in comparison with the perfection of God or with the idea that God had of it when he created it. That is why one feels so imperfect, so unworthy, sees that one's own mistakes are so grave and feels so far from God to the point that it sees that salvation is impossible. One feels certain to end up in hell and has the impression that the confessor, not understanding the gravity of one's sins, can neither understand nor realize their gravity in the right way…

The dark night of the soul as narrated by the Spanish Carmelite saint, confrère of Teresa of Avila, constituted the only measure of comparison and way of comfort for Chiara during that painful period. However, it was the condition of Jesus forsaken on the cross that was uppermost in Chiara's mind, and the awareness that a cross could crush a person, not finding any reasons for hope in the hour of trial, nor consolation in the arms of him who has the power to transform tears into joy.

A typical element of these dark nights consists in ongoing harassment by the devil. The etymology and meaning of the adjective "diabolical" refer to the lack of union with God. There are many witness accounts in the history of sainthood about the temptations of the devil along the path towards contemplation of God. From Frances of Rome to Catherine of Siena, from Teresa of Avila to Maria Maddalena de' Pazzi, from Therese of Lisieux to Gemma Galgani, from Jean Marie Vianney to Pio of Pietralcina.

Chiara too recognized that she had been subjected, along the course of her night, to this type of enticement. They did not consist of direct or physical struggles with the prince of darkness, as happened to many saints, but they were recognized in his subtle incitement to not believe in the concrete love of God. The following account by Eli Folonari refers to it:

> *At that time, I remember something Chiara confided to us. The devil with his logic suggested to her: "You have created a world that does not exist. It's all an illusion of yours this God-Love, this love for neighbor, this reciprocal love. You built yourself a castle in the clouds. Look at the reality of the world outside. Life is something else..." But one day Chiara, seeing Natalia prepare with care something to give to her, said to herself: "How can one not love Natalia?" And she decided to love again. And love returned in her, and the night vanished.*

Pope John Paul II[73] draws from the images that have their origin in the experience of the great mystics when he describes

---

73. "Master in the Faith," December 14, 1990.

the spiritual state of our time and its cultural consequences: "The dark night, the trial that makes us touch the mystery of evil and requires the openness of faith sometimes takes on epochal dimensions and collective proportions." He is talking about an enormous night both of thought and of the soul that affects the contemporary world and humanity "in the abyss of abandonment, in the temptation of nihilism, in the absurdity of many sufferings, physical, moral and spiritual." It is a collective night that led to a loss of confidence, of awareness, and of the prospect of salvation offered by the resurrection.

THE FOUNDATIONS OF THE CASTLE

St. Teresa of Avila outlines her own unitive path in *The Interior Castle* (1577) by using a metaphor which describes the spiritual state of the soul as a castle, arranged in seven concentric mansions. The outer mansion represents the state of sin, that can be overcome by self-awareness, prayer, the sacraments, and conversion. In the next mansion, the soul discovers the need for recollection, silence, and the effort of praying. The third mansion symbolizes the state of intimate prayer yet hides the danger of being perfect only in appearance, where the soul is tempted to consider itself as the measure of the spiritual life. In the fourth mansion, the soul prepares to be welcomed by God. In the fifth, one learns to die, as in a cocoon from which the butterfly emerges, to find life anew in God. The sixth mansion is that of spiritual betrothal, in which the soul learns to leave all behind for the beloved. The central mansion witnesses the celebration of the mystical nuptials, the full union with God and the passive immersion by participation in the Holy Trinity, where like a sponge one is imbued with God, yet maintaining the awareness of one's personal identity. "And all of us, with unveiled faces, seeing the glory of the Lord as though reflected in a mirror, are being transformed into the same image from one degree of glory to another; for this comes from the Lord, the Spirit" (2 Cor. 3: 18).

A great scholar of the history of spirituality, Jesús Castellano Cervera, commenting on St. Teresa's work describing the itinerary of her journey to the center of the soul where God lives, highlights the complementarity between the process of attaining a person's interior maturity and the external aspect of the love for neighbor:

> *The adventure may be even more beautiful and the path easier and more impressive if we were to travel through the mansions of the Interior Castle together, the road of Christian sanctity through which we don't only have a common vocation, but also a communitarian vocation to arrive together to trinitarian communion. This would open a new vision of an interior and exterior castle, personal and communitarian, lived in the key of a spirituality of communion.*

At a magisterial level, one of the clearest references that goes back to tradition and is explicit in regards to the need of a Christian communitarian life and eschatology, is found in the encyclical *Spe salvi* (Saved in Hope) signed by Pope Benedict XVI on November 30, 2007. Referring to the work of the theologian Henri de Lubac and based on many theological references to the vast patristic tradition, he states:

> *Salvation has always been considered a "social" reality. Indeed, the Letter to the Hebrews speaks of a "city" (11: 10, 16; 12: 22; 13: 14) and therefore of communal salvation....This real life, towards which we try to reach out again and again, is linked to a lived union with a "people," and for each individual it can only be attained within this "we." It presupposes that we escape from the prison of our "I," because only in the openness of this*

universal subject does our gaze open out to the source of joy, to love itself – to God (14).

Recalling St. Augustine's writing on the intimacy with God whom we are seeking, he reminds us that:

> Our relationship with God is established through communion with Jesus, we cannot achieve it alone or from our own resources alone. The relationship with Jesus, however, is a relationship with the one who gave himself as a ransom for all (1 Tim. 2: 6). Being in communion with Jesus Christ draws us into his 'being for all'; it makes it our own way of being. He commits us to live for others, but only through communion with him does it become possible truly to be there for others, for the whole (28).

In the same document, the reflection continues, referring to the negative aspect of redemption, when unity is missing:

> Sin is understood by the Fathers as the destruction of the unity of the human race, as fragmentation and division. Babel, the place where languages were confused, the place of separation, is seen to be an expression of what sin fundamentally is. Hence "redemption" appears as the reestablishment of unity, in which we come together once more in a union that begins to take shape in the world community of believers (14).

These reflections relate most clearly to the illuminations that Chiara Lubich had received and shared in 1949, when she proposed a spiritual way of looking at the other with the eyes of God, because it is through his gaze that his love is communicated following a trinitarian model: "Look then at every brother or sister with love, and loving is giving. Then the gift calls for a gift in return. So, love is to love and to be loved: it is the Trinity."

The paths of the soul along which Teresa and Chiara travelled seem to diverge. One is focused on interior recollection in solitude and silence while the other is decidedly oriented towards getting out in the middle of the world. What is most evidently new in Chiara's message is its combining the interior life with that of "meeting the other," weaving the two dimensions into a dialogue. It is a point of equilibrium between interiority and a life lived in connection with humanity and the world, making explicit the need for an "expanded interiority" which is open to a fraternal relationship with the other and within which God-Trinity can dwell.

The "expansion" of this new interiority consists of welcoming the other and of being welcomed by the other, thus creating a unique experience of God. This way, the interior and personal experience reaches the fulfilment and full realization outside of oneself, and in what Chiara has called a "collective spirituality," in which everything is one in Christ. In one of her texts from 1950, she uses the expression "exterior castle," as the kingdom of heaven in which God is amongst us: an image which is closely aligned with the Teresian tradition. However, she re-interprets it dynamically, as she points at the presence of Jesus in the interiority of the person as well as in the interpersonal relationship.

The inspiration and the starting point of this perspective are like the "interior castle." Fr. Castellano Cervera, describing the relationship between the Spanish mystic, Chiara's reflections and the two images of the castle, recalls two passages in the gospel: "The kingdom of God is among you" (Lk. 17: 21) and "For where two or three are gathered in my name, I am there among them" (Mt. 18: 20). He then describes the outcome of this relationship as "a new ideal of communitarian holiness, lived together in the thousand reflections of reciprocity, according to the principle of the trinitarian dynamism of the love that is achieved through the total gift of oneself."

The spiritual experience at a personal level and that as Church are inseparable dimensions and generate a spirituality of communion. The exterior castle characterized by intimacy with the Lord and by his guidance is a spiritual element strongly anchored in tradition, while bringing with it a newness that arises from the collective experience of the spirituality of unity.

Over time Chiara would refine her notion of the exterior castle and would describe it with more precision. In 1961, she compares it with the writings of St. Teresa and observes a mutual "special affinity." She recalls it subsequently throughout her life as a paradigm of the spirituality of unity. As Piero Coda expresses it, in Chiara "the experience of the interior castle (God Trinity who dwells in the soul of the individual) is founded on the groundbreaking experience of the exterior castle (God Trinity who is present wherever two or three are united in the name of Jesus)."

"Into your hands..."
Resignation without detachment

In a letter dated February 9, 1952 Chiara presented her resignation from the leadership of the Movement of the "Focolares of Unity" to Fr. Corrà. The main reason, which was not far from reality, referred to the condition of her health. This was a kind of corollary to the main statement which was her proposal of "remaining a simple focolarina," a statement full of implications, at a juridical level as well, vis-à-vis the will of the Holy Office. The closing phrase above her signature reads: "In Jesus forsaken." She retired for a period of meditation to the Piné Plateau, a few kilometers from Trent, the location of an important sanctuary, and of a popular Marian devotion dating back to the first half of the eighteenth century.

For Chiara, the awareness of doing everything in the name of Jesus forsaken and following his example seems to reach its peak. It recalls Jesus' words "Father into your hands I commend my spirit" (Lk. 23: 46). It recalls the surrender that reiterated the words of the psalmist: "I In you, O Lord, I seek refuge; do not let me ever be put to shame; in your righteousness deliver me. . . . Into your hand I commit my spirit; you have redeemed me, O Lord, faithful God" (Ps. 31: 2, 6). From the writings of Chiara and her behavior during that period, as also expressed by the Psalmist, there shines a total trust, a giving of herself to God with an act of total surrender to the Father. The solitude that she experienced was not due to not being understood by the Church that she loved so much, nor to the fear of not being credible. Like Jesus who, by not saving himself from the cross was not credible to the people who were watching his passion. Had he come down from the cross they would have believed in him, but he would have given a wrong image of God. It would have been a pagan god who conveniently manages and distributes power. Not coming down from the cross, but rather dying on it alone and abandoned, bears witness to the God of life, who is love. He will be faithful till the end of his mission, teaching that only those who lose their own life will save it, gaining the hundredfold. Before appearing in the glory of the resurrection, he pointed to the path of salvation, putting in the hands of the Father his own life and thus bringing forward the presence of the kingdom.

Chiara's prayer during this time is one of abandonment to and trust in the Father, like someone who knows that to understand the mysterious design of salvation, one needs to go through the trauma of the cross of Good Friday and of the loss and disorientation of the tomb on Holy Saturday. Such anxiety does not suppress faith. It makes it mature; it leaves behind the stereotype of faith seen as a state of passive tranquility. The anguished cry of Jesus forsaken is what draws the suffering person to God, just as God, hearing that cry, embraces the suffering of every person. Jesus' final words: "It is finished" (Jn 19: 30) in essence means fulfilment of life and redemption from death.

During those moments Chiara's health mirrored the state of her soul, as she was suffering from strong physical pain. However, her extremely fragile body was linked to a very solid vision, based on the principle of "not separating what should be united."

She knew that her works would have been nurtured by her sufferings. The dark nights, the pain, the sickness, the lack of recognition by the Church, would accompany her throughout her life, marking the main stages of her mission and preceding all her most significant intuitions and achievements …

The frequent exchanges, mainly by letter, with Fr. Tomasi and Archbishop de Ferrari, convinced Chiara to keep a low profile and a distance from the "public" management of the Movement. She maintained, however, the role of the inspirer of all its activities and continued to be a spiritual point of reference. She was being tested both physically and in her soul. However, determined to continue her pursuit of a formal recognition by the Church, she worked with Fr. Tomasi on the drafts of a rule for the Focolare. Giosi Guella assumed the direction of the Movement with constant and discreet support from Igino Giordani. This misalignment during the first years, due to the need to be in line with the will of the hierarchy, did not prevent the Movement from growing and expanding intensely along the line that was being followed until then.

The context of suspension and uncertainty did not prevent the proclamation of the ideal of unity and the endeavor to come together at a personal and communitarian level. Obviously, there was still the need to reach agreement and some protection in the ecclesial circles of the Eternal City. This is the context in which a meeting was being prepared that would be of fundamental importance for the destiny of Chiara, of her Movement and, in certain respects, of the history of the Church in the following decades.

INSIDE AND OUTSIDE THE WALLS

The Secretariat of State

Giulia Folonari was born in Milan in 1926, eldest daughter (out of nine siblings) of a rich family of wine and spirit producers. After graduating in economics from the Catholic University she met the focolarine at the summer Mariapolis held in Tonadico in 1950. The following year, despite her parents' concern, she decided to move to Rome to learn more about the *ideal of unity*. This was soon followed by her decision to enter the Roman focolare where she established a relationship of intense fellowship and absolute trust with Chiara, which would lead to her becoming Chiara's lifelong personal assistant. Giulia modestly explained the reason for that decision and her subsequent role as "I had a driving license, which was rare for a girl in those days..."

Chiara gave her a "new name"[74]: Eli, to remind her always to have before her the God that Jesus lost when He cried out: "My God, my God, why have you forsaken me?" – *Eli, Eli, lamà sabactani?* (Mt. 27: 46). Chiara explained to Giula that, henceforth, for every person she encountered who was suffering, she had to be like the God who was hidden from Jesus in his cry.

Eli's aunt Giuseppina, was married to Ludovico Montini, brother of Bishop Giovanni Battista Montini, at the time (from

---

74. In the Catholic tradition as well as in many other religious traditions, adopting a new name is symbolic of entering into a new place in one's life. Chiara would give internal members of the Focolare a "new name" which reflected her perception of the special spiritual gifts that person had.

November 1952, Pro-Secretary for ordinary affairs of the Vatican Secretariat of State.[75]

Bishop Montini was the son of a prominent wealthy middle-class Catholic family of Brescia in Northern Italy. He had been a key spiritual and intellectual guide for the generation of lay people who helped rebuild Italy after the Second World War. During the twenty years of Fascism he was an assistant to the FUCI[76] – until it was banned in 1933 due to its hostility to the Fascist regime. He was a mentor of different individuals and groups and accompanied many young people in their reflection on politics, economics, and society in the light of the social teachings of the Church. He always imbued his guidance with an intense spiritual experience.

He was an exceptionally fine intellectual, in contact with the most advanced currents of European philosophical and theological thought, and at the same time an accomplished diplomat. In 1937 he was appointed Pro-Secretary of State for the Vatican, from where he was able to follow, often as a direct observer and protagonist, the evolution of the Italian and world political situation that culminated with the tragedy of the Second World War and its results for the international order. At the same time, his sensitivity to the inner workings of the mind and spirit led him to grasp the profound religious needs and to identify the cultural transformations of humanity in the contemporary world. He was also very sensitive to the yearnings for Church reform, assisting and often directing the formalization of important pronouncements and magisterial documents, based on the principles of *"return to the sources,"* the recovery of

---

75. Giovanni Battista Montini was later to be elected Pope Paul IV on June 21, 1963, following the death of Pope John XXIII.
76. Federazione Universitaria Cattolica Italiana – Italian Catholic University Association

the traditions of the early Church, respect for biblical texts and reference to the historical figure of Jesus.

In the Eternal City, in the early 1950s, Roman Catholic Christianity still seemed very robust, with the piazzas full of young people and with large gatherings around Pope Pius XII, the *Pastor angelicus,* who with a "cry" or a "whisper" could gather "an army to the altar," according to the lyrics of a popular 1950s song of Catholic Action.

However, the general situation in the years following the war also forced the Church to confront the problems posed by modernity. These included accelerating the long and tortuous path of recognition of the methods and the many advances in scientific research and acceptance of the secular nature of the state and of democracy (abandoning a mythological vision of a Christian society). Added to these were the recognition of human rights and labor disputes, and full condemnation of war.

The Magisterium of Pope Pius XII, although deeply rooted in traditional theological and ecclesiological understandings and heavily conditioned by the political situation of the war years, adopted some of these new ideas. In a particularly delicate period for the city of Rome, like the one marked by the Nazi occupation and Allied bombing, the encyclicals *Mystici Corporis Christi*[77] (June 29, 1943) and *Divino afflante Spiritu*[78] (September 30) were published. The former changed the traditional perspective of ecclesiology, based on hierarchy. The Magisterium described the relationships that bind humanity to the Incarnate Word in new ways and new words, opening theological reflection that would culminate in the Second Vatican Council and its documents (first and foremost *Lumen Gentium*). The second encyclical, in the wake of the biblical movement that flourished in the first half of the century, established

---

77. The mystical body of Christ.
78. Inspired by the Holy Spirit.

the doctrinal norms for the study of Sacred Scripture, highlighting its importance and role in Christian life. It had a great openness to scientific research on biblical texts, to recognize their nature and promote understanding, without weakening their historical value. At the same time, it freed the evangelical message from literal and mythical forms. It also welcomed the insights of modern biblical theology in the Churches of the Reformation such as those of Karl Barth and Rudolf Bultmann.

These magisterial documents were the sign of a ferment of change that in those years influenced all theological disciplines. There was a renewed attention to sources and a transformation of methods, a return to the spiritual and cultural heritage represented by the most ancient texts of Christianity and patristic literature and a rejection of historical prejudices. Symptomatic of this renewal was the series *Sources Chrétiennes*,[79] published in 1942 and dedicated to the authors of ancient and medieval Christian literature, whose works were published in the original language (Greek, Latin, and Near Eastern languages) alongside their French translation.

As already mentioned, in February 1947 the apostolic constitution *Provida Mater Ecclesia*[80] was published. It approved the General Statutes (constitutions) of secular institutes, which were a new concept of religious life based not so much on vows, life in community, or religious habit, but on a total dedication to God, expressed before a representative of the Church. Their goal was the pursuit of Christian perfection through carrying out one's apostolate within society and in everyday life. Among the first ecclesial realities to benefit from recognition on the basis of this

---

79. *Sources Chrétiennes* is a bilingual collection of patristic texts founded in Lyon in 1942 by the Jesuit scholars Jean Daniélou, Claude Mondésert, and Henri de Lubac.
80. The Apostolic constitution *Concerning Secular Institutes*, recognized Secular Institutes as a new form of official consecration in the Catholic Church.

document were: the *Priestly Society of the Holy Cross* to which *Opus Dei* (founded in Spain by Josemaría Escrivá de Balaguer) was attached; the secular institutes of the *Schönstatt Movement* (initiated in Germany by Fr. Josef Kentenich) who were dedicated to the formation of Christian people and communities capable of freely adhering to God's plan in the world; and the *Institute for Women Daughters of the Queen of the Apostles,* founded by Elena Da Persico, a lay Veronese promoter of the cause of women in society and the Church and canonically constituted by Bishop Endrici of Trent in 1931.

In November 1947, the encyclical *Mediator Dei,*[81] dedicated to the liturgy, was published. This encyclical gave important recognition and strong endorsement to the movement for liturgical reform developed through the recovery of the Benedictine tradition in the monasteries of Northern Europe and the reflection of thinkers such as Lambert Beauduin, Anselm Stolz, Odo Casel, (all Benedictine monks) and Romano Guardini. The encyclical proclaimed liturgy to be an encounter with the living God, detaching it from past formalism and strict observance of rules. The liturgy took on theological and pastoral value. It was an instrument for nourishing faith, as a mystery of Christ that continues in the Church, as God's own salvific action, and as an indispensable reference point for individual and communitarian Christian life.

In 1948 great progress was made by the Ecumenical Movement, dedicated to the recovery of the unity of the Christian world following the great divisions that had punctuated its history, especially during the second millennium. The Movement germinated in Europe in the period between the two world wars.[82] In August 1948, delegates of 147 Christian

---

81. Mediator between God and men.
82. Although many see the *1910 World Missionary Conference in Edinburgh as the*

Churches, gathered in Amsterdam, founded the World Council of Churches: "a fellowship of Churches which confess the Lord Jesus Christ as God and Savior according to the scriptures, and therefore seek to fulfil together their common calling to the glory of the one God, Father, Son and Holy Spirit."[83] The group included the majority of the Orthodox Churches, the Churches of the Anglican tradition and many Protestant denominations (Lutheran, Reformed, Methodist, Baptist...) and also several independent Churches, all meeting together to promote common witness and reconciliation between their different Christian traditions. The Catholic Church did not participate, remaining as an observer. In 1950, however, Pope Pius XII went a step further: in an official instruction he expressly supported the ecumenical movement, emphasizing that the Holy Spirit was its origin.

1950 was a jubilee year, with a great mobilization of Catholic associations and pilgrimages *ad limina Sancti Petri*,[84] which enhanced the popularity of the pontiff. Pope Pius XII published the encyclical *Humani Generis*,[85] which addressed the dangers for theology represented by neo-modernism, historicism and existentialism and denounced dogmatic relativism that threatened the foundations of Catholic doctrine. What was new and significant about the Encyclical was its separation of the themes of the creation of the human body from that of the human soul.

Another document issued in that year was the apostolic constitution *Munificentissimus Deus*, which proclaimed the assumption of Mary, body and soul, into heaven: the first

---

  birthplace of the ecumenical movement.
83. World Council of Churches website: https://www.oikoumene.org/en/about-us/self-understanding-vision/basis
84. *Ad limina Sancti Petri* (literally 'at the threshold of St Peter's), at the seat of the pope
85. *The human genus Concerning some false opinions threatening to undermine the foundations of Catholic Doctrine.*

dogma of faith proclaimed "ex cathedra" since the definition of papal infallibility in 1870.

In October 1951, the first World Congress of the Lay Apostolate declared that "all the faithful, without exception, are members of the mystical body of Jesus Christ." This declaration recognized the presence and organization of the laity who, until then, could not act within the Church except by delegation of the hierarchy or by virtue of a special "mandate" as within the movement of Catholic Action. Two years later, the book by Yves Congar, *Jalons pour une théologie du laïcat*[86] (Milestones for a lay theology) echoed this declaration. On January 23, 1952, to "make the good intentions expressed" during the congress "fruitful and lasting," Pope Pius XII established the Standing Committee of International Congresses for the Apostolate of the Laity (COPECIAL[87]). Also in 1952, Pius XII's famous speech to the Congress of the World Union of Catholic Women's Organizations solemnly affirmed what had already been expressed on other occasions, the recognition of the equal dignity of men and women. The pope emphasized women's civil rights and encouraged Christian women to engage in public life and in the world of work, as "a necessary factor of civilization and progress."

Regarding the Italian political situation and the organization of the Catholic world in the post-war years, the Vatican's Pro-Secretary of State, Montini, often found himself confronted (and clashed) with the clerical culture and the bureaucratic mentality of the Curia.[88] Montini wanted both the Church and the laity to

---

86. "Milestones for a lay theology," published in English as Yves M.J. Congar, *Lay people in the church: a study for a theology of laity*, London, Christian Classics, 1985.
87. Comité Permanent des Congrès Internationaux pour l'Apostolat des Laïcs.
88. The Roman Curia comprises the administrative institutions of the Holy See and the central body through which the affairs of the Catholic Church are conducted.

commit fully to democracy while the so-called "Roman party" of the Curia, obsessed by the threat of (Italian) Communism, advocated ultra-conservative and authoritarian political and governmental solutions. In 1949, the attitudes of the latter led the Holy Office to decree that Catholics who professed "materialistic and anti-Christian Communism" or actively participated in political parties inspired by it were excommunicated as apostates from the Christian faith.[89] In this bipolar geopolitical environment, the same Church circles also considered the Western bloc to be the only one capable of maintaining any semblance of Christian order within society. Their perception of the condition of the Churches in countries of the socialist bloc was such as to render all diplomatic relations and efforts useless.

In this turbulent post-war environment, Montini's privileged collaborator was always Alcide De Gasperi, well-known in Italy from his leadership of the anti-fascist Peoples' Party and his time of 'exile" in the Vatican Library. Montini shared with him, always discreetly, his aspirations and action plans, reflections and projects, anxieties and joys, victories and defeats. They discussed many plans including the politics of potential alliances that would give life to a centrist era and a Christian inspired political party that would be a reference point for the Catholic world. These ideas would subsequently lead to the drafting of a Constitutional Charter for post-war Italy. Other topics they discussed were the possibilities to bind Italy to the Atlantic alliance; grand visions of economic and social reforms; and priority institutional changes necessary to build a united Europe.

But at the basis of Montini's wide-ranging and tireless activity was a true and deep passion for the search for the meaning and destiny of the human person, and a concern for the place of the human person in the contemporary world. According to

---

89. Decretum, July 1, 1949, in *Acta Apostolicae Sedis*, 1949, 334.

Guardini, he nurtured a "deep concern for humanity"[90] and saw the person as the *"way of the Church."* He also affirmed that "one cannot love one's own ideas more than people, lest one becomes estranged from them."

Meeting the successor of Peter

The encounter between Chiara Lubich and Bishop Montini matured through several stages, a clear sign of the diplomatic prudence which the prelate exercised in discerning the nature of the focolare experience. The first of these stages, dedicated to a presentation of the characteristics of the Movement, was requested by Eli Folonari and took place on March 25, 1952. This happened, not without an understandable sense of awe, in the monumental Third Loggia (Logge di Raffaello) of the apostolic palace in the Vatican, where Eli was accompanied by Valeria Ronchetti. The following July there was a long conversation between Montini and Igino Giordani who were long-time friends. They focused on the activities and canonical situation of the Focolare, including the situation with respect to the Holy Office and the need to define statutes with an appropriate juridical basis. This was followed, in January 1953, by a further conversation with Eli and Palmira Frizzera, where Montini expressed his desire to meet the founder, Chiara Lubich. He also assured them that the current examination by the Holy Office represented a guarantee and protection for the Movement. His desire for a meeting was fulfilled the following month, with two meetings on consecutive days attended by Eli and Chiara.

---

90. Romano Guardini, *Ansia per l'uomo (Anxiety for Man)*, Vol. 6 of *Opere di Romano Guardini* (Rome: Morcelliana, 1969).

The latter immediately wrote to her bishop in Trent, summarizing the impression and emotion left by the two talks with the phrase: "We felt in him the love of the Church for us." Montini's feelings had obviously been expressed, with all the subtleties of diplomatic language and juridical vocabulary. He also offered suggestions aimed at directing the Movement's path towards pastoral and political horizons that were particularly dear to the Church's leaders.

The following April 20, Igino Giordani wrote a letter to Archbishop de Ferrari with extraordinary news. Bishop Montini had just informed the Focolare that the Holy Father had granted them a special audience on May 21. The letter specified that they would be received – as formally stated by the pope's secretary – "as members of the Focolare Movement of Unity." This message delighted everyone, especially Fr. Tomasi, who described the invitation as "something truly extraordinary."

The first Focolare meeting with the Pontiff was described in detail in a report written by Giordani (who was not present because he was involved in an election campaign) and signed by all participants (first of all by Chiara and Pasquale Foresi) and immediately sent to the Bishop of Trent. Some thirty or so men and women focolarini, divided into two chambers in the apostolic palace, had met Pope Pius XII, who had welcomed them, listened to them, questioned them, encouraged them and blessed them. He had shown great interest in their work in the communist-dominated regions of Italy, especially Emilia Romagna and Tuscany. To the first group, the pope said: "Continue in your zeal, go forward." To the second, after listening to Valeria Ronchetti's statement: "We want to be the joy of the Church," the pope responded: "And the Church needs it so much." He presented everyone with a souvenir medal and left them with his blessing for all "the people, families, apostolate and benefactors of the Focolare."

De Ferrari greeted the news with immense joy, replying to Foco's letter with these expressions: "My heart cried out its most enthusiastic and joyful 'About Time!' The Holy Father knows and esteems you! What more do you want?" The Bishop of Trent understood how that step marked a point of no return in the long and difficult process of recognition of the Movement. Even though the juridical and organizational aspects – carefully and patiently studied and developed by Fr. Tomasi, in constant contact with the competent ecclesiastical authorities – had not yet reached a synthesis. It still had not been translated into definitive formal measures, but the recognition established by the papal audience represented a milestone in that long process, opening up very positive prospects.

On June 26 the president of the Movement, Giosi Guella, sent Pope Pius XII a letter outlining a strong action-oriented agenda for the Movement. This proposal was probably inspired by the guidelines suggested to Chiara by Bishop Montini. In addition to an overview of the history and spirituality of this organization born in Trent, it sought approval to exercise its apostolate in the countries of the communist bloc. Such availability obviously implied both a recognition and an acknowledgement of the credibility of the Movement which, hitherto, the proceedings in progress at the Holy Office had prevented. This meant suspension of the Holy Office's prohibition on opening new focolares and carrying out public activity.

Chiara's proposals, the fruit of strategic reflection which would decisively orient the destiny of the Movement in the years to come, seemed a response to Isaiah's invitation "prepare the way for the Lord, make straight a road in the desert for our God" (Is. 40: 3). Similarly they seemed a response to the mission of John the Baptist expressed by the evangelist Mark: "See, I am sending my messenger ahead of you, who will prepare your way; the voice of one crying out in the wilderness: 'Prepare the way of the Lord, make his paths straight'" (Mk 1: 2-3). All this in order to look forward to "new heavens and a new earth, where righteousness is at home" (2 Pt. 3: 13).

Against the background of these events, it is useful to look at the tensions within Catholic Action which were affecting the internal equilibrium of the Church in Italy and elsewhere. In 1952 Vittorino Veronese, the General President, was replaced by Luigi Gedda. In the post-war years, the former, had always tried to give Catholic Action a strongly spiritual and cultural focus, being careful to distinguish the religious goals from political options in any concrete action. He sought to avoid any uncritical tendency to support speical interest groups. Gedda, however, concentrated on the organizational dimension, on structures rather than content, with a focus on direct action rather than spirituality and with a decidedly "weak" attitude towards democracy.

In the same year, a debate around council elections in Rome provoked the resignation of Carlo Carretto as president of the GIAC.[91] Carretto had opposed a suggested unprecedented anti-communist alliance between the Christian Democrat Party and ultra-right-wing parties. This alliance was supported by a large part of the Vatican bureaucracy and conservative Catholic circles but was opposed by De Gasperi and Montini.

In those years, the GIAC and the FUCI academics often distinguished themselves by their tendency to rise above the reactionary and subservient thinking and positions of many of the hierarchy. The influence of *nouvelle théologie*[92] and internal

---

91. GIAC (Gioventu Italiana dell'Azione Cattolica – Italian Youth of Catholic Action) was a national Catholic youth organization built around local parish groups.
92. Nouvelle théologie (French for 'new theology') refers to a school of thought in Catholic theology that arose in the mid-twentieth century. Theologians

debates emphasized the need to reconsider the relationship between Church and history, to be more oriented towards an ideal of communion according to which the laity would have a legitimate function in the world from within a Church that no longer saw this relationship as an enemy. This debate, with associated demands for both ecclesial renewal and a renewed approach to political debate and the workings of government, was at odds with the majority in the Roman Curia and the Italian episcopate.

During this period, the life of the Focolare Movement continued to grow with ever increasing vitality. In 1953, the now customary summer period in the mountains of Trent saw a constantly growing number of people being attracted by the ideal of unity. Afterwards, in autumn of that year, eleven adherents were allowed to take a perpetual vow, following the model of that made by Chiara ten years earlier. This vow consecrated and bound them forever to the life of the Focolare. Bishop Montini, who shortly afterwards would leave his Vatican role to become Archbishop of Milan, welcomed and supported a request that Pasquale Foresi, who was completing his studies at the Almo Collegio Capranica[93] be incardinated[94] in the diocese of Trent. After his ordination in Trent, the city of the sixteenth century Ecumenical Council, he remained at the Movement's disposal.

The spirit and characteristics of the Focolare seemed to become clearer and clearer in the eyes of the founder: "the

---

usually associated with nouvelle théologie included Henri de Lubac, Hans Urs von Balthasar, Yves Congar, Karl Rahner, Edward Schillebeeckx and Joseph Ratzinger.

93. The Almo Collegio Capranica is the oldest Roman seminary, founded in 1457. Its alumni include two popes, and some forty-five cardinals and bishops.
94. Incardination in this context, refers to a priest being formally under the authority of a particular bishop while being given permission to work for the Focolare Movement rather than in a diocesan role.

premise of every rule is the presence of Jesus in the midst, where two or more are united in his name." Less clear were the ways of translating these spiritual certainties into statutes that responded to the juridical categories of Canon Law at that time. The draft Statutes that described and regulated the "Focolares of Unity," requested by the Holy Office (and as delivered to Montini) reflected the situation of the moment, with the three branches of the Movement committed to taking "fraternal care in Jesus of all people they were in contact with, whatever their vocation, sex, age, or spirituality," taking Mary, who "served Jesus so that all might be one," as a model.

Chiara and De Gasperi: two minds for unity

It was early August 1953, when in Tonadico, about sixty kilometers from Trent, a gentleman in his seventies, tall and with a distinct bearing, apparently austere and severe but with gentle manners, approached Carlo Casabeltrame to ask directions to the residence of Miss Chiara Lubich. The gentleman was directed to a chalet owned by the Brunet family where, for the previous five years, the founder of the Focolare Movement had spent the summer months, accompanied by an increasing number of people who either belonged to the Focolare Movement or were simply attracted by the prospect of an experience of sharing an evangelically inspired life. At that moment, Carlo did not recognize the person who asked him the question... It was Alcide De Gasperi who, from 1945 and until a very few days before had been Prime Minister of Italy, leading the country in the exceedingly difficult years after the war.

De Gasperi had arrived at the slopes of the Dolomite mountains to meet Chiara. He had come up from nearby Sella

Valsugana where he used to spend his summer holidays in a small villa owned by the family of his wife, Francesca Romani.

The previous months had been particularly turbulent for both Italian and international political life. The statesman from Trent was tired and dispirited and clearly felt that his public trajectory was on the way down. On January 20, 1953, Harry Truman's presidency had ended, and with him the government of the United States of America had changed considerably. Gone were those with whom De Gasperi had frequently interacted and woven close relationships with during his intense political career in the years that marked Italy's return to democracy and the reconstruction of the country. Two months later, on March 5, Stalin died. He had been the secretary general of the Communist Party of the Soviet Union and the symbol of the Soviet bloc which had confronted the Western world in the context of the Cold War. The following July 27 saw the armistice which ended the Korean War, a confrontation between the two powerful blocs which had stirred up the specter of a global nuclear war.

The process of European integration, inspired and initiated over previous years by De Gasperi and other political leaders who shared a common ideal of peace and unity among peoples and nations of the European continent, was proceeding slowly. On February 10, 1953, under the ECSC Treaty,[95] a common market for coal was opened. In March, the European Court of Justice began its work. The same month Paul-Henri

---

95. The European Coal and Steel Community (ECSC) was an organization of six European countries created after World War II to regulate their industrial production under a centralized authority. It was formally established in 1951 by the Treaty of Paris, signed by Belgium, France, Italy, Luxembourg, the Netherlands, and West Germany. The ECSC was the first international organization to be based on the principles of supranationalism and started the process of formal integration which ultimately led to the European Union.

Spaak[96] handed over to Georges Bidault, President of the ECSC Council, a draft treaty establishing a European political community, drawn up in previous months with the help of representatives of the various countries.

In Italy, in the elections of June 7, 1953, the Christian Democrat Party suffered a sharp drop in support. It got around 40% of the vote, but this nevertheless represented a loss, mainly to the right, of about two million votes compared to five years earlier. The coalition of governing parties did not reach the 50% necessary to govern under the new electoral laws. De Gasperi was commissioned to form his eighth government, a minority Christian Democrat government, which did not, however, win a parliamentary vote of confidence.

The day before entering the Chamber of Deputies[97] to face the vote of confidence, De Gasperi had read a text inspired by the Gospel story of Luke 6: 12, suggested to him by one of his daughters. It said: "Lord, you go alone to the mountain to pray, tired of the crowd, tired even of us, your disciples, who understand you so little, and make you repeat the same things over and over again, without understanding. . ." Next to the passage he had written: "reminds me of our 1953 crises." And on July 29, Giulio Andreotti, De Gasperi's close collaborator, wrote in his diary: "Returning to Caprarola, President Einaudi, who was even more upset than De Gasperi in accepting his resignation, told us: 'Never forget the Gospel, which reminds us that we are all useless servants.'"

Within a year De Gasperi would die. His spirit, ever vigilant and continually straining in search of the common good, was worn out by the difficult task of living for others and from those

---

96. Belgian statesman who was prime minister during several periods and Belgium's Foreign Minister for eighteen years between 1939 and 1966.
97. The "Lower House" of the Italian Parliament.

final frustrations, disappointments, and betrayals. In the last days of his life he confided to his daughter, Maria Romana:

> You see, the Lord makes you work, lets you make plans, gives you energy and life, then when you think you are necessary and indispensable to your work, he suddenly takes everything away from you. He makes you understand that you are only a tool. He tells you that you can go now... Our puny human minds need to finish things and do not resign themselves to leaving to others the object of our unfinished passion.

But let us return to his visit to Chiara in Tonadico in August 1953... De Gasperi had gone there because of a bond of profound spiritual communion with Chiara and the Focolare Movement. The origin of this goes back to March 1950 in Rome, with a meeting organized by their mutual friend Igino Giordani. Contact with the Focolare continued through the group of members of parliament close to the Movement, organized by Giordani and Graziella De Luca, and through some meetings at the home of Alvino[98] and at the villa of friends on the beach in Fregene.[99]

The two were united by their Trentine origins, by their natural predisposition (each in their respective fields of activity) to work for the good of others and by their vision of life and the world which both saw from a perspective of unity. Their personal histories had been marked by suffering: material suffering through poverty and because of the war, but above all interior suffering, the result of misunderstandings and rejection, often on the part of those whom they had believed to be their closest friends.

---

98. Luigi Alvino, editor of the Italian weekly newspaper "La Via," and his wife Elena, met the Focolare in 1948. Chiara and the focolarini were often guests at their home in Rome.
99. Fregene is a village on the Mediterranean coast near the mouth of the Tiber River.

But the friendship and closeness between Chiara and De Gasperi was moved above all by a profound understanding at the level of the spirit. He had grasped the value and the relevance of the gospel message proposed by the Movement. He drew hope and serenity from the spirituality throughout those years marked by divisions and conflicts, suffering and misunderstanding. Their shared understanding resided in the same faith in Christ and fidelity to his Church (lived intensely in their role as laity), in their deep knowledge of biblical texts and sincere Marian devotion, in their love for the common good and in their commitment to the unity of the human family. But probably their most fundamental element of communion arose from their understanding of Jesus' mysterious cry on the cross, "My God, my God, why have you forsaken me?" Both recognized the reality of suffering-love as the indispensable way to achieve *ut omnes unum sint* (may they all be one). Both deeply believed that true consolation for earthly sufferings and misunderstandings is fulfilled in Jesus Christ and his grace. Both knew well the gospel account of Jesus' proclamation in the synagogue of Nazareth, according to which God's promise to his people was fulfilled in him (Lk. 4: 21-30) but which also provoked a widespread reaction of skepticism, hostility, and rejection among those present. Jesus shows us how mysteriously the message of grace is always associated with rejection and resistance ... and precisely by those who are first called to listen to and welcome him. It is a dimension of grace to be rejected, thereby confirming that grace is for everyone ... it is always given freely but without the necessity to be accepted by us.

In some particularly difficult moments of his political life, De Gasperi confided in Chiara through letters, always seeking support and comfort in the prayers of the Focolare in the face of his fatigue and suffering. This trust shows in the letter of April 21, 1951, in response to the wishes received for his seventieth birthday (he was born on April 3, 1881):

The feeling of being united under the wings of divine fatherhood gives me a sense of serenity and trust, even in this hour of tribulation. And I am certainly troubled ... the man who has responsibility for government is gripped by fierce doubt: bitter days are in store for our country and we are not ready to face this tragedy with the necessary solidarity and unity. If I were not obliged to accept my responsibility for this part of history that Providence has entrusted to the free will of mankind, I would withdraw, but always resigned to the will of God. For the Christian who recognizes that politics is a dimension of one's faith and above all a work of social fraternity – and hence a fundamental duty towards one's brothers and sisters and our common Father – this anguished torment becomes an inexorable duty. I do not want this torment of mine to burden you or impact the ardor of your spiritual life which rises above such sad temporalities; but I want to explain to you my state of mind and, in thanking you for your good wishes, to tell you how precious and useful are the prayers of so many brothers and sisters, like you and like many whom I meet everywhere in our country and who are aware of this worrying responsibility of mine.

THE SUMMER MARIAPOLIS

The context in which the meeting in Tonadico between Chiara Lubich and Alcide De Gasperi took place, as recounted in the previous pages, was that of the so-called *summer Mariapolis*,[100] which grew from an idea born in 1949 during the period when Chiara was graced with profound mystical experiences. The Mariapolis, born and developed without any precise plan or orga-

---

100. Mariapolis (plural Mariapoli) literally means "City of Mary."

nizational criterion, was a gathering of people, men and women, from different social strata, of all ages and from the most varied vocations. During the summer months the Mariapolis became like a temporary small town characterized by all its inhabitants trying to live the "New Commandment," the very touchstone of Jesus' teaching, "Just as I have loved you, you also should love one another." (Jn 13: 34).

The entire territory of the Alpine Arc of Northern Italy, as well as the network of parish churches in almost every village, is dotted with religiously inspired artifacts, built over the centuries to bear witness to faith and popular devotion. From the valley floors to the highest peaks, the landscape is dotted with chapels, shrines, devotional paintings, and hill-top crosses. These works reflect popular piety and community devotion, signs of a faith rooted in the history of the mountain people. Shrines and monasteries, often rich in art and in full harmony with nature, complete this geography of "pathways of the infinite," which traverse and unite villages and valleys, bringing them together in the boundless dimensions of the spirit.

As the twentieth century unfolded, the mountains were gradually populated with other structures, designed for recreation and rest, for moments of recollection and reflection, and to accommodate families and youth groups. It is a kind of "religious tourism," which in many cases has integrated, if not replaced, the traditional concept of "pilgrimage." Promoters and stakeholders of this phenomenon included dioceses, parishes, religious orders, and the world of lay associations (like Catholic Action and the Scouts). There can be various practical and spiritual reasons why the mountain environment is such a preferred choice for such activities. Mountains can be seen as places of transition, immensely greater than ourselves, subconsciously considered closer to God, and as environments that naturally favor the ascending motion of the spirit. They often represent an idealized symbolic backdrop to the pilgrim condition rooted in the nature of the human person, whose journey is a response to the need for the absolute, spiritual nourishment, inner change, peace, and happiness. In the mountains, in addition to meditating and praying with greater ease, one walks and struggles, one learns to overcome difficulties – often helping one another – and not to give in to tiredness and temptations. You can share the exchange of experiences between the generations and on returning home you can sense to be more "whole" than when you left.

To date there has been little research into the importance of these summer experiences in the mountains, these places of encounter and sharing between groups of different origins, between generations of members of the same local church or of associations founded on a particular charism, between leaders and spiritual guides, between leading figures from the ecclesial world, culture and politics, and between the people responsible for pastoral ministry. Similarly, just as little thought has been given to the extent to which these experiences, as well as invigorating the body and the spirit, have often been a place for developing and planning policies and strategies or projects and activities to be carried out once participants return to their respective homes.

The example of the Focolare Movement's summer Mariapoli suggests these (and many other) characteristics. Certainly unique to the Focolare are the ways in which these experiences were born and developed during the 1950s, and then evolved towards other forms of assembly and activities of a more permanent nature that would spread throughout the world. The absence of planning is a first obvious fact. From the "first event" in 1949 until 1959, these experiences were characterized by great spontaneity and a lack of attention to the organizational dimension. Only two Mariapoli were not held in Tonadico. The move to the nearby Val di Fassa in 1954 and 1955 was motivated by purely logistical reasons. The number of participants grew from year to year and managing moments of communal prayer and sharing experiences, even though they were carried out in fairly large groups, suggested moving to an area with greater hotel accommodation and where there were more houses for rent. However, another reason, perhaps the most important one, was of a "disciplinary" type. The move was also necessary to comply with the directives of the official Visitor from the Holy Office, Fr. Enrico Corrà, who had ordered a strict separation of the accommodation of the focolarini (men) from those of the focolarine (women). Accusations of promiscuity, even if made in bad faith and with other motives, had been leveled at the Focolare Movement, and required careful attention to avoid any possible criticism during the difficult path of canonical recognition. Obviously, the separation was only physical, and was largely compensated for by the principle and the guarantee of always having "Jesus in the midst."

The experiences and impressions of the participants in those Mariapoli were many and so too were the motivations that drove people to enter more deeply into the focolare spirituality. All those who had lived even a few days in a Mariapolis left with similar impressions. They were aware of having experienced true life so that they could leave everything else behind and follow the Lord. They felt the push to become "evangelists" with something precious to announce. They felt that God had come remarkably close, that he had abolished the distance between himself and humanity, and that he had come to seek out every sinful person. They had the certainty that Jesus had again climbed into Peter's empty boat to announce salvation to all and that, just as Peter and his companions would leave from there to share this announcement of salvation with humanity, so would they.

Chiara intuited that the Mariapolis would take root in different places scattered throughout the world, with the characteristics of a town:

During one of these Mariapoli, admiring from a hilltop the green expanse of the valley, I seemed to understand that one day the Lord wanted, somewhere, a little town similar to the one that was being built here, but on a permanent basis. In my imagination, I already saw a valley populated with houses and cottages.

This new project will be discussed in one of the following chapters.

THE GREAT ATTRACTION

Everyone realized that the experience of the Mariapolis had enormous "attractive" potential, since it satisfied people's deepest and most natural spiritual desires, yearnings and needs, especially in our contemporary era characterized by the Nietzschean assumption of the "death of God," killed by indifference and fear of the infinite.

This "great attraction" would become the title of one of Chiara's densest and deepest spiritual meditations, capable of summing up the charism of unity and expressing it in an ever new and timely way. It provides an interpretation of our relationship with the absolute which seems to foreshadow many traits of postmodernity and of the "liquid society,"[101] firmly maintaining the reference point of universal fraternity and full communion with God. The text was written by Chiara on November 12, 1958, published in *Città Nuova* on November 20 and the following year in the book *Meditations*.

---

101. The "Liquid Society" was a concept coined by Polish-British sociologist, Zygmunt Bauman, who described the general traits of the "liquid modern" man as he flows through his life like a tourist, changing places, jobs, spouses, values, political allegiances and even sexual orientation.

> *This is the great attraction*
> *of modern times:*
> *to penetrate to the highest contemplation*
> *while mingling with everyone,*
> *one person alongside others.*
> *I would say even more:*
> *to lose oneself in the crowd*
> *in order to fill it with the divine,*
> *like a piece of bread*
> *dipped in wine.*
> *I would say even more:*
> *made sharers in God's plans*
> *for humanity,*
> *to embroider patterns of light on the crowd,*
> *and at the same time to share with our neighbor*
> *shame, hunger, troubles, brief joys.*
> *Because the attraction*
> *of our times, as of all times,*
> *is the highest conceivable expression*
> *of the human and the divine,*
> *Jesus and Mary:*
> *the Word of God, a carpenter's son;*
> *the Seat of Wisdom, a mother at home.*[102]

Many years later, the journalist and politician Sergio Zavoli, an admirer of the Focolare, would comment on this text defining Chiara "a mystic of the unity between heaven and earth," saying that she had made a turning point in trinitarian mysticism:

> *Allowing God to dwell in the intimacy of one's soul is making him live among us through communication between – I repeat Chiara's words – God in me and God in my neighbor. It is not by chance that Chiara Lubich's thought challenges us to put*

---

102. Chiara Lubich, *Essential Writings* (New York: New City Press, 2007), 169.

together the fragments of what is inseparable, the human person, and to recompose the fractures of what can be shared, that is the community.

The passage dedicated to Mary, who is simultaneously *seat of wisdom and a mother at home,* indicates the other fundamental criterion for understanding the charism of unity and the work of its founder: to be a mother, a generator of life, capable of transforming the lives of thousands of people through the spirit of communion, to bring about fraternity, the unity of the human family. This generative experience allows us to see reality in a completely new way, like Mary who, after her personal encounter with God in the annunciation sings of a new world with her *Magnificat.* She sings of the world as she now sees it, in relation to Christ and his salvation given to the lowliest servant. Mary can be considered as the masterpiece of God's imagination. The Lord who always chooses the humblest to carry out his works, makes Mary his most immediate collaborator.

BEYOND THE WALLS

Religious and theologians

Noting the visitors to the summer Mariapolis and the relationships that the Focolare Movement was able to build within the ecclesial environment of Rome and of the cities where the first communities were created, it is clear that, compared with the hierarchy and the secular clergy, it was mainly men from religious orders who were among the first to perceive the value of this new, and in many respects, alternative approach to traditional consecrated life.

Beginning from its early days in Trent, Chiara's charism had developed in the spiritual context of the Franciscan Third Order and in the Capuchin environment. Its value had been recognized in the early 1940's by Archbishop de Ferrari (a Stigmatine religious) and by his confrère Fr. Tomasi. Soon after, the potential of the Movement had been grasped by Franciscans like Leo Veuthey and Bede Hernegger, founders and animators of lay movements on an international level, and by Raffaele Massimei, provincial of the Conventual Franciscans in Rome. The spread of the Movement was marked by allegiances, openness, friendships, declarations, and acts of support from the world of the religious orders. The network of communities and monasteries, of connections inside and outside the ecclesial world, and the traditionally open and positive attitudes of the three Franciscan families (Minors, Conventuals and Capuchins) in responding to new signs of the times, were the fertile ground on which the first focolarini could begin to discuss and develop their own particular ideal of evangelical life.

Later, members of mendicant and contemplative orders, Jesuits, Dominican friars, Benedictine monks, but also Servites, Camillians, and Pallottines were added to the list of the Focolare's "friends in high places" (the "allies at the heart of the system" according to the classic definition proposed by sociologist Bernhard Callebaut). Religious orders, although quite different one from the other, are by nature more sensitive and receptive than the institutional church to new religious phenomena, to proposals for spiritual renewal and to the emergence of charisms. Their founders are usually animated by charismatic experiences, and their statutes, especially the initial versions, are a mirror of such experiences. The same is true of the mottos that summarize the spirit of these various vocations: *Ora et labora* (Pray and work) for the Benedictines, *Pax et bonum* (peace and goodness) for the Franciscans, *Contemplativus in actione* (contemplative also in action) and *Ad maiorem Dei gloriam* (for the greater glory of God) for the Jesuits, *Contempla aliis tradere* (hand down to others the fruits of contemplation) for the Dominicans, *Stat Crux dum volvitur orbis* (The Cross is steady while the world is turning) for the Carthusians, and so on.

For the most part, compared to the secular clergy, the religious orders showed greater interest and fewer fears concerning the new phenomenon confronting the ecclesial structures and mentality of that time, especially the fact that lay people were independently giving birth to a spirituality and an apostolate at the service of the laity and all believers. The well-established ruling clerical hierarchy with a clear distinction between the roles of the clergy and the laity and the vertical relationship between the former and the latter, were suddenly challenged by this tension towards communion. They found it more difficult to accept the creation of authentic and fraternal relationships within the believing community and the overthrow of passive customs and spiritual individualism. These challenges anticipated the development of principles such as the common priesthood of all believers and the concept of the Church as the people of God, which have since matured theologically and which were solemnly and definitively formalized with the Second Vatican Council.

The networks constituted by the organizations and relationships across the various religious families and third orders (starting with the Franciscan Third Order which had "hosted" the birth of the Movement) acted as intermediaries, facilitators and often opened the road for the spread of the ideal of unity. Of significance here is also the "political" importance of religious orders in the Roman environment, which hosts the general headquarters or governing bodies of all the orders. The Vatican departments and offices there have always employed numerous friars, monks, and nuns, often in senior positions. Each congregation usually has a cardinal "protector" and the religious, well inserted in the "Roman world," found direct access to the pope often easier than it was for a bishop.

Also, one cannot ignore the impact of the reports from superiors of the various religious orders concerning the involvement—indeed membership—that many of their members had in the spirit and activities, of the Focolare Movement. They observed the growing climate of collaboration and the spiritual development among their members. They witnessed a growing fraternity among the religious orders, while respecting the individual founding charisms, which overcame age-old prejudices, exclusiveness, and feelings of competition or rivalry. This influence exercised by lay people on religious circles, improving relations and stimulating apostolic zeal and pastoral mission was considered something new and extremely positive. It was a moral influence, detached from the hierarchical dimension, which immediately aimed at deepening the spirituality of fraternity. As such it would soon lead to an increase in the capacity for mobilization and efficiency in the Church's response to the needs of the time; to the accomplishment of missions where hitherto they had been unsuccessful; and in unprecedented pastoral projects.

The interest in the Focolare's lifestyle and mode of action was not limited to religious circles or the pastoral dimension. Prominent figures in the world of theological research, for the most part active in the Roman Pontifical Universities and often leaders or consultors in important offices of the curial apparatus, met the Movement. They were probably attracted, more or less consciously, by the witness of these young lay people who were drawn to the original experience of Christianity, built on the relationship between Jesus and the apostles as described in the Gospels. This original experience in all its freshness and simplicity was often barely perceptible within the refined theological and canonical corridors that led the Church's journey through history, its confrontation with human civilization and culture, and constituted the basis of its institutional dimension and governance.

These contacts and exchanges were with minds who felt the first breaths of the breeze that in a few years would blow strongly into the sails of Peter's boat at Vatican II. They perceived the need for necessary changes in the Church. They were elaborating the basic theological cues and reflections which soon would inspire and guide the reforms that would find expression in the Council. They sensed how much new forms of spirituality, originating through intuitions and charismatic experiences, would profoundly change the religious feeling and the relationship of multitudes of people with the absolute.

In those years, theological studies in many areas, saw new contributions that made a powerful impact on the self-understanding of the Church, especially regarding the human person and the contemporary world. Hans Urs von Balthasar, one of the greatest theologians of the twentieth century, published

Schleifung der Bastionen: Von der Kirche in dieser Zeit (*Razing the Bastions: On the Church in this Age*) in 1952. In this book he speaks about the need for the Church to demolish the defensive walls that keep it separated from the modern world and its culture, and argues for the right of theology to rethink Revelation (without pretending to exhaust its meaning) and to apply its meanings to the conditions in which it finds itself. In 1956, the Jesuit Karl Rahner launched a new edition of the *Lexikon für Theologie und Kirche* (*Lexicon of Theology and the Church*). The unwritten rules of theological research had been mainly based on the deepening of knowledge of the mysteries but were now being directed towards a reflection on faith in view of its proclamation to humanity. The supremacy of the scholastic method which proceeded deductively from abstract formulations, was progressively being replaced by an anthropological approach which proceeded from below and sought a correspondence between truth and life. On the moral front, in 1954, the work of the Redemptorist theologian Bernhard Häring, *Das Gesetz Christi – Moraltheologie für Priester und Laien* (*The Law of Christ – Moral Theology for Priests and Laity*) proposed a doctrine centered on the Bible, Christology, liturgy and life, moving beyond a legalism that makes God a controller and judge rather than a savior. Moral judgment was no longer considered to be the simple application of a general principle to a particular case. Rather, the primacy of conscience was recognized and the capacity, under the guidance of the Holy Spirit, to intervene on a case-by-case basis, according to the principle of situation ethics. In 1955 the Jesuit Pierre Teilhard de Chardin (1881-1955) died. His scientific research in the fields of paleontology, anthropology, and world evolution had gone so far as to interpret the universe philosophically and theologically in new and, for the times, disconcerting terms. His research looked at the possibility of reconciling a passionate and legitimate love for the cosmos, that is being discovered as more and more grandiose, with the search for the kingdom of God, recognizing Christ, who died and rose again, as the center of the universe and the *omega point* of reciprocity between God and humanity.

Hans Urs von Balthasar got to know the Focolare Movement and had encountered its spirituality. His writings underline the *Marian profile* of the Church, which helps to recognize and understand the charismatic experiences coming from God's people. They also focus on its relationship with the other profiles, especially the *Petrine profile*. "Mary," he says, "is Queen of the apostles, without claiming the apostolic powers for herself. She is both different and more." Another was Gabriele Maria Roschini, of the Order of the Servants of Mary, an expert in Mariology and a consultant to the Holy Office, who understood the charismatic phase that the Movement was going through in those years, and its potential. There was the Benedictine theologian and future cardinal Paul Augustin Mayer, teacher in priestly formation and rector of the Pontifical University of St. Anselm; the Jesuit, Jean Beyer, canonist and scholar of lay and secular life; and Augustin Bea, biblical scholar, pioneer of ecumenism and Jewish-Christian dialogue, cardinal and among the leading figures of the Second Vatican Council.

During the summer Mariapolis of 1958 another significant encounter with an academic theologian who would have a strong influence on the history and development of the Focolare Movement in subsequent years and decades: the priest, theologian, and philosopher Klaus Hemmerle (1929-1994). At the time he was the director of the Catholic Academy of Fribourg. Over the following years he was to have a brilliant university career and, in 1975, he was appointed Bishop of Aachen. The main object and fruit of his research was trinitarian ontology and the mystery of love of God-Trinity. His encounter with Chiara and the charism of unity, he said, "was an experiencing of the kingdom of God among people, of the risen one who becomes present where two or more are gathered in his name (Mt. 18: 20). And at the same time it was for me the 'revelation' of Jesus crucified and forsaken as the 'place' and the 'way' of God's trinitarian giving of himself to us and of us to him, and to one another." From that moment on, and with ever greater intensity and insight, the light of the charism of unity would inform his theological reflection.

Light and Darkness
New Sufferings and New Horizons

On January 2, 1954, Fr. Tomasi died. This loss was a profound disruption for Chiara and the history of the Movement. He had been placed alongside the Focolare Movement from its early days in Trent to accompany the difficult path of its spiritual and organizational development and of the juridical recognition and integration among the lay realities of the Church. On the face of it, the loss of their ecclesial mentor could have been a potentially mortal blow for the Movement.

Tomasi's death had a strong impact on the physical and psychological health of Chiara, who, with the loss of her wise and far-sighted fatherly mentor, fell into a state of severe depression. A dark night of the soul seemed to thicken over her. It was, however, a period marked by the interweaving of darkness and light. The first phase of the investigation by the Holy Office had ended without any definitive decisions. This situation was not ideal. Nevertheless, it could still allow for a positive outcome of the canonical process. In the meantime, the spread of the Movement proceeded beyond all expectations and with the prospect of expanding into other relevant areas. There were also many innovations on the organizational level. In addition to the initial division into female and male branches, the married focolarini had been added and was organized by Igino Giordani. Also, possibilities were developing that would soon generate the priestly branch of the Movement and branches for men and women religious. The seeds had also been planted for another branch of the Focolare, a lay movement that would take the name of "Volunteers of God."

A young Franciscan priest, Fr. Andrea Balbo, was chosen to replace Fr. Tomasi. This new assistant had a quite different profile from his predecessor. Born on February 8, 1923 in a village near Vicenza, he had entered the Franciscan College at Chiampo, near Venice, at thirteen years of age. He took his perpetual vows in 1947 and was ordained a priest in Bethlehem on July 3, 1949. Having shown remarkable intellectual gifts, he dedicated himself to the study of natural sciences at the Sorbonne in Paris, with the prospect of continuing in the world of research and teaching. Having come into contact with the Focolare Movement and having met Chiara during the Mariapolis of Tonadico in 1953, he soon earned the esteem and affection of the focolare community in Paris and of other groups which were in closer contact with Chiara (especially in northern Italy). According to the focolare custom, the founder proposed a new name for him, "Fr. Novo," to underline the newness of life that must be understood and then lived according to the Gospel. This was a name inspired by the passage of St. John which narrates the conversation between Jesus and Nicodemus: "no one can see the kingdom of God without being born from above" (Jn 3: 3).

Chiara's request to Fr. Balbo to replace the late Fr. Tomasi in his role as ecclesial assistant was totally unexpected. Nevertheless, having obtained the permission of his provincial, the young Franciscan left Paris to travel by train to the Eternal

City. He went to the focolare in Via Tigré, where Chiara lived, simply saying: "I am here. I have arrived." He was found a place at the men's focolare in Via Vigliena, where there also was Pasquale Foresi, who was about to finish his studies for the priesthood at the Almo Collegio Capranica and was shortly to be ordained in Trent on April 4 of that year.

Fr. Novo himself was filled with doubt and trepidation as he witnessed Chiara's inner torment and weakened physical condition. He recognized the delicate path the Movement was going through with respect to the directives of Vatican authorities, and became aware of Chiara's inexperience and lack of preparation regarding the issues she had to deal with, and understood the difficult situations Chiara was confronted with. At the same time, however, seeing Chiara's suffering and being faced with her severe anxieties, turmoil, and inner darkness, made him fully understand his function as an assistant and allowed him to recognize the light inherent in the mystery of Jesus forsaken. That mystery of pain and passion was capable of changing one's life; it gave new meaning to both absolute and abstract values; it enriched them with more real and vital perspectives; it allowed one to open one's heart and mind to the hidden secrets of God's work. "The trials to which God subjected her," said Fr. Novo, "were to refine her soul and make it docile and more transparent to his light." During this "dark night" Chiara felt as if God had withdrawn from her and she no longer felt his presence neither within her nor in the world around.

The new phase of investigations by the Holy Office was entrusted to another member of the Franciscan family, Fr. Alfonso Orlini, replacing Fr. Corrà. The new Visitor dedicated himself with great zeal to his office, collecting testimonies and working on a statute which would provide for the Movement to be called the Focolare Movement for Christian Unity and for its provisional leader to be a non-Focolare priest. From the perspective of canon lawyers, his proposal seemed to provide a solution to the controversial and "difficult to regulate" dimensions of the nature and features of the Movement. Of special concern were the presence in the Movement of priests and of consecrated married men and women – the married focolarini.

This branch of the married focolarini was conceived by Igino Giordani as early as 1951 but did not become a reality until his own personal act of consecration in November 1953. With the establishment of this last branch the Focolare became aware of a profound sense of openness to humanity and of a new path to holiness. This we find expressed in the following words of Chiara, from a special conversation with Giordani and some single focolarini and focolarine, who made their consecration in front of Fr. Tomasi:

> *Foco was with us focolarine, and there, in front of us, he was saying things that really touched us. They were words of an utmost humility. It was as if his soul was at rock bottom, whilst he contemplated the mountain top of the greatness of the vocation of virginity to which God calls particular souls in the Church. Foco could not follow this path, because he was married. However, forgetting himself and struck by God's grace, he glorified God for what God had done here on earth in our midst. Perhaps because of this humility – because humility always attracts God's attention – I remember that we said: "Listen, Foco, what is it, after all, that you lack? If you love Jesus forsaken, you are detached from everything; you do not attach yourself to anything; you are detached from your fields; you are detached from your family; you are detached from your ideas, from your books, from your life, from your age. If you love Jesus forsaken, if Jesus forsaken is everything for you, you are empty of yourself and you are full of God. If you are full of God, you are living charity. If you are living charity, God lives in you: and then who is more virgin than you?" And I remember that I said to him: "Look, it is not physical virginity that counts: there will even be virgins in hell. It is*

spiritual virginity that counts and where God is – God is always virgin – where God is there is chastity, where God is there is obedience, where God is there is poverty....Why don't you make this consecration to Jesus forsaken, to be love, why don't you also put this on the altar, why don't you also offer your vows to this Ideal from this point of view?"

The priestly ordination of Pasquale Foresi, on Passion Sunday 1954 in the church of the Sisters of the Holy Child Mary in Trent, opened another "front" in the panorama of the Movement. Ever since her mystical experiences in 1949, Chiara's vision for the Movement included the establishment of a branch for priests. Chiara felt the need for the Church to renew its understanding of the role of the priests, less tied to the institutional dimension but rather anchored in ideas that would anticipate concepts such as the people of God and the universal priesthood of the baptized which within the decade would find an expression in the reflections and decisions of the Vatican Council. She envisaged priests who were apostles of unity, who were asked to bring the spirit of the Gospel to parishes, seminaries and ecclesial structures, without controlling or interfering with diocesan organization and liturgical discipline, but charged only with spreading and bearing witness to the yeast of unity.

The autobiography of Fr. Andrea Balbo (Fr. Novo) is quite clear regarding the new ideas that the Focolare Movement was proposing for the priesthood. Its model was the "priesthood of Mary," avoiding any form of clericalism, positions of authority or of being put on a pedestal but striving to be accessible to all and for all and close to the people. Priests should be seen as equal to other people and only come to the fore at the right and opportune moments. This way of living should also be reflected in the "habit," leaving the cassock behind to dress in normal civilian clothes so as to blend in among all, to be one among all. This was important because the Work of Mary had to reflect the love of the Mother of God for all, including those farthest away from the Church. Therefore, the apostolate of the focolarini had to be discreet, with a reserved attitude, including the external signs of belonging to the clergy.

This idea was obviously daring and well in advance of its times, especially for the Church hierarchy. At that time, it was just too radical for Church authorities to understand and assimilate. Officials appointed to judge the nature and work of the Movement misunderstood and misinterpreted the structures, and in any case, were not always willing to interpret things in the right light or even try to understand the new things inspired by the charism of unity. Accordingly, some wise counsellors suggested to Chiara that she should not push the "cassock question" too strongly.

In any case, priests in contact with the spirituality of unity found themselves living as brothers among their (lay) brothers and sisters, since the basis of their ministry was what united them with all the other baptized, namely, the common condition of being disciples of Jesus. Only in this way could their specific gift of the priesthood stand out and their vocation be renewed by experiencing that "circulation" of the different states of life (priests, religious, laity) that characterizes Church-communion and by highlighting the universal vocation to holiness. To show how every vocation should relate to the others and be at each other's service, as a model for priests Chiara has always proposed Jesus' act of washing the feet of his apostles as recalled in the liturgy of Holy Thursday. She invited them not only to be builders of unity within the Catholic Church, but also to become creators of dialogue that is open to Christians of other Churches, to followers of other religions, and to people of non-religious convictions. She would remind them that the only priestly vestment recorded in the Gospel for the mass celebrated by Jesus on Holy Thursday night is the rough cloth that surrounds his hips to dry the disciples' feet.

Years later a great bishop, poet, and man of peace, Tonino Bello (1935-1993), would write about the meaning of this act of humility in relation to the Eucharist:

> There is not a Eucharist on the inside and a foot washing on the outside. The one and the other are complementary operations to be expressed together in the places wherever the disciples of Christ gather and live. Outside, if anything, there is only the logic of those gifts: fruits that ripen fully only in the warmth of the Gospel greenhouse. In conclusion, the jug, basin, and towel must become sacred vessels to be arranged at the center of every community experience. I hope that they will not be seen simply as ornamental items... because, since we are so slow to convert, that jug is exposed to sacrilege no less than the Eucharist itself.

In December 1955 Chiara formalized the practice of the *Word of Life*, the cornerstone of the spirituality and community life of the Focolare Movement ever since the time of its origins. Hitherto its practice, derived from small beginnings, had been spontaneous and unscripted. However, from this time on the passage from Scripture that would be preserved in the heart of each one and that would inspire daily life, was now to be illumined by a commentary from the founder, Chiara herself (with other authors added later on) and sent out every month throughout the Focolare Movement. This practice would be one of the catalysts for the start of a monthly magazine of the Movement, which would be born but a few months later.

That year Chiara sent a Christmas letter to all the focolare communities which expresses this program:

> *Dear friends,*
>
> *Driven by a variety of circumstances, we came up with the idea of living a specific "Word of Life" each month. We would like this practice to be as regular as possible and we would like everyone to take it very seriously. This is also an opportune time,*

with Christmas just around the corner, which all Christians look forward to with joy.

... Jesus, as the Gospel shows, has a way of understanding, of loving, of wanting which is all his own, unique, and so superior to the way of life of us Christians. For every age he knows how to extract from the Gospel "something" that will serve humanity of that era; and century after century that "something" will appear so new and revolutionary as to seem at first as if it had been ignored up to that time.

Now, we want to make Jesus' way of living our own. And nothing seems more appropriate to achieve this end than the periodic "emptying" of ourselves and our souls to let the Gospel enter. If we do that we will become more and more like Jesus. And what more splendid and concrete way is there of making him be reborn in us – for the benefit of humanity – than to truly celebrate Christmas? It will be a Christmas that will continue throughout the year and more.

We are certain that God will like our efforts. We can rejoice to think that, amidst so much darkness across the world, with so much confusion and hallucination caused by false ideologies that deceive people and threaten to tear apart even portions of the mystical body, nothing could be more effective than to give birth to the light of the Gospel alive in us and around us. If God has spoken through Jesus, we must have faith that those Words contain the fire mentioned by him and the divine energy to overcome the world....

In closing there is also an explicit reference to the situation of the "living martyrs" of the Churches behind the Iron Curtain and to the "Church of silence," whose forced muteness has to be opposed with a strong proclamation of the "Word that is Christ."

A PARTICULAR CONSECRATION

During the summer Mariapolis of 1953 a young Jesuit priest had discreetly approached the Movement, observing and following its activity. He was Pavel Hnilica, of Slovak origin, who had recently moved to Rome. This meeting would have a particular impact on the future development of the Focolare, inserting it into the delicate diplomacy of relations between the Catholic Church and the Eastern Orthodox Churches and into the global dynamics of international politics and the balance of power in the Cold War.

In the post-war period the countries of the communist bloc had established a homogeneous political, social, and cultural system which identified Moscow as its epicenter. Rome, a religious reference point for the West, but also for part of Eastern Christianity, witnessed the emergence of an ideological spirit which threatened to reach the heart of Christian Europe, and with which it would do battle for the whole of the twentieth century. This gave rise to an antagonism and opposition that would characterize the following decades, maintaining its own logic until the end of the 1980s. It impacted the religious and political life of millions of people and deeply scarred the ecclesial culture, debate, and mentality.

The Church of Pope Pius XII had chosen the path of absolute and definitive condemnation of Communism and every country that pursued the communist system. The Church took the path of refusing dialogue, refusing recognition or diplomatic relations, and rendered any encounter impossible. The Vatican's attitude is expressed (but also tempered in its intransigence) in the words of the Pro-Secretary of State Montini, who in 1948 spoke of "the policy of patience. A firm patience without illusions but which never wearies."

The story of the so-called *Church of silence* is a story of suffering and martyrdom. From the years immediately following the Second World War, Christians in Eastern European countries belonging to the communist bloc suffered heavy abuse and repression. As early as 1946 the Soviet authorities imposed the annexation of the Ukrainian Greek Catholic Church with the Orthodox Patriarchate of Moscow, forcing those who remained faithful to the Ukrainian Catholic Church to worship "underground." Two years later the same fate would befall Romanian Greek Catholics, who were forced to submit to the authority of the Bucharest Patriarchate. This persecution took the form of arrests, summary trials, torture, internment in the gulags, and ideological re-education programs, aimed above all at the clergy and bishops of the Catholic Church in its various rites.

The Catholic Church, with the Vatican as its spiritual and political reference point, was considered by the communist propaganda to be the international center of resistance and the main ally of the capitalist world. Because the Catholic Church proposed an anthropology based on the primacy of the human person, it was considered the main enemy of every state system that tries to control individual freedom and conscience.

Repressive measures became normal and widespread practice in the USSR, Czechoslovakia, Hungary, Romania, Bulgaria, and Poland, albeit with some exceptions, thanks to the action of the Polish primate Stefan Wyszyński. Nunciatures were closed because they were seen as possible observation points and channels for passing information to the West. Seminaries too were closed, and Catholic schools, parishes, and convents suppressed. The most respected bishops and priests were arrested on charges of espionage or offences against the state. The most striking case was the trial of Cardinal József Mindszenty in Budapest, who in 1949 was sentenced to life imprisonment.

If on an official and diplomatic level the Church reacted with silence, throughout the 1950s it engaged in many clandestine forms of action. In the face of the repression of local hierarchies and police control of every pastoral activity, the Holy See activated independent channels with local churches and implemented specific, and often decidedly original, solutions of Church leadership and government. For example, it granted great autonomy and extraordinary powers to certain bishops, some of whom were secretly consecrated.

Fr. Pavel Hnilica (1921-2006) was one of them. Ordained a priest of the Society of Jesus in 1950, the following year he was consecrated bishop by the apostolic administrator of Rožňava (Slovakia), Róbert Pobožný. The exercise of his clandestine ministry cost him imprisonment and an ideological "re-education" program, such that in 1952 he had to flee to the West. He settled in Rome and started working to support his brothers in the faith at home and to raise awareness of the spiritual and material situation in Eastern Europe among the public in the West.

Seeing the communist system as a sort of "atheistic mystical body," he was convinced that the only effective remedy would be Christians intensely living their reality as the mystical body of Christ. Encouraged by his Jesuit confrère Lorenzo Del Zanna, Hnilica observed and gradually approached the Focolare Movement. Some sources (to be confirmed) suggest that a meeting with Chiara took place in Trent during the Christmas holidays of 1953. They certainly met and discussed matters during the summer Mariapolis of 1954 – then called *Giapoli*, the city of Jesus forsaken – which was held in the Val di Fassa with the town of Vigo at its center. Their dialogue took place one morning, after Mass at the ancient church of Pieve di San Giovanni, in the presence of Pasquale Foresi, Fr. Novo, Antonio Petrilli, Enzo Fondi, Aldo Stedile, and two focolarine. Hnilica revealed his identity and dignity as bishop to those present and invited the Focolare to be "an instrument God wants to use to bring a breath of new life into Christianity and to save the world from the danger of Communism." He invited the Focolare to direct and dedicate the activity of the Movement to supporting the Church of silence and to the conversion of communist countries. Chiara voiced her concern that the Focolare Movement had no particular purpose other than to live the Gospel and to do God's will, and that their spiritual commitment was steadfastly oriented towards dialogue rather than opposition, so that "all may be one."

However, Chiara immediately understood that an activity along these lines could be a positive outlet for the future of the Movement, directing it towards a precise ecclesial mission. It was an opportunity to be considered seriously, building around it a vision to promote and spread the charism of unity where God seemed to have no refuge. This would show the ecclesiastical authorities that the Focolare was a reliable and discreet resource to ensure an "unofficial" presence in countries where the institutional Church was impeded or forbidden. Last but not least, such availability to the Church could help foster a positive outcome to the long process of formal recognition and approval of the Movement.

Chiara did not respond directly to Hnilica's proposals, but proposed a pact similar to the one made with Igino Giordani in 1949: to consecrate themselves to the immaculate heart of Mary so that Mary would be the one to enlighten and guide the designs that God had on the Movement. The consecration was held in the church of Vigo on August 22, the day on which the liturgical calendar commemorates the immaculate heart of Mary. Only those present at that first meeting knew the reason for this pact, and the act that followed of offering their lives to the immaculate heart of Mary. Given the bond of secrecy that accompanied this it was called "the conspiracy."

THE DRIVE TOWARDS THE EAST

The work of Fr. Hnilica in support of the Church of silence was obviously not limited to his involvement with the Focolare Movement. In agreement with the Vatican Secretariat of State he had undertaken to organize a sort of secretariat for the study of the problems of the communist East, which was given the name, the *Mystici Corporis* Committee. József Gawlina (1892-1964), originally from Silesia, and who had been bishop to the armed forces in Poland since 1935, was appointed head of the committee. During the war he held the same office with the Polish government in exile, first in France and then in Great Britain, and after the conflict he was appointed bishop for the Poles in exile, which involved a lot of missionary activity world-wide. The years following Stalin's death, the rise to power of Nikita Khrushchev and the twentieth congress of the Soviet Communist Party, had shown faint signs of openness and relaxation between the Soviet bloc and the West. The Church, at the official level, confirmed the line of intransigence in condemning the communist system and institutional incommunicability, but it set up and maintained confidential contacts and clandestine channels. Cardinal Alfredo Ottaviani, Secretary of the Holy Office, proposed sending "priests disguised as merchants" to Eastern Europe, exploiting the opening to trade.

The commitment of Fr. Hnilica, secretary of the Committee, generated support for the initiative, especially among the religious. Among them were the general provost of the Jesuits, Jean-Baptiste Janssens, the superior general of the Franciscan Conventuals, Vittorio Maria Costantini, Agostino Sepinski of the Friars Minor, and Fr. Arcadio María Larraona Saralegui of the Society of St. Paul, at the time Secretary of the Congregation for Religious in the Vatican.

Everyone knew and appreciated the activity of the Focolare Movement and agreed with the idea of involving them directly in missionary activity in the communist world. From then on, a period of preparation began which was conducted in a variety of ways. A group of lay people did courses of formation at pontifical universities, with the aim – kept secret – of being ordained to the priesthood and exercising their ministry in Eastern countries. Others organized a program of public meetings to raise awareness of the situation of the communist countries in various Italian cities. At the service of this project, a focolare for priests and religious was opened in Via Capocci in Rome, at the disposal of the *Mystici Corporis* Committee. Initially it was made up of Pavel Hnilica (to whom Chiara had given the name "Fr. Maria"), a Jesuit, the Friar Minor Fr. Andrea Balbo (Novo, who had returned from a stay in Lebanon and Jerusalem), the Conventual Angelo Beghetto, the Pallottines Fr. Giuseppe Savastano and Fr. Giuseppe Leonardi. They were joined by many others who went on to form the League of Priests and Religious. "Days of awareness" regarding the situation and the problems of Christians and churches in the countries of the communist bloc were held in dioceses and parishes. These were led by "teams" of activists composed of a focolarina, a focolarino, a married focolarino and a diocesan priest or a religious. The meetings were planned meticulously, with conferences, testimonies, and debates coordinated by the lead team and supported by other members of the Movement mixed with the audiences. The contents, the communication strategy, and the style of presentation were based on a positive proposal of evangelical life with a strong social element. The approach was never aggressive, nor was there any criticism of communist militants. In fact, they were considered brothers and sisters, united by a sensitivity for justice and a desire to free humanity from all slavery. The spread and success of the initiative was remarkable and local leaders had to be identified – all belonging to the League – to oversee maintaining and regulating relations with the local churches. Fr. Giuseppe Savastano was appointed for the Rome area; Fr. Angelo Lazzarotto of the Pontifical Foreign Missions Institute was appointed for

Milan; Fr. Beghetto worked in Trent; Fr. Andrea Balbo, because of his connections with France, was appointed to follow the meetings held in Grenoble and Chambéry.

Through this and many other activities of the League, many religious and priests, students from international colleges, and missionaries destined for evangelization in many parts of the world were approached. The Augustinian Diederik De Muynck became the contact person for Belgium, the Benedictine Mariano Costa Rigo for Brazil, Joseph Taschner for the Philippines, Fr. Angelo Lazzarotto of PIME in Hong Kong.

This mission, officially authorized and supported by the ecclesial authorities, offered the Focolare a great opportunity and considerable space for spreading their spirituality, lifestyle, and witness, starting from the Gospel and the Word of Life. Guidance by a priest gave official status to the activity, while the animation by the laity of the Movement gave them the possibility to spread the ideal of unity in the freshest and most effective way. All of this conveyed an image of the Church totally focused on building the mystical body of Christ with constant reference to the principle of unity. The Gospel account – especially that of Luke – of Jesus' entrance into Jerusalem, seems to express this image. Upon entering the holy city, Christ seems to disappear, making the Church appear in his place, sent to announce to all the Passover of its Lord. The verb "to send" expresses here the meaning of the mission. As when he sent his disciples among the people to bring the good news that the kingdom is near, Jesus sends two of his disciples to the Mount of Olives to take the colt on which he will enter the city, instructing them how to do it, justifying it by saying "The Lord needs it" (Lk. 19: 31).

Among the many new things induced by this project was the collaboration of religious belonging to different congregations who, going beyond their tradition and discipline which normally saw them working separately, now came to live together in function of a common project. The secretary of the Congregation for Religious, Fr. Arcadio Larraona, commented:

> *Ever since I was young, I dreamed of such collaboration between religious orders. How beautiful the Church would be if there were this unity among all the orders. I have worked so hard for it. Now seeing you, who are so young and who have this soul, it's like a dream come true. Do not be afraid of difficulties. Difficulties will come, and many, but do not be afraid. This is the right way.*

The collaboration between the Congregation and the superiors of the orders lead to the establishment of the Union of Superiors General.

Only twenty years previous, the expression *Drang nach Osten* ("drive towards the East") was the slogan to support the aims and the policy of German expansionism in search of *Lebensraum* ("living space"). It had been one of the ideological triggers of one of the most tragic pages in the history of the twentieth century, culminating in the Second World War. Now this motto represented a new responsiveness of the Church, committed to bringing the Gospel to the countries behind the iron curtain. One of the symbolic characters of this was certainly Guido Mirti, who was part of the first group of young Romans who entered the Focolare in 1949. Born in 1921, he worked in the administrative offices of the Ministry of the Navy. Chiara gave him the name "Cengia" ("ledge"), because of his solid character and his attitude of support for others, like a rocky ledge which is a sure point of support for the mountaineer. On September 8, 1955 he was the first focolarino to go behind the Iron Curtain into Eastern Europe (starting from Czechoslovakia). Officially he went there as a sales representative for the OIE company, which had been established ad hoc to specialize in the import-export of various items between countries on both sides of the Iron Curtain. He had a mandate directly from the pope which was to be delivered in absolute secrecy to the bishops who exercised their ministry in hiding. Guido was to be the first thread destined to compose the network of relations and activities that, over the years, would be built up in support of the clandestine churches in the communist countries. He was to keep in contact with the churches of Western Europe, ensure the sustenance of relationships and guarantee the flow of information in support of the future Vatican Ostpolitik. During his first mission to Bratislava he met a Jesuit bishop, to whom he reported the pope's wishes and blessing and the "special faculties" that were given to that underground Church. After having given all the messages, the bishop made Guido kneel and ordained him a priest, with the mandate to serve the Church of silence.

For eight years Cengia carried out his very delicate task with the utmost determination and confidentiality, until his arrest in Prague in January 1963, his trial, and his expulsion from the country. In the minutes of the criminal proceedings brought by the Prosecutor General's Office of Prague against Guido Mirti and the Jesuits Peter Dubovský, Josef Hnilica (Pavel's brother), Dominik Kalata and Vladimir Klestinec, one can read the motivations that led to the accusation of "attempted overthrow of the Republic" and the consequent conviction of the defendants. The file shows how the "enemies of the Czechoslovakian socialist regime" had engaged in "anti-state propaganda" activities, in an "attempt to create among Catholic believers, distrust of the people's democratic regime in order to re-establish a bourgeois regime." The report meticulously reconstructs the movements and activities of Guido Mirti, responsible for transmitting "economic, religious and political news" about Czechoslovakia to the West.

Cengia was a modern Nicodemus who, in John's account (3: 1-21), went secretly at night to listen to Jesus. After Jesus' death he went with Joseph of Arimathea to the cross to wrap him in a sheet and lay him in the tomb from which he would shortly rise again.

Guido Mirti's, story has still largely to be reconstructed and recounted, but it is probably decisive in understanding the role of the Movement at the service of the Church in this complex situation. It is also fundamental in grasping the importance of this mission for the road to recognition of the Focolare by the Church.

After Stalin's death, forms of dissent against the strict political control exercised by the USSR had spread in various Eastern European countries. In Hungary, this intolerance took the form of student protests and peaceful demonstrations against the dictatorial regime of Mátyás Rákosi. On October 23, 1956, demonstrators occupied the most important institutions and brought Imre Nagy to power. He declared that he wanted to disengage the country from the Warsaw Pact and appealed to the UN for arbitration. The Soviet reaction was immediate and violent, with the military occupation of Hungary and the suppression of all dissent. The clashes resulted in 3,000 deaths and 250,000 Hungarians were forced to leave the country. Cardinal Mindszenty took refuge at the US embassy, where he remained for many years. Imre Nagy was tried and executed in 1958. The new government was entrusted to the secretary of the Workers' Party, János Kádár, (a position he would keep unchallenged until 1988), who restored the status quo.

In the anterooms of the Kremlin, the worry about a domino effect became a central issue. Demonstrations in support of the Hungarian uprising had been recorded in Poland, Romania, and Czechoslovakia, and even in Moscow many students and teachers had taken to the streets against the intervention. In the same days of October 1956, international political scenarios were shaken and threatened by another event that affected and compromised the ever-precarious balance between Eastern and Western blocs. This conflict broke out in the Mediterranean when Britain and France, allied with Israel, invaded Egypt, allied with the Soviet Union, because of Egypt's nationalization of the Suez Canal, a vital trade route between East and West. The world was suddenly one step away from World War III. As with the Hungarian crisis, Moscow tackled the issue with an iron fist. Defense Minister Bulganin threatened to use nuclear weapons if France and Britain ignored the ceasefire ordered by the UN. The crisis ended only the following year with the sending of a peacekeeping force under the aegis of the United Nations to "keep the borders in peace while seeking a political agreement."

Europe watched the events with bated breath. In Italy, a group of intellectuals close to the Communist Party, in open contrast to Secretary Togliatti who was siding with the Soviets, spread the Manifesto of the 101 in support of the Hungarian insurgents. For the first time there was an attack from the inside on the ideological orthodoxy of the Italian Communist Party, a sickle and hammer blow against the wall of Marxist-Leninist totalitarianism. Gino Lubich, Chiara's brother, a former partisan and at the time editor of the Communist Party newspaper *L'Unità*, also joined that protest movement, returning his membership card and resigning from the newspaper.

In a radio message on November 10, 1956, Pius XII's appealed to the world in "the name of God, source of all rights, justice and freedom ... as a synonym of peace, and a banner for men of good will." Chiara took up this appeal, stressing the need for the presence of authentic disciples of Jesus and his love in the world. This gave birth to the "Volunteers of God," lay people of the Movement committed to building a new society with love as their rule of life.

The need to spread the ideal and maintain relations with the already established communities as well as those emerging in Italy and Europe was at the root of the publication of *Città Nuova*, a fortnightly magazine of opinion at the service of the Movement, for which Gino Lubich now began to write. A short time later, the *Città Nuova* publishing house was born. Pasquale Foresi was head of the editorial board whose aim was to build a new civilization based on a sense of unity and belonging to the one human family. The first book, published in 1959, was a collection of Chiara's spiritual writings entitled *Meditazioni* (Meditations).

Speaking with "God's microphone"...

The conclusions of the scrupulous investigations into the condition and conduct of the Movement conducted by the Visitor Fr. Orlini and conveyed to the Holy Office through a detailed report, did not produce the desired effects, so much so that the Franciscan, assisted by the Jesuit Augustin Bea (close collaborator and personal confessor to the pope), sent Pius XII a reminder specifically on this matter.

In the meantime, Fr. Foresi, Fr. Hnilica, and Fr. Beghetto, and the lay focolarini Giulio Marchesi and Enzo Fondi, had encountered the Movement for a Better World, founded and animated by the Jesuit Riccardo Lombardi (1908-1979). They aimed at building a new society centered on the Christian message, focusing on promoting the dignity and freedom of the person and so creating an alternative to totalitarian regimes. A community-based group inspired by the Magisterium of Pope Pacelli (Pius XII), it had spread to about thirty countries. It centered on proclaiming the Gospel, interpreting the need for reform in the Church, and offering formation for "Christian leaders." Similar and complementary to Lombardi was the Oasis Movement founded by another Jesuit, Virginio Rotondi. Oasis focused on the apostolate of youth and the spiritual concept of serving out of love.

Trained on the editorial staff of the Society of Jesus' magazine *La Civiltà Cattolica,* and a qualified and authoritative voice on Vatican Radio, Lombardi became famous for his powerful oratory and his vast extent of public preaching. He strongly promoted a Christian vision of the world in opposition to Communism, an opposition that accompanied the electoral campaigns, the great mobilizations of the Catholic world, and the political battles following World War II. Lombardi's vocation was summarized by Gianfranco Zizola in the title of Lombardi's biography: *God's Microphone.* The pastoral project of the Better

World Movement began with the intention of reforming the Church, starting from the top, and establishing a new ruling class. In practice it produced a renewed community mentality and a spirituality of communion which quite naturally fit with the sensitivity of the Focolare Movement and stimulated collaboration and the search for a common purpose and the means to pursue them. In the Focolare Movement Lombardi saw a reform from the bottom up and rejoiced at the thought of welding the two together.

It was a harmony that between 1956 and 1957 seemed to be leading to a real fusion between the two movements. The continuous examination on the part of the Vatican Supreme Court seemed to postpone indefinitely the status of the Focolare Movement. The Italian Episcopal Conference and some of the bishops were not much in favor of the Focolare and things were moving in the direction of its dissolution. All this led to Fr. Lombardi writing a letter to Cardinal Ottaviani, speaking of "a fusion of the two efforts into a single work," that is, the aggregation of the Focolare Movement with the Movement for a Better World.

The idea was discussed in depth with the leaders of the Holy See. As well as to Ottaviani, Lombardi brought the matter to the attention of the cardinal prefect of the Apostolic Tribunal, Giuseppe Pizzardo, and the substitute for the Secretariat of State, Bishop Angelo Dell'Acqua. This was eventually communicated by Fr. Rotondi to Mother Pascalina Lehnert, the personal secretary of Pope Pius XII. The Jesuit also participated in the Summer Mariapolis of 1956 and 1957 at Fiera di Primiero, sitting among the guests of honor. It is not clear exactly whether his intention was to absorb the Focolare Movement in order to have adequate strength to implement the aspirations for reform he had in mind for a Church paralyzed by bureaucratic immobility; or whether he sincerely wanted to share in the spirituality and ideals of Chiara Lubich. Probably both elements contributed to Lombardi's promotion of his project with all the passion and decisiveness that had made him famous, which also attracted envy and dislike within the highest ecclesial institutions and in those who watched over the orthodoxy of the faith.

The Archbishop of Trent, de Ferrari, took a clear position on this situation. He was constantly updated by frequent correspondence with Chiara, Giordani, and Foresi, and he expressed his reservations about the prospect of the merger. The policy of *non movere et mota quieta*,[103] which until that moment had been his way of dealing with the problems relating to the Movement born in his diocese, but now he temporarily abandoned. His authoritative opinion was valued in Rome and so he went to investigate the confidential files in the Vatican. In the summer of 1957, when Chiara was recovering from a serious road accident that she had in May of that year, a new Visitor was appointed, the Jesuit, Giacomo Martegani, former director of *La Civiltà Cattolica* and an expert on the Focolare Movement. He too agreed that merging with the Lombardi Movement was not a good idea, so he proposed to draw up a statute that would clearly reflect what the Focolare had built up until then, following the founder's intuitions. The Jesuit's position is summed up in a dialogue with his confrère Lombardi, who had written it down in his diary: "Such mergers... have never been successful, nor does God perform such miracles to generate a head there and a body here to unite them."

The report Fr. Martegani sent to Cardinal Pizzardo on April 3, 1958 mentions clearly and analyzes critically all the problems linked to the Focolare Movement, including the issues that provoked the greatest criticism, such as the so-called "matriarchy" exercised by Chiara on its members. He also mentioned doubts

---

103. *Quieta non movere et mota quietare* is a popular Latin language motto that can be translated as "Don't shake what is calm, rather calm what is agitated."

on the doctrinal level, identified more as the result of the "prevalence of the heart and sentiment." He did not point to any danger of deviation from orthodoxy and emphasized how at the basis of the spirituality of unity there was conformity to the "genuine doctrine of the Church." He emphasized the Movement's practice of living "the love that comes from above" in the mystical body of Christ. Regarding the "temporary" status into which the Movement had been forced for years, he invited the authorities to bring it into a "normal status" of life, activity, and development through an *ad experimentum*[104] regulation. This direction was summarized in the Notes to the Rule of the Work of Mary, which described the three groups of consecrated persons with "distinct tasks, in the one call." One family divided into three branches: one male, one female and one married. Besides them there was the wider lay movement and the League of Priests and Religious, both animated by the same spirit of "unity in charity to be brought into the Church and into the world."

This approach seemed to be in line with the will of the pope. Having heard that news through a personal friend, Chiara, on May 8, 1958 wrote to the Archbishop of Trent: "Our Movement did not survive the Holy Office because it was recommended by someone, but because it is the Work of God." De Ferrari replied the following day, rejoicing at "the very explicit and decisive expressions of the Holy Father in person." He added: "We are now entering the full stage of life." He finished his letter with a blessing and signed it: "Carlo, Archbishop / honorary focalarino."

Over the following months both trepidation and optimism increased, as news filtered through that the formal recognition of the Movement was passing from the examination of the Holy Office to the much less "dangerous" one of the Congregation for

---

104. *Ad experimentum refers to a decision for a given period of time and subject to revision.*

Religious. There were still a few hiccups regarding the regulations of the involvement of the priests of the Movement.

Pius XII died on October 9 in the papal residence at Castel Gandolfo, at the age of 82. The living symbol of a Church strongly committed to defending the values of the faith and to building the new Christian order – a beacon in a world in the grip of a profound spiritual and moral crisis— was lost. Pope Pacelli, in his apparent solitude, had produced an authoritative magisterium, which seemed to be open to innovative trends which faced up to the challenges of the contemporary world. At the same time, the Church of Pius XII seemed to lack communication with the world. The time was now right for the great season of renewal that would come with the Second Vatican Council and the implementation of its reforms.

From the Vatican to the Italian Bishops Conference... and back...

In this situation, the "Focolare dossier" returned to lie on a desk somewhere in the sacred buildings, waiting for the approval of the Church. According to the founder's wish, in the statutes of the Work of Mary (the name of the Movement which had matured from its common name "Focolare Movement" to one from ecclesial authorities) every detail had to be an expression and the fruit of communion which lies at the basis of the life of the association and is set as a condition for every other rule. And the name "Work of Mary" indicated the role of the Movement whose function was that of giving Jesus back to humanity today.

The events following the death of Pius XII marked a turning point, a new and significant phase in the history of Catholicism.

On October 28, 1958 Cardinal Angelo Giuseppe Roncalli (1881-1963), Patriarch of Venice, was elected to the papal throne and took the name John XXIII. Pope Roncalli was the son of peasants from the Bergamo countryside and had a long diplomatic and pastoral career, in which he had shown singular human, cultural, and political talents. He was educated in Rome at the beginning of the century, in the lively and fertile climate of the anti-modernist struggles and the social question. He had been secretary to the Bishop of Bergamo, Giacomo Radini Tedeschi, and very much involved in the social ferment of the world in those years. He was an army chaplain during the First World War, then Apostolic Visitor to Bulgaria, Apostolic Delegate to Turkey and, from 1944, Apostolic Nuncio to Paris. In 1953 he was nominated Cardinal and Patriarch of Venice by Pius XII.

The election of Roncalli at the age of 77 made many people think that it would be a "transitional" papacy, after the twenty years marked by the strong imprint given to the pontificate by Pacelli's personality. His good-natured and simple attitude immediately led to him being called the "good pope." He was like a parish priest who speaks to people with simple gestures and language, with a deeply human warmth. Equally special were other aspects of his personality, in particular his deep religious sense and his perception of the history of the Church. He also had an extraordinary capacity to listen to the expectations of the world and to the cry of the weakest.

Only three months after his election, on January 26, 1959 in the Basilica of St. Paul Outside the Walls, John XXIII amazed the world by announcing an ecumenical council for the universal Church. This event was to be epochal for the Church (and for the whole of humanity). It urged the Church to grasp the signs of the times, to immerse herself in historical reality and to open to the world and dialogue with it. It looked for the elements of union among peoples, cultures, and religions to overcome divisions, while looking to the future with optimism, not wasting time in useless comparisons with the past. The structures of the Church as defined by the Council of Trent and by Vatican I were to be radically changed. A process of profound transformation of Catholicism had begun, aimed at recovering sources and models from the most ancient Christian tradition.

In this period, defining the canonical status of the Focolare Movement did not look imminent, and a positive solution seemed even less obvious.

Between the end of 1958 and the early months of 1959, a campaign of hostility towards the Focolare Movement developed within the Italian Episcopal Conference. The Italian bishops very strictly interpreted a directive of the Holy Office regarding the vigilance to be exercised over the activity of the Movement within diocesan boundaries. The protagonist of this campaign was the national ecclesial assistant of Catholic Action, Bishop Mario Jsmaele Castellano, supported by Cardinal Giuseppe Siri and the Archbishop of Verona (and later Patriarch of Venice) Giovanni Urbani. Already in 1957, at a meeting of the heads of local episcopal conferences, they expressed their concerns. They were worried about the threat of Communism in Italy, and felt threatened, for example, by the theses of French thinkers such as Emmanuel Mounier and Jacques Maritain, whom they accused of "mortifying the hierarchical charism of the Church, in favor of the charismatic aspect, exaggeratedly distinguishing the temporal from the sacred."

Fr. Foresi's activities in defense of the Movement's position and a clarifying intervention by Cardinal Pizzardo seemed to bring back the "crisis." John XXIII's decision to put the study of the Movement into the hands of the Italian Bishops Conference (CEI) seemed to put everything into question again. Pope John made this decision in the light of his desire to promote a greater sense of collegiality and synodality. This decision also had a more political character with respect to the historical moment that the Church was experiencing, close to the celebration of the Council. He wanted to evaluate the internal positions of the various ecclesial bodies (first among which the college of cardinals and the Italian episcopate) and wished to downsize Roman "centralism."

In October 1959 the presidency of the CEI had passed from the Archbishop of Turin, Maurilio Fossati, to his colleague from Genoa, Giuseppe Siri, known as a convinced and intransigent defender of the doctrinal and liturgical tradition of the Church, as well as for his concept for the laity, to be considered mere "executors of superior directives." The question of the Focclare Movement was immediately addressed by the General Assembly and most of the bishops demonstrated opinions and positions, more or less, negative towards the Movement. Par reservations were expressed about the priests and religious belonging to the Movement and, above all, the preponderance of the presence and influence of women within the association. The role of women as spiritual guides was particularly contested. The discussion on the role of women took on different tones and positions, which came to conclusions and proposals – like the one formulated by Bishop Adelchi Albanesi, Bishop of Viterbo – such as: "If they get rid of the women, they can get back on the right track."

Following the discussion, Cardinal Siri decreed that diocesan clergy should not have any contact with the Focolare, and that the participation of priests in the Mariapolis should be subject to permission issued by their respective ordinaries. In January 1960 a commission of five bishops was established, presided over by Enrico Nicodemo, Archbishop of Bari, charged with ascertaining the rectitude of the doctrinal principles at the basis of the Movement and the existence of its possible "charismatic direction" (to be condemned). The commission requested from all the bishops a report on the situation of their respective dioceses with respect to the presence and activities of the Movement and that the restrictive measures, such as the prohibition of the clergy, were implemented.

Chiara and all the focolarini welcomed this further suffering with obedient and trusting abandonment, but continued to work intensely with the bishops (especially the Bishop of Trent) and the members of the hierarchy considered friends, to ward off the worst case scenario. Giordani and Foresi worked especially hard, being experts on the inner workings of Roman offices on both sides of the Tiber, on the languages and customs used in those environments and in many episcopal seats of local churches.

At the plenary assembly of the CEI held in Rome at the Domus Mariae between November 17 and 19, 1960, the extensive report drawn up by the commission was presented and discussed. It contained very heavy judgments and notes on the work and orthodoxy of the "so-called Focolare Movement." It spoke of the lack of a "clear and organic spiritual doctrine"; of the distortion of the "true Catholic doctrine about fundamental points," such as grace, sin, Church and hierarchy; of a "distrust, in recent times less openly manifested, towards ecclesial control"; of an "excessive familiarity between the two sexes." The commissioners considered the Movement to be "infected by a pseudo naturalistic mysticism," such that it could not be corrected, concluding with an explicit invitation to dissolution.

The prospect of suppression was not, however, shared by Cardinal Montini, who with his intervention produced an "authoritative minority," composed of fellow Archbishops of Turin, Maurilio Fossati and Bologna, Giacomo Lercaro, Corrado Mingo of Trapani, and Giovanni Ferro of Reggio Calabria. Although they did not discuss the remarks made by the episcopal commission and espoused its concerns, they considered some statements about the impossibility of reforming the Movement too severe and opposed the drastic therapy proposed to remedy the problem, namely the suppression of the Focolare Movement.

The action of Montini, Archbishop of Milan, the fruit of his experience and diplomatic finesse, made sure that the Archbishop of Trent, who was not well enough to participate, was involved in the process. Montini asked his confrères in the episcopate to exclude any measure of censorship without first consulting de Ferrari. His intervention had made it impossible to reach a final decision of suppression.

However, after the CEI assembly, the prospects for the survival of the Movement were such that there seemed to be "no margin for deterioration." The whole question was once again put to the judgment of the Holy Office, with results that could not differ much from those of the Italian bishops.

At this point, de Ferrari's intervention, made possible by Montini's "opening" in the assembly, was very incisive and positive, if not decisive. He wrote to the Secretariat of State, to the Holy Office, to cardinals and bishops, but above all to the pope. The archbishop was linked to Roncalli by a longstanding friendship. In addition to attending the assemblies of the bishops of Triveneto, the former Patriarch of Venice used to spend part of the summer on the plateau of Folgaria, near Trent. The letter to the Pontiff of November 24, 1960 speaks of the life of the Focolare "characterized by divine charity and by a social and religious intent of unity." It states that "if a focolare could be planted in every inhabited center, a hearth of holiness would truly be lit, suitable for the new times and capable of acting deeply in the social body." He closed by asking for an end to the "painful suspension that for more than seventeen years has kept hundreds of people, all dedicated to God, between life and death," allowing them to "work for the Holy Church with the zeal that already animates them."

The above activities demanded probably all de Ferrari's physical and moral energies. A few months later, heavily burdened by his illness, he saw himself flanked in the diocesan government by an apostolic administrator, the Bishop of Brixen, Joseph Gargitter, who was to govern the Church of Trent until the death of the prelate on December 14, 1962.

Expansion, towards the world

During the years in which the long and complex canonical processes were carried out and the skirmishes within the ecclesial institutions about the recognition of the Work of Mary were being fought, the movement founded by Chiara Lubich lived a phase of powerful vitality and diffusion outside Italy. While always keeping alive their interest and delicate activities towards Eastern Europe, the second half of the 1950s saw an intense flourishing of their apostolate and the opening of the first focolares throughout Western Europe. First in France and later in Germany, Belgium, the Netherlands, Great Britain, Austria, Switzerland, Spain, and Portugal. Before this expansion Chiara had made a trip to Jerusalem, in 1956. After having been to the places of Christ's Passion and at the Holy Sepulcher, she wrote:

> *Jesus, here I want to plant once more my cross, our crosses, the crosses of those who know you and those who don't know you.*
>
> *I came out of the tomb with something very different from before, with the confidence, full of hope, that the skies of Jerusalem, which now cover also a multitude of brothers and sisters far from us, will one day hear again the angel's words to Mary Magdalene: "He is risen, he is not here," addressed to someone in search of a brother or sister who is not yet fully united.*

1957, the year of the Treaty of Rome, which gave new substance to the process of European integration, saw the first focolare mission on German soil, starting from Münster. Chiara and Aldo Stedile were hosted by the rector of the seminary, Hans Heillkenbrinker, who organized many meetings for them to present the ideal of unity. He also brought them into contact with some religious from countries behind the Iron Curtain.

That year, the summer Mariapolis saw the participation of many people, among whom several bishops, and some high-profile priests. Apart from Fr. Riccardo Lombardi of the Movement for a Better World, there was Fr. Werenfried van Straaten (1913-2003), a Dutch Premonstratensian.[105] He was known throughout Europe for his humanitarian work through the international Catholic association he founded, Aid to the Church in Need, which in those years was focused on helping refugees from the Eastern European countries. This contact bore fruit the following year, with an invitation to Brussels for the inauguration of the International Expo. He also invited the focolarini to come and work with him in the Belgian abbey of Tongerlo. The first focolarina who went was Valeria Ronchetti. Following the visit to Brussels with its marvels of human ingenuity produced and exhibited by the various nations and admired at the international exposition, the summer Mariapolis of that year was called the "Expo of God." The idea was to "create an exposition of God present among us, with a show of fraternal love, where everyone is a servant to the other, where positions are considered nothing, and where the beatitudes are being sung."

While the canonical investigations of the Focolare and the developments of the international situation weakened the official activities of the *Mystici Corporis* Committee, which was formally suspended, a new phase began of exploration towards possible destinations of expansion in other continents. On October 26, 1958, the feast of Christ the King, Lia Brunet, Ada "Fiore" Ungaro

---

105. Premonstratensians are also known as the Norbertines and, in Britain, as the White Canons

and Marco Tecilla set out on their first journey to Latin America. They left from Ciampino airport cheered on by many members of the community of Rome, without any knowledge of the local language and with few points of reference about the itinerary that awaited them overseas. The first stop was Recife, in north-eastern Brazil. They immediately went to bishop João Batista Costa, who gave them a warm welcome. This is how Marco Tecilla remembers it:

> The bishop wanted to know about our life, about the Movement and the reason for the trip. He said, "this is an ideal for the times we live in," adding words that proved prophetic: "what is being born in Recife, sooner or later will be born in other places in Brazil. The presence of God will accompany you everywhere." And he made a recommendation: "Don't leave now! Stay here until you leave behind a well-formed group. Those who have given life to this Movement will have to come here several times, because we need your presence."

The three then visited Belo Horizonte, Rio de Janeiro, Sao Paulo, Montevideo, Buenos Aires, Santiago de Chile, meeting missionary priests and religious, lay people and former students from Roman colleges, communities of Italian emigrants, collecting testimonies and evaluating the potential for spreading the ideal of unity throughout the Latin American continent. On their return, in the spring of 1959, they arranged for four girls and a priest from Recife to come to the summer Mariapolis in the Dolomites. At the same time, the bishop invited the focolarini to set themselves up permanently in Recife.

The Mariapolis of that year had more than ten thousand participants, causing some complaints from the locals who were accustomed to the tranquility of the alpine valley. There were lay people and priests from all over Europe and from several non-European countries (27 in all) where the first focolarini had established communities. On October 25 eight focolarini embarked at Genoa for Brazil. Leading the "expedition" were Marco Tecilla, the first focolarino, and Ginetta Calliari, one of Chiara's first companions, who would spend the rest of her life there, until her death in 2001.

Throughout this period Chiara maintained a detached and barely visible position compared with the vibrant activity that characterized the life of the Movement. She had been ordered to do so by the ecclesial authorities who were making a close study of the Movement with a view, possibly, to shutting it down. Chiara's way of living this moment was obviously dictated by prudence, but it also gave confidence to the members of the Movement and space for new ideas. This situation, combined with courage and faith in God's plan, would bear fruit. Meanwhile, *Città Nuova* published the first anthology of Chiara's spiritual writings, entitled *Meditations*. Over the years it has become a best seller, currently with twenty-seven editions in Italian, twenty-eight translations and over one million printed copies.

In 1959 the experience of the summer Mariapolis in the Dolomites came to an end. The hostility shown by the majority of the members of the Italian Episcopal Conference and some Vatican circles towards the Movement was too evident to continue to organize an event of that magnitude in Italy, where at any moment negative decisions could have been made about the future of the Focolare Movement.

In the rest of Europe, however, relations with ecclesial authorities, religious congregations, and lay groups were much less unstable and much more open to a fraternal collaboration. In 1960 the first European Mariapolis was held in Freiburg, Switzerland. Chiara, speaking to the many participants from all over the world, encouraged people to apply the evangelical law of love and the ideal of unity to relationships between peoples and nations. Her proposal was to "love the homeland of others as one's own" (a formula coined and promoted in the Mariapolis of the previous year). There was a change of perspective and a widening of proportions in the vision of the united world and in the activity of the Movement, grasping the positive characteristics of each people and putting them at the service of the good of humanity.

In the same year a special meeting was organized in West Berlin. Chiara and Pasquale Foresi, assisted by the Oratorians Hans Lubsczyck and Joseph Guelden, laid the foundations for the spread of the Movement, meeting about two hundred people from Eastern Europe. These people were the fruit of the "missions" (for example those in Leipzig under the pretext of visiting the Trade Fair) carried out by Aldo Stedile, Valeria Ronchetti and other focolarini in various East German cities. Mentor of the meeting (and of the subsequent ones) was the Cardinal Archbishop of Berlin Julius August Döpfner. He invited Chiara to open a focolare to serve as a point of reference for the Christians of East Germany. That first small community at Bundering-37 was the beginning of the spread of the Focolare in Eastern Europe.

From there, visitors from the other side of the Iron Curtain (which would soon materialize with the construction of the Berlin Wall) returned to their homes and communities with the announcement and the vision of a new life, based on the love of Christ and their brothers and sisters, and with the certainty that the silence of the Church of Rome towards the "Church of silence" was only an official one, required by the political-diplomatic needs of the day. It was a highly active and eloquent silence that was interpreted, deciphered, and translated by a long chain of contacts made up of nunciatures, bishoprics, monasteries and even focolares. Pope John commissioned people of the caliber of the Archbishop of Vienna, Franz König, and the Undersecretary of State, Agostino Casaroli, to start a new approach toward international politics of the Holy See. They established a growing dialogue with international organizations with a courageous openness towards Eastern European states, aimed at reopening spaces of religious freedom for their citizens and an organized presence for ecclesial institutions.

In July 1960, the German Bishops' Conference gave its unreserved approval of the activity of the Focolare in their dioceses, while in Italy the CEI was thinking along completely different lines. The support of the German bishops also served to balance the opposition of the Italian Episcopal Conference and proved to be key in opening the way to the recognition of the Movement. At the time, most of the Italian ecclesial circles were still anchored in their traditional theological and pastoral ways and were surely not seen as an example of doctrinal innovation. In the archives there are comments from German prelates of the time that can be summarized in this statement: "If the Focolare Movement has difficulties in Italy, this means that it contains something very interesting." The German bishops and their theologians were at that time among the drivers of liturgical, biblical, patristic, and ecumenical renewal and they had no difficulty in recognizing the prophetic and innovative charge of the charism of unity as a possible catalyst for the reform of the Church.

Cardinal Döpfner, aware of the problems the Movement was experiencing "at home," wrote to the Vatican expressing his admiration and full support for its work. Following the example of his Berlin colleague, the Bishop of Leipzig, Otto Spulbelk, promoted the presence of the Focolare Movement, so much so that in early 1962, Natalia Dallapiccola arrived there with two companions, one a doctor the other a nurse. After a long interrogation they were allowed to remain in the country. Shortly after, they were joined by Anna Fratta and Roberto Saltini, both doctors. The shortage and the need for workers in the healthcare facilities and hospitals of Eastern Europe was an excellent opportunity to enable the presence of focolarini. Many of them had done training and university courses so that they could treat the physical (as well as spiritual) problems of their brothers and sisters behind the Iron Curtain. Health care professions demand both scientific and human skills. They need the ability to observe and analyze so as to recognize the symptoms and to know how these symptoms will develop. They need expertise in diagnoses and confidentiality in the treatment of data in order to formulate adequate prognoses and respect the dignity of the people. They need to create deep and sincere relationships of trust and mutual respect... In other words, it was a good basis for talking about unity and achieving it.

Meanwhile, in Rome, after the pope's announcement of the ecumenical council, they were taking the first steps of preparations. It was to be a council without a pre-established model that entrusted to the bishops the task of designing the future of the Church and of drawing up criteria and norms for pastoral reform. The preparatory commission presided over by the Secretary of State, Domenico Tardini, started to consult the world's episcopate, obtaining 2,019 responses out of 2,594. The hopes and proposals for reform coming from the bishops were mainly aimed at changing the canonical and liturgical discipline of the Church, but some ideas looked at the arrival on the ecclesial scene of non-European countries and cultures (especially African and Asian) and emerging nations. They also looked at the differences between the concepts of the human being present in the various cultures and religions, the impact of Christian values on civil society and the secularized world and the influence of materialist political doctrines and new theological trends. In January 1960 the Roman synod, which should have constituted a sort of "dress rehearsal" for the Council, ended in failure. In June, with the motu proprio[106] *Superno Dei nutu,* John XXIII set up the ten preparatory commissions: the theological commission; the

---

106. *Motu proprio, literally "on his personal initiative" is an edict issued by the pope personally to the Church.*

commission of the bishops and the government of the dioceses; for the discipline of the clergy and the Christian people; for the religious; for the discipline of the sacraments; on liturgy; on study and the seminaries; for the Oriental Church; for the missions; and the commission for the lay apostolate, for all questions relating to Catholic, religious and social action. The Secretariat for Promoting Christian Unity was established and entrusted to Cardinal Augustin Bea.

In the wake of all this activity and in virtue of its relations with other Christian denominations, the Focolare Movement looked at its ecumenical vocation in relation to the principle of *ut unum sint*, and the unity of the mystical body of Christ. Until then, Chiara had not thought much about ecumenism. Things began to change for her during her visit to the Holy Land in 1956, when, seeing the Holy Sepulcher being disputed between the various Churches, she realized the urgency of healing the divisions within the mystical body.

A few years later, in the climate generated by the pontificate of John XXIII and the imminent opening of the Council, the ecumenical commitment of the Focolare Movement formally began. In 1961 in Darmstadt, Germany, there was an important meeting between Chiara and several pastors and sisters of the German Lutheran Church who wished to know more about the evangelical spirituality of unity. Fraternal contacts with the Church of England started through Canon Bernard Pawley (later an observer at Vatican II representing the Archbishop of Canterbury), who understood the potential of the spirituality of unity to facilitate the encounter between Christians of the various denominations.

In Rome, Centro Uno was founded, directed by Igino Giordani, and dedicated to the establishment of full communion among Christians. Through meetings and "ecumenical weeks" organized since 1962 in Rocca di Papa, contacts and systematic discussions began with representatives of the various Orthodox Churches, the confessions inspired by the Reformed Churches, Anglicans, Armenians, and Copts. These meetings would build a basis for dialogue, mutual trust, and theological reflection essential for the progress of relationships between the Churches in the years and decades to come. This passion for unity, in time and according to the spirit of the Council, would be extended to relations with other religions, with people of non-religious convictions and, more generally, with contemporary humanity and the world.

SPRINGTIME OF THE CHURCH AND THE MOVEMENT

GAUDET MATER ECCLESIA[107]

At the start of the 1960s, the destiny of the world seemed divided between great prospects for progress and imminent dangers capable of bringing humanity to extinction. On the one hand there were the technological advances and the space race, and on the other the specter of nuclear war and the confrontation with the immense disparities between peoples. There was a "new frontier" envisaged by the election of John Fitzgerald Kennedy as President of the USA and the awareness of the rigid division of the world into two opposing blocs, epitomized by the construction of the Berlin Wall. There was the hope and widespread perception in much of the Western world of great economic and civil progress underway, juxtaposed against great social conflicts. There was the "Cuban missile crisis" that led the world just a step away from total confrontation and the first agreements for the detente and interruption of nuclear tests. There was the break in relationship between the USSR and Maoist China and the maturation of the process of decolonization, with the reaching of independence by peoples and nations once ruled by the great Western powers. There were the beginnings of various confrontations; one that would lead to the war in Vietnam and another towards attempts of reconciliation between the two Germanys by Willy Brandt.

---

107. *Gaudet Mater Ecclesia (Mother Church Rejoices) is the opening declaration of the Second Vatican Council.*

Political debate in Italy was polarized over the Christian Democrat's opening out towards the socialists. The idea of a "center-left" coalition, even given all the precautions imposed by the Atlantic alliance and taking into account the suspicions of many ecclesial circles, was progressively gaining ground, starting from some local administrations and arriving at the national government.

On May 15, 1961, John XXIII issued the encyclical *Mater et Magistra*,[108] through which he addressed developments in relation to social justice, considering new international perspectives and in particular the relationship between rich and poor. In December, the assembly of the World Council of Churches, meeting in New Delhi, welcomed representatives of Orthodoxy from the countries of the Soviet bloc, while Roman Catholics continued to participate as observers. In that year the Dominican theologian Marie-Dominique Chenu published the article *La fin de l'ère constantinienne*, dealing with the theme of the separation between Church and state. It appeared in the series *Un concile pour notre temps*, published by the magazine *Informations catholiques internationals*. This article placed the imminent event of Vatican II within the history of its days on the basis of the principle that "there is not the Church on the one side and the world on the other, but there is the Church in the world." At the same time the Church recognized that it could no longer be at the helm of civilization, but that her task was once again, more simply and even more authentically, that of "spreading the Gospel leaven into society, into the structures of humanity."[109]

The pre-conciliar debate reflected the orientations and cultural atmosphere of the various ecclesial circles and the tensions

---

108. *Mater et magistra* (mother and teacher) is the encyclical written by Pope John XXIII on the topic of "Christianity and social progress."
109. M.D. Chenu, *Un concile à la dimension du monde*, in *Témoignage chrétien*, October 12, 1962.

between old and new. The conservative and curial wing was moving, as Church historian Hubert Jedin observed, "on the tracks of tradition," while the progressive component of the episcopate sent numerous indications expressing the desire for renewal. Among these was the speech by Cardinal Frings of Cologne, given in Genoa on November 19, 1961 (and written by the young theologian Joseph Ratzinger) which expressed the expectations for reform caused by the imminent ecclesial assembly in a good part of the European episcopates. There was the debate on the episcopate and papacy promoted by Montini in Milan in February 1962. Yves Congar's report to the ecumenical meeting in Chevetogne in 1959, (published in Italy in 1962) spoke of the urgent need to focus on the issue of episcopal collegiality and to reconsider the relationship between Scripture and Tradition. Jedin's "Short History of the Councils" (*Breve storia dei Concili*, 1959, published in Italian by Herder in 1960) called for a return of the synodal tradition. Hans Küng's book, *Reform of the Church and Christian Unity*, published in 1960 gave impetus to the ecumenical question.

The Second Vatican Ecumenical Council was convened on December 25, 1961 with the constitution *Humanae salutis*. On February 2, 1962, with the motu proprio *Consilium*, the day of its beginning was fixed for October 11. On August 6, the regulations were published. On October 4, 1962, the feast of St. Francis, John XXIII went on pilgrimage to Loreto and Assisi, because Pope John wanted to place the Council under the protection of Our Lady and the Poverello (=St. Francis: God's pauper). It was an important moment. No pope had made such a journey for more than 100 years, visiting the places that, before the unification of Italy, marked the northern borders of the Papal States. This journey also represented the Church's desire to open to the world and be reconciled with it.

On Thursday October 11, the Council Fathers present for the opening of the Second Vatican Council solemnly processed across St. Peter's Square and into St. Peter's Basilica. At the end of the celebration, the proceedings were opened by Pope John XXIII starting with the words *Gaudet Mater Ecclesia* (Mother Church Rejoices). His address clarified the aims of the assembly that was about to begin, stating that "As all sincere promoters of Christian, Catholic, and apostolic faith strongly desire, what is needed is that this doctrine be more fully and more profoundly known and that minds be more fully imbued and formed by it. What is needed is that this certain and unchangeable doctrine, to which loyal submission is due, be investigated and presented in the way demanded by our times."[110] The Church, in countering errors, should "use the medicine of mercy rather than the weapons of severity." He invited the Church to be wary of the many "prophets of doom" capable of seeing "only ruin and calamity in the present conditions of human society" and of behaving "as if they have nothing to learn from history, which is the teacher of life, and as if at the time of past Councils everything went favorably and correctly with respect to Christian doctrine, morality, and the Church's proper freedom."

On the evening of the same day, seeing the crowd gathering in St. Peter's Square by torchlight to celebrate the event, the pope improvised the famous "moon speech," where, in addition to his invitation to give the pope's caress to the children, he concluded with a speech bathed in spirituality and poetry calling all to brotherhood and spiritual fatherhood, giving a preview of the results of universal communion that Vatican II intended to achieve.

The following morning the 2,540 Fathers (1,041 Europeans, 956 Americans, 30 Asians, 379 Africans), flanked by experts, lay auditors and observers from other Churches, started the work of

---

110. This is a translation from the official Latin version of the opening speech to Vatican Council II by Pope John XXIII.

the general assembly. There had been a long phase of preparation to give voice to unexpressed hopes and requests in the greatest gathering of equals on earth. It was an assembly where no one had the right of veto. The image and model of a Church no longer defined by power but by communion, which would give a place of existence for the genuine communities and local churches within a historical perspective of salvation.

The first session discussed the outline of the liturgy, the media, the Church, and Christian unity and closed on December 8, with general and cautious optimism, but without the approval of any document. At the same time, a majority (led by Cardinals Lercaro, Montini, Suenens, Léger, Döpfner, Frings, König, Alfrink and Liénart) supported the pope's wishes for an adaptation of the languages in which doctrine was expressed, greater freedom in theological and exegetical research and greater synodality in the government of the Church. A minority (which came from the curia and Cardinals Ottaviani, Siri, Ruffini and Browne) was more concerned with the integrity of the "deposit of faith" and respect for tradition. The start of the Council's work produced a stiffening of positions in Catholic theology, measuring the relationship of strength between the so-called "Roman school" and the most advanced points of theological renewal. For Yves Congar, one of the protagonists of the Council debate from the theological and ecumenical point of view, the convocation of the Council had come at least twenty years too early. In his *Mon Journal du Concile* he noted: "things have been moving for too little time; ... in twenty year's we might have an episcopate composed of men with proper biblical formation, based on a return to the sources, and with realistic missionary and pastoral awareness."

The birth of the Work of Mary...
AD EXPERIMENTUM...

In the preparatory phase of the Council an important work was carried out by the commission *De laicatu catholico* (Concerning the Catholic laity), with particular regard to the need to establish a body responsible for promoting lay apostolate. An outline was drawn up that would animate the work of the Council from the first session onwards, involving the heads of the international Catholic organizations and the lay apostolate.

Probably, the Focolare Movement also benefited from this. At the Holy Office a commission, presided over by Bishop Pietro Parente and formed by his colleague consultor Bishop Pietro Palazzini, the Dominican Paul Philippe and the Capuchin Agatangelo da Langasco, worked intensively on yet another draft of the statutes presented by Chiara and her colleagues.

Following their debates, on March 23, 1962, the approval arrived of the first statute of the Focolare from the Church of Pope John, the Church of "mother and teacher" *(mater et magistra)*. It was established as the "Men's Pious Association Work of Mary," whose statutes were in conformity with canons 684 et seq. of the Code of Canon Law and in conformity with other prescriptions and directives of the Holy See. The following year came the ratification of a similar provision for the women's branch. In the two documents, married focolarini would be considered as "aggregates," among those who "aspire to Christian perfection." Christians of other denominations were mentioned in the statutes as "sympathizers," a term that, taking away the legal language and compared to the relations between the Churches of previous centuries, could rightly be considered revolutionary. The approval was, however, *ad experimentum*, that is, for a period and subject to revision. It did not yet sanction the unity of a work that was based precisely on the ideal of unity.

In any case, the mutual and continuous charity that makes the presence of Jesus in the community possible, constituted for Chiara, "the norm of norms, the premise of every other rule." It was canon law that was not yet capable of contemplating, recognizing, and institutionalizing what the charism had already conceived and brought about. It struggled to translate into norms and juridical language the various vocations and branches of the Movement reflecting its nature, its development, and its expansion.

The juridical nature of the Work of Mary was therefore seen as an association overcoming the approach (until that moment pursued by the ecclesial authorities and dictated by the encyclical *Provida Mater Ecclesia*) that had tried to fit it into "secular institute." That approach had proved an almost impossible task for a Work that had as its rule the presence of Jesus in the midst of its members, as its main purpose the *ut omnes unum sint,* and Jesus forsaken as the model of the life of unity. This, too, is a sign of the times that the atmosphere of the Council made it possible to let this come about.

While the first session of the Council was taking place, the world went through a moment of very strong political tension between the two blocs, caused by the Soviet intention to install nuclear weapons in Cuba and the consequent military reaction of the United States. Faced with the possible outbreak of war, John XXIII set up intense diplomatic activity and launched an appeal for peace, contributing to the easing and resolution of the crisis. The pope cultivated relations with the countries of the communist world with caution and determination. In February 1963, as proof of good will, he obtained the release of the Ukrainian archbishop Josyp Slipyj, detained in a Siberian gulag. The thaw with the Kremlin continued the following March, when Rada Khrushchev, daughter of Soviet President Nikita Khrushchev, was received in the Vatican with her husband Alexei Adjubei. The new Vatican Ostpolitik was based on respect for the person, which considered the communists as individuals and not as an expression of an ideology or political movement. From that moment on, the threads of the Holy See's diplomatic network, woven until then in an informal and clandestine manner, reached Eastern Europe, succeeding in creating new spaces of religious freedom and a dialogue on the themes of peace and human rights. The Secretariat of State translated into formal steps the progress derived from Pope Roncalli's teaching: value what unites and not what divides.

On April 9 the encyclical *Pacem in Terris* was published. It proposed to the world the ideal of peace, resting on the four pillars of truth, justice, freedom, and love. The document, addressed to "all men of good will," marked a real turning point. The Council received many stimuli and suggestions from it to guide the Church's mission in its dialogue with the modern world. It presented to the whole world the great human values that God had made sacred by becoming human, and so collaborating with all human beings towards their fulfilment. The encyclical also pointed to three great signs of the times that show the evolution of humanity's journey in history and that can assist in the assimilation of the truth: the advancement of women, the social and political development of the world of work, and the independence within a democratic context of exploited nations. Equally important is the distinction made in the encyclical between sin and sinner. *Pacem in Terris* was the spiritual and political testament of John XXIII, who died on June 3, 1963.

The conclave convened on June 19 led to the election, after six ballots, of Cardinal Giovanni Battista Montini, Archbishop of Milan. He took the name of Paul VI. Among his first acts was to declare his intention to continue the Council opened by his predecessor.

Within these great changes in the history of humanity and Christianity, the micro-history of the Focolare Movement proceeded in the furrow traced by its founder and dictated by the will of God and the Church. Full canonical recognition also followed this line, which saw a fundamental milestone in the private audience granted by Pope Montini to Chiara on October 31, 1964. His simple question on the state of the Movement was followed by his advice to create a *trait d'union*, a link, that would enshrine the unity between all its manifestations and in the variety of its composition, beginning with the two pious associations that had already received approval. It needed to bring together the form dictated by canonical legislation (in which "consecrated life" related only to members of religious orders) and life (born of the Gospel and inspired by the Holy Spirit) which took the form of a lay work and which included all vocations. Paul VI's suggestion was to make provisions for a collegial body (a Coordinating Council) headed by a layperson, to represent all the members and manifestations of the Movement.

On December 5, 1964, the Work of Mary was definitively approved by a decree of the Sacred Congregation of the Council,[111] which declared the closure of the apostolic visitation to the Movement and provided that it would continue its activities according to the statutes and with the guidance of its own superiors.

The presidency of the Movement was entrusted to Chiara. Fr. Foresi became its ecclesial assistant. Even with some formal adjustments during its first years of life, the contents, and especially the spirit of that statute would be maintained over time, updated with the changing times, law and ecclesiology. The ability to listen and read the signs of the times, revealed by Paul VI, and his trust in the laity would allow the Church to write new pages of her own history, invading with the breath of the Spirit fields hitherto unknown or little ploughed.

---

111. The Sacred Congregation of the Council was the congregation of the Roman Curia responsible for overseeing matters regarding priests and deacons not belonging to religious orders. At that period there was no Congregation specifically relating to the laity.

Part IV

LOVE IN AND FOR THE WORLD

WHAT KIND OF LOVE…?

THE BOND OF LOVE OF THE TRINITY

The itinerary of Chiara Lubich's earthly life and its narrative is characterized by the frequent use of the word "love." Every moment, every intuition, every achievement is inspired by the occurrence and presence of this dimension, which creates a constant tension towards transcendence and a continuous dialogue with humanity.

"Jesus answered him, 'Those who love me will keep my word, and my Father will love them, and we will come to them and make our home with them'" (Jn 14: 23). These words spoken during the Last Supper prefigure the new coming of Christ after Easter and define anew the nature of our life as inhabited by the life of God, which is summed up in the relationship and communion of love between the Persons of the Trinity. Jesus comes to dwell in our true home, which is to say, in the love of the Father. The work of salvation begun at Easter is fulfilled with this coming and is summarized in the new commandment "Just as I have loved you, you also should love one another." (Jn 13: 34). The events and all the achievements that will accompany Chiara Lubich's life will always be inspired by and conformed to this notion of love, which will take the form of works (first among which, the Focolare Movement itself), intuitions, writings, human and spiritual relationships, etc…The spirituality expressed over time by this approach has been defined as collective and communitarian, taking us back to Pentecost which made people into a community, and oriented them towards the fulfilment of *ut omnes unum sint* (may they all be one). Chiara summarized this spirituality in twelve points which are very much integrated with one another: God-Love; the will of God; the Word; our neighbor; mutual love; Jesus in the Eucharist; unity; Jesus forsaken; Mary; the Church; the Holy Spirit, and Jesus in the midst.

The spirituality of unity, in every one of its points, never seems to be the implementation of a project matured in Chiara's mind, nor the fruit of a reflection, or a cue from spiritual theology, drawn from more or less known historical examples. It flows from her mystical experience which, according to the definition of the Dominican theologian Albert Nolan, "is an experience of God that takes place without words, names, ideas, or any knowledge at all."[112] It is a spirituality that calls for a total and practical commitment involving all aspects of one's life and which invites all around to do the same.

In the spirituality of unity there surely exists the experience that the individual has with God and which in God is unique and unrepeatable, but alongside this indispensable personal spiritual experience, the community component of Christian life is being emphasized as coming directly from the words of the Gospel. In this sense what is new is essentially represented by the recovery of an original and ancient dimension, which exalts the communitarian aspect of the pilgrimage to God. This was done by drawing from the examples of the first Christian communities as described in the Acts of the Apostles. But also from other experiences, such as those recounted in the writings of St. Basil regarding his communities, up to the Franciscan ideal which revolutionized and permeated medieval Christianity and the following centuries up to the present day,

---

112. Albert Nolan, *Jesus Today: A Spirituality of Radical Freedom*. Obis Books, Maryknoll, 2006.

demonstrating the capacity for renewal over time, remaining faithful to the original inspiration. Chiara Lubich brought this sensibility to our days, responding to the thirst for spirituality and interpersonal communion, while both distinguishing herself from and at the same time dynamically integrating herself with traditional spiritual ways of a predominantly individual nature and approach.

This type of spirituality, so ancient and so new, had been anticipated by some great Christian thinkers and mentioned in the documents of the Second Vatican Council, which directed its fundamental reflections towards the understanding of the Church as the body of Christ and as the people gathered together in the bond of love of the Trinity.

The great theologian Karl Rahner, speaking of the spirituality of the Church of the future, thinks of it as "fraternal communion in which it is possible to have the same basic experience of the Spirit." He said:

> *We older people have been spiritually individualists because of our background and formation. . . . If there is a community experience of the Spirit, it is clearly the one of the first Pentecost in the Church, an event – it must be assumed – which did not consist in the casual gathering of a sum of individualistic mystics, but in the experience of the Spirit by the community . . . I think that in a spirituality of the future the element of fraternal spiritual communion, of a spirituality lived together, can play a more decisive role, and that slowly but surely we should continue along that path.*

Visiting the international center of the Focolare in Rocca di Papa on August 19, 1984, John Paul II defined Chiara's spiritual experience as "a radicalism that discovers the depth of love and its simplicity, that discovers all the demands of love in different situations and that tries to make this love triumph in every circumstance, in every difficulty."¹¹³ This definition speaks of many dimensions: upward in contemplation, full of spiritual depth, and horizontally extended towards relationships and communion with every neighbor.

The great mystery of love as expressed by Jesus consists of two main actions, which are equal and opposite. They can be represented as a descending and an ascending action. As described in the form of a hymn in Paul's letter to the Christians of Philippi (Phil. 2: 6-11), the first is the descent from the divine condition to that of a servant and sharer in our humanity, to the point of death through the infamous cross; the second is the ascent, where he is exalted by the Father and where all creatures of heaven, earth and the underworld will kneel before his name. These two motions are known as the *kenosis*, that is the "emptying" of himself of his divine prerogatives to share the condition of humanity. There can be no ascent and glory without descent and humiliation, just as there can be no resurrection for those who have not first humiliated themselves through death.

The resurrection reminds us every day that pain and death are only the penultimate words about life, because after them there is love. It is the love of Jesus crucified and forsaken, whose pain remains but is overcome by the glory of the resurrection.

Some twentieth century philosophical and theological thought has emphasized the dialogical dimension of human existence and its dynamic relationship with the understanding of the Trinity. They abandoned the purely conceptual dimension of the Trinity and its merely assertive descriptions, and reflected more on the human experience, overcoming the idealistic understanding of the person, and proposing perspectives based on relational and community concepts. They went beyond

---

113. Pope John-Paul II to the members of the Focolare Movement, Mariapolis Center, Rocca di Papa, 19.8.1984.

both the medieval concept of the person as a substance, and the modern one as a "self-conscious subject." According to them, the Cartesian *"cogito"* was no longer sufficient to define the ego, but that the fact of being acknowledged by the other and to be questioned by them was an essential requirement. These schools of thought were founded by philosophers such as Ferdinand Ebner, Martin Buber, Franz Rosenzweig, Emmanuel Lévinas and – with reflections on the theological dimension – Romano Guardini, Hans Urs von Balthasar, and Gisbert Greshake.

The work of the Jewish philosopher Martin Buber (1878-1965) sees the solution to the crisis of our self-understanding in the need for interpersonal and communal relationships, allowing us to recover the authentic reality from which we had departed. He asserted that "We become who we are in contact with the other." He presents contemporary culture with the idea that life is an encounter and should be understood as an inter-subjectivity (so much so as to affirm "In the beginning there is relationship"). In this way, the "we" becomes an interpersonal unity and communion.

It is the essence of dialogue that characterizes the human being, who fulfil themselves only through communion with fellow human beings, with creation and with the creator. Here too the love for humanity leads to love for God and vice versa. This reciprocity makes the encounter and dialogue between human beings authentic when it is shared by the divine presence. In this way, through dialogue, we face up to the reality of the other and we take it into account in our own lives.

The Catholic philosopher Emmanuel Mounier (1905-1950) started the debate regarding the person in the community, centered on the development of the person: "The first experience of the person is the experience of the other. The you, and therefore the we, comes before the I, or at least accompanies it....One could almost say that I exist only to the extent that I exist for others, and that in the end, to be means to love."

In later theological reflection, the Trinity and the relationship between the three Persons would become the model and source of harmony and fraternal human encounter at all levels. In the intimate truth of the Trinity, summarized in the doctrine of *pericoresis*, the three Persons are each for and in the other two. A passage from John (16: 12-15) brings us directly into the relational and communitarian dimension of the Trinity. When he speaks of the Holy Spirit, Jesus offers a description of the relationships being lived out within the Trinity, where he speaks also of himself and of the Father. Each of the three Persons does not have an individual consciousness, with themselves at the center of their horizon. Nothing is definitively possessed by anyone. What is of the Father is also of the Son, and what is of the Son is "taken" by the Spirit so that he may "make it known" to all. This is because life within the Trinity is essentially a life of love. This model of life contains a message for us to live our life equally expressed as love and as mutual gift, so that all may be one...

The theologian Piero Coda does not hesitate to recognize in the charism of unity the proof of "an all-embracing shift in the history of Christian spirituality. A shift from the primacy of the individual to a balance between person and communion and in line with the Council's expectations and the demands of the signs of our times."

The greatest and most intricate mystery of Christianity, a source of infinite interpretations and disputes over the course of more than two millennia, however, can be explained in all its depth and simplicity with the use of a simple mathematical formula used as a metaphor. This image is the fruit of the imagination of the spirit of a bishop, in love with the least, a prophet of peace, and a master of the use of the word that comes from the heart and forms a synthesis of which only poetry is capable. Tonino Bello, recalling a conversation with a priest friend recounts:

> *Do you know how I explain to my gypsy friends the mystery of the one God in three persons? I don't speak of "one plus one plus one," because that makes three. I speak of "one for one for one": and that makes one. In God, there is not one Person who is added to the other and then to the other. In God every Person lives for the other. And you know how I conclude? I say that this is a kind of family trait. A form of "hereditary character" so dominant in "Trinity House" that even when he descended to earth, the Son manifested himself as "the man who is there for the others."*

We, created in the image and likeness of God, are an icon of the Trinity and, as far as love is concerned, we are called to reproduce the pure "life-spring" of the Father, the radical welcoming of the Son and the outpouring freedom of the Spirit.

Agape

Dear brother, my Lord is on the cross and you are asking me why I am crying? . . . Even if we put all the rivers and seas together there would not be enough tears to weep over the pain and love of my crucified Lord. Love is not being loved! How can we love one another if we don't love Love?

With these words St. Francis of Assisi, one of the main inspirations behind Chiara Lubich's spirituality, showed his own inner turmoil regarding our attitude towards God's love, repeating "Love is not being loved." Jesus crucified and forsaken, the expression of "the power of God and the wisdom of God"'(1 Cor. 1: 24), calls us to contemplate the mystery of unloved Love and imitate it by pouring our mercy on the world. The cross, symbol of defeat and death, thus becomes the tree of life, and through it we are led to overcome indifference and to distribute love.

Pasquale Foresi, in his reflections on *agape*, insists strongly on this Greek word, used by the apostles John and Paul to represent God's love and to explain the life lived in God's light. *Agape* is never just a feeling, but always a free choice, an act of the will and a decision that occurs whenever there is interaction. Therefore, it is a love based on reciprocity, called for by the Gospel invitation to love God and neighbor: "love one another as I have loved you" (Jn 15: 12). As typically Christian love, the distinctive characteristic of *agape* is its ability to sum up both *eros* and *philia*, and at the same time transcend them both, because it includes gratuitousness. *Agape* is an active, concrete, gratuitous and creative love, which leads people to be projected outside themselves, turning to others and provoking a kind of action that can be called *"agapic."* This idea is being expressed in John's first letter: "We love because he first loved us. Those who say, 'I love God,' and hate their brothers or sisters, are liars; for those who do not love a brother or sister whom they have seen, cannot love God whom they have not seen. The commandment we have from him is this: those who love God must love their brothers and sisters also" (1 Jn 4: 19-21).

This is an almost systematic approach, where through love for God, which unites heaven and earth, the immanent and the transcendent, and people with their neighbors, we are being re-united to God ever more deeply thanks to this reciprocity. In the spirituality of unity, love-*agape* leads us to God together with and through each neighbor, with each person with whom a relationship is being established. It therefore has both a personal dimension in the here and now and a universal dimension. Chiara summed it up as follows:

> *Love everyone. And, to achieve this, love your neighbor. But who is my neighbor? We know it: we don't have to look far; my neighbor is the person who passes close to me in the present moment. We should... love this person now. So it is not a platonic love, not an idealistic love. It is an active love. It is necessary to*

love, not in an abstract way or in the future, but in a concrete way in the here and now.

Jesus crucified and forsaken is the model that shows us the intensity of this love. His love reached its climax on the cross in his ability to give up his life. In Chiara's words:

> Jesus said this is my commandment: "love one another," but he did not leave us without a model, because he added: "as I have loved you." And he did not leave us without an explanation, when he added: "No one has greater love than the one who gives his life for his friends." Yes, Jesus crucified and forsaken is the model of how to love one's brothers and sisters.

This is the concept of a God who becomes our companion, who suffers with us and needs our help, as was also mentioned by Etty Hillesum[114] in her diary: "If God does not help me to go on, then I shall have to help God."[115]

Vera Araujo, Brazilian theologian and sociologist, describes the meaning of love for Jesus forsaken as follows: "It does not mean living in suffering, but going beyond suffering out of love, transforming every encounter with pain, with limits, with conflicts, into an opportunity to love, which then leads to the fullness of joy."

Mutual love among people reflects the intimate nature of God, as expressed in the Trinity, the image and place of the loving relationships between Father, Son and Holy Spirit. For this reason it also takes on a social dimension by becoming the source and the guiding star of all relationships between people. It is a

---

114. Esther "Etty" Hillesum (1914-1943) was a Dutch author who wrote of the persecutions of Jewish people in Amsterdam during the German occupation. In 1943 she was murdered in the concentration camp of Auschwitz.
115. *Etty – The Letters and Diaries of Etty Hillesum, 1941-1943*, edited by Klaas A. D. Smelik, translated by Arnold J. Pomerans (Ottawa: Novalis, 2002).

concrete love, immersed in the polyphony of life, in the delight expressed by many, which generates relationships and arouses hope, which disdains individualism and selfishness. Jesus in his preaching has always referred to the love of the heart, where the fire burns and the loaves and fishes multiply. In this way love becomes the new law.

As a consequence we see the fulfilment of Isaiah's prophecy:

For as the rain and the snow come down from heaven,
 and do not return there until they have watered the earth,
making it bring forth and sprout,
 giving seed to the sower and bread to the eater,
so shall my word be that goes out from my mouth;
 it shall not return to me empty,
but it shall accomplish that which I purpose,
 and succeed in the thing for which I sent it. (Is. 55: 10-11)

Light and colors

The modern scientific theory of the composition of light and its dispersion into the colors of the rainbow was first described by Isaac Newton in the second half of the seventeenth century. Throughout the ages, all civilizations and cultures have been fascinated by the natural phenomenon of the rainbow. From the Greek myths, which saw it as the path traced by the messenger Iris to join the earth to the home of the gods, to the books of the Bible, which always depict it in poetic and dreamlike ways. In Genesis it is mentioned as the sign of God's benevolence and his covenant with Noah after the punishment of the flood. Sirach invites us to observe the rainbow and bless the one who created it in its splendor. Ezekiel, at its appearance in the clouds of rainy days, compares it to the glory of the Lord. In Revelation, it encircles the forehead of an angel and wraps around the throne of God.

Since the truths of religion often exceed the capacity of our intellect and the mystical experience anticipates their rational understanding, the aphorism from G.K. Chesterton can be applied to them: "They are like the sun; we cannot see inside them but you see everything else in its light."[116]

Love as a rule of life was expressed by Chiara through the image of light and of the colors that make up this light. Each color is a single and different part of light, and together they are a symbol of communion. The light of the Gospel, which flows from the understanding of Jesus crucified and forsaken, is like the white light that passes through a prism or a drop of water, and is then reflected in the seven colors of the rainbow, illuminating the world and its relationship with God. The seven colors are seven expressions of love, and they sum up all its infinite nuances:

> *So the Lord helped me understand that just as light splits into seven colors, those of the rainbow, it is still always light: red, orange, yellow, green, blue, indigo, violet, so also love is always love. It makes us put everything in common; this can be called the red of love. It makes you win over souls: the orange. It unites you more and more to God: yellow. It makes you healthy in the mystical body: green. Not only spiritually healthy, but also physically. It makes you to be Church, that is gathering, an assembly: blue. It gives you a culture that comes from heaven, it makes you wise: indigo. This is an understanding, a seeing of things as from within the very Word of God who is within you, and in front of the Word of God you can well imagine how small our human reasoning is. It makes us all one body: the violet. In short, we seemed to understand that the Lord had ordered our life as a rainbow. What God*

---

116. Gilbert K. Chesterton, *Orthodoxy*, Munich 1909, 28.

has done in nature, in which you can recognize the imprint of the Gospel, is very similar to what in there is in the supernature.

It is the same light. It passes through the pupil of the eye and splits up leaving an impression on the retina, allowing us to see and understand the world, both the earthly and the divine world.

And in her notes from 1949 she writes:

Jesus is Jesus Forsaken. Because Jesus is the Savior, the Redeemer, and he redeems when he pours the Divine upon humanity through the Wound of his Forsakenness which is the pupil of the Eye of God upon the world: an infinite Void through which God looks upon us, the window of God thrown open upon the world and the window of humanity through which we see God.

JESUS IN THE MIDST

"For where two or three are gathered in my name, I am there among them" (Mt. 18: 20). This passage from Matthew, often the subject of commentary in the patristic literature of the early centuries, again came into prominence in the twentieth century[117] in the context of the theological reflection of the liturgical movement. It registered a flowering of attention during the time of the Second Vatican Council. During that period, the exploration of the mystery of the Church and the new approach to its intimate nature, based on communion, found its expression in *Lumen Gentium* which describes the divine and communitarian vocation of humanity (called in Christ and in the Church to a life of love

---

117. That is, in the Roman Catholic Church. Already in many of the Churches of the Reformation it had become a central issue of their spirituality. (Editors' note)

and unity that reflects the Trinity, and defines the Church as "a people made one by the unity of the Father, the Son and the Holy Spirit" (LG 4). Also the fruit of this approach is the document's systematic exposition on holiness: all the faithful are called to holiness, which is essentially union with Christ; this one holiness is presented in many forms, where alongside the traditional models we have a growing number of saints coming from a wide variety of backgrounds (LG 50).

Matthew's passage, which speaks of the presence of Jesus in the midst of his people, was mentioned in the Council papers and in various documents dealing with the questions concerning the renewal of the Church: *Sacrosanctum Concilium* (on the liturgy), *Unitatis redintegratio* (on ecumenism), *Mysterium fidei* (on the Eucharist), *Perfectae Caritatis* (on religious life), and *Apostolicam actuositatem* (on the apostolate of the laity). Such attention regarding this point on the part of the Magisterium had not occurred since the time of the Council of Chalcedon in 451.

Christ is always present in his Church in the liturgy (in the sacraments, in his word, in prayer and in praise), which opens us up to the fullness of the Christian life in order to make the new people of God into the holy temple of his presence. With the new ecumenical vision, prayer in common is extended outside the strictly Catholic liturgical sphere, and the Council document that speaks of it says that the soul of ecumenism lies in the conversion of the heart, which is an effective means of bringing about the grace of unity. In this respect, Chiara wrote:

> Since we cannot yet be united in the Eucharist with most of the other Christian Churches, we feel we can already be united, when the necessary conditions are in place, through the presence of Jesus among two or more.

Christ is present to his Church in the sacrament of the Eucharist. The Belgian Dominican Edward Schillebeeckx, a protagonist of the theological debate of those years, noticed how the new understanding of the eucharistic presence tends above all to set it in the context of the real presence of Christ in the believer and in the assembly of the community of believers. In this way the ancient Christian view regains its fullness: the eucharistic presence is directed towards the realization of the intimate presence of Christ in each individual believer and in the entire believing community.

Christ's presence is real both in the assembly gathered to pray and praise, and in the daily experience of faith.

Life is shared, following the example of the early Church in which the multitude of believers was of one heart and one soul, and everything was shared among them (Acts 4: 32). They were nourished by the teachings of the Gospel and by the food of life from the Eucharist, persevering in fellowship, in the breaking of bread, in prayers and in unity of spirit (Acts 2: 42). The spirit of Mt. 18: 20 with "Jesus in the midst" was also taken up in the context of the apostolate as in the decree of *Apostolicam Actuositatem* published on November 18, 1965, which reminded the faithful that "man is naturally social and that it has pleased God to unite those who believe in Christ into the people of God (1 Pet 2: 5-10) and into one body (1 Cor. 12: 12)" (AA 18). Therefore, the apostolate that goes with it is seen as a sign of the communion of the faithful and of the unity of the Church in Christ. The enormous power deriving from unity was here being affirmed: it is Christ present among its members who attracts and wins over other people.

Already in 1950 Chiara wrote: "Jesus in the midst was like a fire that melts down two metals into a third, which has different qualities from those of its two components" A clear reference to the Trinitarian dimension, where souls are at the same time equal and distinct, but integrated by love.

LOVE AND JUSTICE

Chiara Lubich's ideas, the Focolare's intimate social vocation and their achievements in various fields of human activity, especially in the social field, inevitably lead to a comparison between love and justice. We see this clearly in the thought of Paul Ricoeur, one of the greatest philosophers of the twentieth century, who dedicated an important book to the relationship between the two terms, with ample references to biblical exegesis.[118]

The French philosopher countered the somehow abstract idea of love, often relegated to the sphere of human passions, and the formalism of justice, with a dialectical principle according to which love teaches us to "enter" the order of justice. In this way we become a generator of virtuous coexistence, activating community experiences and social set-ups capable of rectifying inequalities in forms that can serve as a model and can be copied. He goes so far as to say that "love propels justice to be directed towards the culture of giving." Throughout history, institutions with beneficial aims have been created through the application of this principle and have become part of society and of the civil order, such as hospitals, schools, banks, and cooperatives. Love also goes beyond justice, thanks to its prophetic gaze and its supplementary character in situations, though legal, marked by selfishness and inequality, so generating authentic justice.

Even though they have a conflicting internal logic, love and justice can and must complement each other. It is possible to arrive at a correct balance between them, however it is challenging. Ricoeur says: "To incorporate an additional degree of compassion and generosity, slowly but tenaciously, into all our

---

118. EG., Paul Ricoeur, *Love and Justice*, Philosophy & Social Criticism, vol. 21, 5-6. 1995.

ways of doing things is a perfectly reasonable, though difficult and interminable task."

The commandment of love in Luke's version of the Sermon on the Mount ("love your enemies," Lk. 6: 27), would in this way be complemented by the "golden rule," which is a symbol of justice ("do to others as you would have them do to you" Lk. 6: 31). Clearly Jesus' words are not laws to be taken literally, they are not articles of a rigid code, but are defining images that contain demanding messages. Christians must be ready to reach the point of absolute and unconditional love for their neighbors. They must learn to love as God loves them, that is, totally and unconditionally. Therefore, the righteous person *par excellence* is none other than the Good Samaritan who had compassion for the injured man on the road to Jericho, while everyone else turned their back on him. Jesus, who was not a priest, wanted a people of priests capable of loving, and not a priestly caste to guard the law. As the biblical scholar Alberto Maggi says, "Jesus did not come to purify the temple, but to eliminate the temple categories," to eliminate the Pharisaism of so many of our practices and control by means of the law. When, faced with the choice between law and love, and we do not know what to do, let us remember that we are facing two choices. If we favor a presumed law of God, we do not know if it will prove useful to our neighbors and therefore make them happy and fully alive. If we choose the path of love and the good for our neighbor, even if it is apparently contrary to the law taught or handed down, we can be sure that we are doing God's will.

Mary, *Theotókos* and *Hodegetria*

The prologue of the Gospel of John says, "And the Word became flesh and lived among us" (Jn 1: 14). This verse sums up the full and indissoluble unity between the divine and the human nature of Jesus. The "great things" that God accomplished in Mary (Lk. 1: 49) and that culminate with the Incarnation is part of the patrimony of faith of every believer.

In 431, the Council of Ephesus solemnly proclaimed that "he was begotten before all ages from the Father in his godhead, the same in the last days, for us and for our salvation, born of Mary the virgin, according to his humanity." On November 21, 1964, at the conclusion of the third session of the Second Vatican Council, Pope Paul VI declared Mary "Mother of the Church," that is, of all the Christian people. Summing up the Council's work, he said: "This is the first time that an ecumenical council presents such a comprehensive synthesis of Catholic doctrine regarding the place of Mary in the mystery of Christ and of the Church."

This title has ancient and deep roots in the Church. St. Augustine already used to say that Mary is the mother of the members of Christ, because she cooperated through her charity with the rebirth of the faithful in the Church. St. Leo the Great called Mary the mother of Christ, who is the Son of God. He also called her the mother of the members of the mystical body of Christ, that is, of the Church. Both Fathers anchored their reflections in John's passage (Jn 19: 26-27) that describes the episode of Mary at the foot of the cross, where Christ entrusted to her John, the beloved disciple, with the words "Here is your son." In his pontifical decree of March 3, 2018, Pope Francis says:

> *Our Lady accepted her son's will and embraced everyone in the person of this disciple as children to be regenerated to the divine life. In this way she became the loving guardian of the Church that Christ on the cross, by emitting the Spirit, generated. And Christ, in the beloved disciple, chose all his disciples to become stewards of his love for his mother, entrusting her to them so that they would welcome her with filial affection.*

The Council had proposed a new understanding of who we are as immersed in the mystery of God. Mary had also been described in more human and concrete ways, without diminishing her individuality. In this new Marian hermeneutics,[119] as expressed in *Lumen Gentium*, the most important aspects of our faith were brought together and reflected upon. It is in the Daughter of Zion that the Church, all Christians, and humanity as a whole, find their identity and fulfilment.

These hermeneutics are fully expressed in Chiara's charism of unity as embodied by the Movement, whose official name is "Work of Mary." During an interview with Vatican Radio on June 4, 1987, Chiara said:

> *This is how we live the Marian spirituality: our spiritual way, our spiritual itinerary is also called Mary's way (Via Mariae), and it seems to us that all the adherents of our movement travel their holy journey of life following in the footsteps of Our Lady. . . . For example, when our new ideal was announced to them, which was the announcement of a charism that has entered into the Church for the good of many, there is a certain similarity with the Annunciation. It was announced to Our Lady that she would become the mother of Jesus and that Jesus would begin to be born within her.*

From her very first "yes" to the Archangel of the Annunciation, Mary was the first to live the Christian vocation, which is a vocation to love. This love cannot be lived without knowing and loving the cross. In Mary's sorrow at the foot of the cross, love is manifested in its maximum expression. Mary's desolation, her *stabat*[120] is her identification with her crucified son, showing us

---

119. Hermeneutics is the branch of knowledge that deals with interpretation, especially of Scripture.
120. This refers to Mary as remaining standing at the foot of the cross in the greatest moment of her sorrows as expressed in a thirteenth century hymn

how to connect with Jesus forsaken, and how the way of the cross is the way of Mary.

This is how Igino Giordani describes Mary desolate:

> *Restrained and firm against the storm, at the decisive hour, there were only Mary and the cross: the two supports to the Redeemer offered in holocaust. It was then that the virgin mother rose as queen of the universe, both in power and beauty, against the darkness and against death. There was no mother on earth more to be pitied, a creature more tormented. This single woman was the only representative of the servitude of men and of the kingship of God.*

In that moment of utter desolation Jesus seems to release Mary of her motherhood in order to entrust her to the beloved disciple, symbol of humanity. It is the moment in which Mary becomes the mother of the Church. In the loneliness of her loss, the plan that God had for her is fulfilled, bringing her to a universal motherhood. In her Diary 1964-1965 Chiara published a meditation that condenses this vision of Mary and her role in the divine plan of salvation. Her desolation in front of the cross makes it possible to achieve this full identification with Jesus:

> *I have only one mother on earth:*
> *Mary desolate.*
> *I have no mother but her.*
> *In her is the whole Church for eternity,*
> *and the whole Work of Mary in unity.*
> *In her design is mine.*
> *I will go through the world reliving her.*
> *Every separation will be mine.*
> *Every detachment from the good I have done*

---

called *Stabat Mater*.

> will contribute to building up Mary.
> In her "staying" (at the foot of the cross), my "staying."
> In her "staying," my "going."
> Hortus conclusus, enclosed garden,
> Sealed fountain (see Sg 4:12);
> I will cultivate her most loved virtues,
> so that on the silent nothingness of myself
> her wisdom may shine.
> That many, all her chosen children,
> those most in need of her mercy,
> may always find her maternal presence in another little Mary.[121]

Chiara described Mary once as "only word of God" and "all clothed with the word of God," to underline her total adherence to the Word, which conveys to her the will of the Father. In this regard, the theologian Marisa Cerini commented how "this profound relationship of Mary with the word of God enables her to be acknowledged and loved by all Christians of the most varied denominations. And her being an 'absolute emptiness,' and therefore invincible, fascinates the believers of other religions."

To the many attributes of the Virgin that Christian spirituality has coined over the course of two millennia, Chiara added another, the title of one of her meditations during the summer Mariapolis in 1959, which is of great theological and poetic charm: "Transparency of God." In this meditation Chiara uses definitions such as "the protagonist of all humanity," "the greatest design that God-Love could invent," "marvelous shade that contains the sun," "lofty silence that is silent no more," "a scene majestic and fair as nature," "rainbow of virtue that says 'peace' to the entire world," "creature first thought of in the mysterious abyss of the Trinity and given to us," "masterpiece of the creator, on whom the Holy Spirit delighted to bestow all he invented,

---

121. Chiara Lubich, *Essential Writings*, New York New City Press, 2007, 139.

and poured out so many of his inspirations," concluding with: "about her we can never say enough."[122]

In this new understanding, Mary is both *Theotókos* (mother of God) and *Hodegetria* (she who points the way). She is a bridge between heaven and earth, to be contemplated and imitated concretely, so that we become a presence of her on earth and almost a continuation. This understanding is summed up in Article 7 of the statutes of the Work of Mary: "The Work of Mary ... places itself under the special protection of Mary most holy, venerated in her splendid prerogatives, imitated as a model to which all can conform, loved as mother of the Church and of every human creature, and invoked as the mother of unity."

The title of "Mother of the Church" is very much rooted in the theological reflection of the twentieth century, in particular that of Hans Urs von Balthasar, assisted by the mystical ideas offered to him by his friend Adrienne von Speyr, to whom he was a spiritual director. These reflections emphasize Mary's role in salvation history and the link between her maternal and spiritual experience with the Church's maternal experience. This great Swiss theologian described the profound relationship between Our Lady and the Church as a "Marian principle," which intersects with the four existing vocational models in the life of the Church the Petrine principle (the institution), the Johannine principle (love and charism), the Pauline principle (the evangelizing and missionary impulse) and the Jacobite principle (tradition, memory, roots). In particular, the Petrine principle and the Marian are complementary, united in origin and purpose, but different in roles and tasks. Institution and charism, office, and holiness, are inseparably united in the same origin and purpose. The true point of convergence between them is the Holy Spirit since they both serve the unity of the Church and the Church's mis-

---

122. *Mary Transparency of God*, New City, London, 2003, 11 – 14.

sion of unity in the world. Mary, through her "yes" pronounced at the moment of the Annunciation and with her "yes" at the foot of the cross, represents the model for the Church and the people of God through which to carry out their mission. Mary is a symbol of charismatic logic, as we can see during the wedding feast at Cana, where she realizes that the guests have no more wine (Jn 2: 3). Charisms see further ahead and before anyone else (especially before the institution...) because they look at history with different eyes, grasping the problems, sensing opportunities, and proposing solutions. Looking at Mary in the light of Scripture, the Marian profile consists in welcoming God's gift in faith and love, and so becomes generative too.

Von Balthasar calls Mary "the all in a single piece," because she sums up the entire economy of salvation, the divine revelation of trinitarian love and God's way of acting in history; a God who chooses to work in humble people like Mary, the human creature in whom humility appears in all its beauty.

AFTER THE COUNCIL

Nostra aetate

At Christmas 1961, Pope John XXIII signed the Apostolic Constitution formally announcing the Second Vatican Council. His signature was accompanied by a strong call for a "new Pentecost" for the Church. This implied the need to discern, accept and favor the work of the Holy Spirit in history, and to become the interpreters and protagonists of the possibilities offered to the Church and to humanity. It was about the recognition of the *kairos* (opportunity of change), the awareness of an unrepeatable and providential occasion that was being offered regarding salvation. The conscience of humanity and Christianity were urged to grasp this *kairos*, as an event of grace to be recognized and lived to the full.

Hence the message about the *signs of the times,* taken directly from the page of Matthew's Gospel, where Christ invites us to discern "the signs of the *kairos*" (see Mt. 16: 3).

An invitation to welcome "the *kairos* of Christ" – always imminent – is frequent in the texts of the evangelists and in the Pauline letters, because every moment of the *new age* which the Lord inaugurated with his death and resurrection, offers us the opportunity to attain salvation: "now is the acceptable time [*kairos*]; see, now is the day of salvation! " (2 Cor. 6: 2). It was an invitation to seize the opportunity offered and to respond to God's will in this precise moment of history. This brought together many people in the Church in the period before, during and after the Second Vatican Council, in which they invested a lot of time on the key words of "conscience," "renewal," and "dialogue," and drawing up and dictating the guidelines for a future, still largely to be deciphered, discovered, and lived.

The utopian and revolutionary buoyancy that had invaded the world, especially the young, of the 60s and 70s, also affected the Church, theological debate, and religious life with its crises sometimes localized and momentary, and at other times more spread out. The ecclesial protest and dissent was a widespread and multiform phenomenon, marked by strong and traumatic choices, involving issues that were limited to small groups but at times had global implications ranging from new forms of spirituality to anti-institutional religious proposals. These ranged from the primacy of conscience to the authority of the Magisterium; from civil disobedience to the analysis of the profound and evangelical needs of the people; from the Vietnam war, to social justice, from human rights to divorce, abortion, and celibacy.

A general cultural climate, permeated with various forms of materialism and ideologies, provoked a kind of alienation from Christianity and some of its traditional moral foundations, and made them the object of free choice.

In the general radicalization of the discussion within the Catholic world, perspectives regarding conscience and the secularization of laws and ethics became more diverse, especially with the publication of the encyclical *Humanae Vitae* in 1968.

Phenomena like feminism and religious pacifism, grassroots communities, debates on ethics and sexuality, and the liberation movements with a strong political focus started to be formed around some people who had powerful and prophetic charismas.

In that symbolic year, the theologian Johann Baptist Metz published the book, *The Theology of the World*, inaugurating a current of political theology, which was aimed at correcting the prevailing tendency of reducing the Christian faith to a private matter, and took on the task of developing instead the social implications of the faith, freedom, peace, justice, and reconciliation as critical and liberating requirements.

A few years later, in 1976 in Tanzania, the Ecumenical Association of Third World Theologians (EATWOT), through the document "Theology from the other side of history" (also known as the Manifesto of Dar-es-Salaam), inaugurated the path of *Third World theology*.

The reaction to these movements led to situations such as that of the French bishop Marcel Lefebvre, who reproached the Church of Rome for giving in to modernist ideas, thus creating a schism that has not yet been recomposed.

Paul VI, who was the target of strong theological and pastoral criticism from many quarters because of his way of conducting the work of reform following the Council and because of many of his decisions, looked at the protest with great attention and foresight, opposing nihilism with hope, so much so as to spell it out at the General Audience of January 15, 1969, where he said:

> *Humanity has acquired the consciousness both of the shortcomings in which their life unfolds, and of the prodigious possibilities with which new means and forms of existence can be produced. They are no longer at peace: a frenzy has engulfed them, a dizziness exalts them, and at times a madness invades them which directs them to overturn everything (here is the global protest) in the blind trust that a new order, a new world, a palingenesis still not predictable, is about to fatally arise . . . We will not be the ones to challenge completely this protest, this need for renewal, which for many reasons and in certain ways is legitimate and necessary.*

The world of the clergy and religious was also marked by deep tensions, with animated debate on the traditional understanding of the priesthood and on the rationale for consecrated life in the light of these new ideas. In the general framework of the 1970s, the Church was aware that it was necessary to establish a dialogue with the world regarding "re-evangelization."

It was an important moment for the Church, one that was brimming with ferment. In particular there was the question of "discernment of gifts" present within the Church and lively debate, stirred up by the same Spirit, on the co-essentiality between the hierarchical and charismatic gifts. This dialogue proved to be a key factor in the revision and renewal of Christian life.

In those years, alongside the traditional associations which were experiencing crises, often deep crises, new movements and associations were being born, frequently from the same roots and often with a strong lay profile. They had their specific characteristics and aims, sometimes with a more national dimension and outlook, and other times much wider.

Among the best known of these are, in addition to the Focolare Movement, Communion and Liberation, the Community of Sant'Egidio, communities born in the context of the Charismatic Renewal (Emmanuel, Béatitudes, Chemin Neuf, Shalom, Cançāo Nova...), the Cursillos de Cristianidad and the Neo-catechumenal communities. They are all quite different in their charisms, pedagogy, structures of community life and missionary practice, in their service to the Church, and in their relationship with the broader cultural and religious horizons that make up the globalized world.

It was the "moment of the movements," which were seen as fruits of the Holy Spirit, concentrated in various clusters, to renew tradition while springing from the same wellspring. They wanted to reform the Church through a renewed radicalism which proposes new forms of communion and evangelization in the surrounding secularized culture.

The emergence of charisms seems to be a recurring phenomenon at certain crossroads in history and in many epochal turning points, especially when the survival of the Christian message seems deeply questioned. To mention some of the best known examples of this, we can recall the great mystics and reformers of religious life in the late Middle Ages, such as Dominic de Guzmán and Francis of Assisi; or, at the beginning of the modern age, Ignatius of Loyola and Teresa of Avila. The different realities born out of such charisms often represented unexpected, sometimes disruptive innovations that inevitably raised questions and caused discomfort and tension in the Church. Before being grafted onto the ecclesial structure, of which the movements were part, and being able to exercise a fruitful exchange with other realities in the Church, time was needed for discernment, patience, and charity, along with the courage to experiment. Such a process continues to the present day...

In the decades following the closure of the Council, up until today, the geography of the world has profoundly changed. This is true regarding local and national boundaries and political structures, social and cultural environments, within the religious sphere, and the perception of the future. Also, the situation of Christianity has radically changed. What were once the "peripheries" of Christianity are today witnessing significant growth, albeit in ways totally different from the past.

Europe and the western world, which for two millennia constituted the heart of Christianity, have become severely affected by secularization, with the consequent desacralization and de-Christianization, as well as a sharp reduction in the number of believers. All this dramatically impacts the Church's consciousness vis-a-vis the ways of dialogue between Christian Churches and other religions, the encounter with civilizations, religious freedom, and the secular nature of relations between religions and states. This situation exposes an urgent need for Christians to become authentic witnesses and to seek new forms of dialogue that overcome ideological barriers and rivalries between cultures and religions.

There has been a change in the very landscape of contemporary life regarding the future of religion, secularism, and the whole of humanity, which makes it essential for the Church to reorient itself carefully.

The Council's invitation, in particular through the constitution *Gaudium et Spes* regarding a renewed relationship and a new encounter with modernity, represented only a provisional and partial beginning of a theological project, a rough draft of a humanist vision which to "the people of God," together with all humanity, confidently entrusted every subsequent interpretation and way forward.

The concept of "the people of God" has a clear biblical background, which refers to God's covenant with Israel and identifies the Church as the new Israel. It enshrines fundamental equality within the Church and emphasizes the community as opposed to individualism, and the ordinary people as opposed to the elite. It depicts the identity of the Church as an effective historical subject, capable of becoming tangible.

Charismatic experiences like Chiara Lubich's are recognized as such by their ability to understand, interpret, and live *kairos*, often ahead of the times (of both humanity and of the Church). What was intuited, thought out, shared, sown, and lived, often without being understood by a good part of the hierarchy and the faithful, before the "Springtime of the Council," was destined to develop powerfully and to accompany the complex years of the initial reception of the contents of Vatican II by the people of God. In particular, it was destined to follow the paths of dialogue with the modern world and its rapid evolution towards a secularized post-modernity which would prove to be the fundamental expression of the last remnant of the second millennium and the dawn of the third.

The Church of Christ, in her catholicity, has always been a model of globalization, but at this time, in her historical-institutional dimension, she was called to face a world that itself had recently become global. Deeply anchored in euro-centric cultural models, she had to rethink many of her constitutive interpretations of the world. She had to take up the challenge of inculturation in large regions of a rapidly changing world epitomized by the end of the colonial period.

At a theological and pastoral level, the Church had to redefine its ideas of what is the center and what the periphery, revising an organizational model that for almost two millennia had been based on the territorial criterion of diocesan structures.

The new globalized village presented itself as increasingly less regulated by its juridical systems and more by the laws of the market. It was increasingly less defined by its cultural and ideological affiliations and always more by the movement of information and migrations of people. It was less defined by political boundaries and religious identities, but more organized by the geography of its emotions and communication networks. This global complexity resulted in the Church having to rethink its identity and presence in the world, aiming at the proclamation of the spirit of the Gospel and at being a leaven. She now had to begin to identify herself as a creative, prophetic minority, without fixed borders, with an inclusive vision that addresses itself to the "people," identifying it as the whole of humanity.

The proclamation of the Council's decree, *"Ad Gentes,"* dedicated to missionary activity, indicated that the Church should embrace the cultural heritage of peoples, purify and enrich it, thereby improving herself and advancing towards the fullness of her catholicity. The pontificate of Paul VI considered the Latin

American continent as a true laboratory for redefining a new model of the Church, for spiritual regeneration, and the affirmation of the "civilization of love," that should characterize the renewed dialogue between faith and modernity.

In 1966, announcing "the hour of Latin America," he mentioned how the world was waiting for the Church's "witness full of energy, of wisdom, of social renewal, of concord and peace, a renewed witness of Christian civilization."[123]

The meetings of the Latin American and Caribbean Episcopal Conference (CELAM) held in Medellín in 1968, and in Puebla in 1978, redefined the features of theology, ecclesiology, and pastoral care in the new world. They affirmed the preferential option for the poor, the liberation of people from all forms of oppression, the relationship between evangelization and human promotion, the religiosity of the people, inculturation and indigenous traditions, and religious pluralism.

These ideas influenced the drafting of the Apostolic Exhortation of Pope Paul VI, *Evangelii Nuntiandi*, in 1975. This stated that the proclamation of salvation is the reason for the Church's existence, and that therein lies its contribution to the liberation of humanity. The fruits of a local, synodal and creative reception of the conciliar texts became, for the first time, part of a pastoral proposal addressed to the universal Church. Despite many delays, revisions, and corrections due to the attitude of the successive papacies and the unfolding of history, this would bear fruit in the CELAM conference held in 1992 (the 500th anniversary of the discovery of America) in Santo Domingo and, above all, in that of 2007, in Aparecida, Brazil.

The focolarini first traveled to the South American continent between 1958 and 1959. In 1961 Chiara herself visited Brazil

---

123. Pope Paul VI, homily, May 22, 1966: Celebration of the 75th Anniversary of *Rerum Novarum*.

for the first time. Starting from Recife, their presence in Latin America had grown rapidly, even though they experienced difficulties as they implemented their traditional European-style methods and models for both evangelization and in their social justice activities. However, all this made them aware of their limitations.

They patiently observed the world around them, listened to the people, discovered new ways of living in contact with the infinite outskirts of physical and existential peripheries. They saw the impoverished and marginalized rural areas and had to re-invent the meaning of the original community as described in the Acts of the Apostles (2: 44-45): "All who believed were together and had all things in common; they would sell their possessions and goods and distribute the proceeds to all, as any had need." Only in this way were they able to understand the flexibility of the ideal of unity and develop new forms of dialogue and collaboration with the theological and social situations in those places and in that climate. It was a form of evangelical poverty as a constitutive element of the Church and her mystery. So they found an intrinsic link between Christ, the poor, and those who suffer, all rooted in the mystery of the Incarnation, a fruit of the *kenosis* and of the abandonment on the cross.

Dialogue with liberation theology (a term coined in 1969 by the Peruvian theologian, Gustavo Gutiérrez), with its aspirations of building a more just and fraternal society, the enormous social disparities with moments of revolutions and dictatorships would accompany the Focolare's journey in Latin America with ever new experiences of life, and with the development of the charism. The Brazilian theologian Leonardo Boff, the main exponent of liberation theology, appreciated their work and their collaboration in the promotion of local churches, in the love for the poor and for justice, and in the dialogue with all the various religious bodies present in the continent. These experiences led, in the 90s, to the development of the project of the *Economy of Communion,* born precisely in Brazil. This will be discussed later in the book.

The Focolare's aptitude for dialogue also made it possible to understand the phenomenon and the theological basis for the rapid expansion of new religious groups, largely of Protestant origin, and the neo-Pentecostal movements. These were seen not as enemies but as a challenge and a stimulus to identify Christian life on the Latin American continent. This hermeneutical challenge called into question the ecumenical dynamics of the traditional Churches of Latin America.

The first focolarini arrived in Africa in February 1963, at the request of Julius Peeters, Bishop of Buea, in Cameroon. When this Dutch prelate was in Rome for the Council, he met Chiara and Pasquale Foresi. The bishop asked them for a missionary presence in his diocese, which was needed to revive a local hospital that needed doctors. The answer was yes, and three focolarini left for Cameroon: Nicasio Triolo, a pediatrician; Danilo Gioacchin, a veterinarian; and Lucio Dal Soglio, a dentist. The following year the first three focolarine went as well. They too were involved in health care, and many others were to follow.

It was the time of decolonization and of independence for many African states. The Church quickly followed with a delicate transition from a structure marked by the presence and authority of missionaries to the building of local churches with an African identity and hierarchy. In August 1969 during his historic journey to Uganda (the first time a pope visited Africa) Pope Paul VI said: "You Africans are now your own missionaries."

Chiara went to visit Cameroon in 1965, where she set in motion the development of one of her "little towns" (of which we will speak later) in a remote location called Fontem, an area inhabited by the Bangwa people.

King fon Defang met her the following year, to talk about the construction of a hospital and other social projects. Chiara commented at that time that she had the impression that the people there had "a strong sense of the divine in their hearts" and a special sense of community and unity, and believed that "God had a special plan for that place."

She sent her friend Marilen Holzhauser from Trent as the responsible for the focolarine, and told her: "Go to Africa, listen to everyone, don't talk for six months. It is an extremely sensitive moment. We must not impose religion, nor Western ways of seeing things, but try to learn, try to understand. In this way a Christian-African people will emerge, and not just an African one."

From that moment on, starting with the town of Fontem, projects were developed for the whole of the continent, dedicated to health care, education and vocational training, catechesis, and local pastoral work, often in the absence of any priests. They built relationships with local religious traditions and forms of worship, often animist in nature, based on dialogue and understanding, and the possible integration of their respective principles. The model of Jesus forsaken, who lost everything to give us his kingdom and culture that exist wherever Christ is present among his own, was expressed in the relationship with the Bangwa people, who responded beyond all expectations. Fontem became a little town – a light for the irradiation of the spirit of unity throughout sub-Saharan Africa.

In all her public interventions over the next decades, Chiara made at least one reference to that first African experience. In 1992 she inaugurated a "school for inculturation" in Kenya, based on the principle "cutting with the roots of one's own culture, in order to be able to grasp and appreciate all that my neighbor wants to express." In 2000, from Fontem she launched an evangelization project based on "the witness of a united community" and said that "the works we do should be a confirmation that the love we preach is true."

On this continent of joy and love for life, yet with the most appalling injustices, intolerable violence, systematic exploitation by the global capitalistic system and the scene of new regional and religious wars, Chiara had initiated a new process that opened the door for the manifestation of God in history.

The northern and eastern regions of the African continent are inhabited by populations who have Islamic religion and culture. They are in close contact with Mediterranean Europe and the Arab nations. They are places of encounter and exchange. An ideal laboratory of convergence towards one another, to encourage one another to the truth of knowledge, drawing everyone into the search for the one God. These are the lands of the encounter between St. Francis and the Sultan, which took place after a dangerous journey, facing both the prejudices of their opponents at home and the resistance and opposition of those who did not understand the reason for their encounter and dialogue.

The beginning of our new millennium has been characterized by a strong temptation to see the world as a clash between Christian and Islamic civilizations and to regard religion as a source of conflict. This needs to be countered by showing that it is possible to meet, to respect each other and to have dialogue. It is necessary to show that even within the diversity of their cultures and traditions, the Christian and Islamic worlds can appreciate each other and together protect common values such as life, the family, the sense of religion, a peaceful coexistence and much more...

Lay People in the Church and in the World

In a strong and unprecedented way, the Second Vatican Council explored the question of the identity of the lay person in the Church. However, it did not necessarily resolve it, since the acceptance of what it contained requires a critical and in-depth rethinking of its future possibilities, which, for the most part, has yet to happen.

However, the Council's most innovative insights generated a tension of positive expectation regarding the role of the laity in the Church, and in the world. From then on, theological exploration tried to address and interpret the multiplicity of meanings linked to the terms "secular," "lay," "laity," and directed these terms more and more in their use within an inter-ecclesial context, and in the dialogue between believers and secular humanism.

In this regard, the talk given on the theme of Christian unity by the lay auditor, Jean Guitton, who spoke to the bishops participating in the Council on December 3, 1963, represented a symbolic moment and one of fundamental importance for the development of the ecclesial understanding of the laity.

He recalled the ideas the Church had of the laity during the first centuries, citing clear biblical and patristic sources, such as Augustine who defined the faithful of Hippo as a "living church" and the fathers of the family as "co-episcopi" (fellow-bishops); John Chrysostom who considered the monk and the Christian living in the world, as having the same obligation of striving for perfection; and Ignatius of Antioch who defined lay people as "fellow travelers bearers of God, bearers of the temple, bearers of Christ and of the Holy Spirit."[124]

---

124. The Epistle of Ignatius to the Ephesians, Chapter 9.

The medieval juridical tradition, expressed in the *"Corpus iuris canonici"*(Canon Law), is strongly dependent on the formulation of the *"Decretum Gratiani"*[125] which, quoting a text of St. Jerome, identified two categories of faithful *(Duo sunt genera christianorum)*, and emphasized the clear distinction between clerics and laity. The gradual denial of the role of the laity in the Church of the second millennium had its main cause in the ecclesial determination to defend its freedom and its mission from political interference, accentuating beyond measure the power of the clergy.

The Council of Trent, in the face of the explosion of the Protestant Reformation, dedicated many of its reflections and conclusions on the role of the clergy and the importance of ecclesial mediation between the laity and God, stressing the distinction between the ordained priesthood and the community of the faithful. The former had an active role in the life of the Church *(populus ducens)*, the latter in a decidedly subordinate position and passive function *(populus ductus)*.

In the ecclesial regulations of the first half of the twentieth century (in particular the Code of Canon Law of 1917) laypeople were defined in a negative way, for what they are not, that is, the one who is not a priest or religious.

The encyclical of Pius XI *Ubi arcano* (1922) uses the term "layperson" in reference to a group of the faithful and their mission in the apostolate, and points at the flowering of lay organizations and movements to which we have already referred in these pages.

Vatican II, after an intense period of reflection, had a rethink regarding the role of the layperson in the Church and in the world. In almost all the Council documents reference is made to the vocation, character, mission, and responsibilities of the laity.

---

125. The *Decretum Gratiani is a collection of canon law compiled around 1140 as a legal textbook.*

Its ecclesiology is based on two pillars: the community, understood as a key expression of the presence of Christ; and the fact that all believers, whether lay people or members of the hierarchy, are equal in dignity (LG 32).

This ecclesiology is Eucharistic, based on communion and a trinitarian relationship, which unites all the baptized, and intertwines human history with the very mystery of God, and leads them to eschatological fulfillment.

The laity is no longer seen as being subordinate to the hierarchy, but as belonging to the same people of God and having the same dignity as the "kingdom of priests" (LG 10). This is a Church with diversity of ministry but unity of mission, proper to the people of God and never exclusive.

The layperson, by virtue of his or her secularity, has the primary vocation to seek the "kingdom of God by dealing with temporal things" (LG 31), sanctifying themselves and the world in which they live. The Church, body of Christ and people of God, is a pilgrim in human history going towards its fulfillment in the glory of God, in which all the baptized, in their common dignity as Christians, share in the priestly gift of Christ according to a diversity of ministries, charisms, and functions, all called to holiness.

The resulting ecclesiology inseparably links the vertical dimension of communion with God to the horizontal dimension of communion among people. Ecclesial communion is expressed in the liturgical celebration as an act of the whole Church, to which the constitution *Sacrosanctum Concilium* is dedicated. This communion is shown in *Lumen Gentium*, which speaks of the possibility of understanding the truth of God, enabled by the Holy Spirit, and of the call to holiness for all the baptized. *Dei Verbum* invites everyone to read, listen to, and meditate on the Scriptures. *Gaudium et Spes* speaks of the common mission to make the world more human. *Unitatis Redintegratio* speaks of ecumenical commitment, and *Ad Gentes* of missionary zeal.

Chiara Lubich, through the light she received in the 1940s, the insights and achievements of which she was the protagonist, was well ahead of the times in defining many traits of the role of laypeople in the Church and in the world.

The Focolare Movement, through its spirituality and action, anticipated and inspired some of the conclusions reached by the Council, stimulating an in-depth study and offering a patrimony of experience and "wisdom," which then became indispensable in developing the theology of the laity.

This contribution continued in the post-Conciliar period, with participation in all the aspects of the complex reception of Vatican II amid the tensions deriving from implementing its openness and reforms. It involved the issues of collegiality, liturgy, ecumenism, morality, and coping with all the divisions, corrections, setbacks, and the different hermeneutics.

The experience of the Movement certainly contributed to overcoming the dialectics between hierarchy and laity, to the rethinking of an ecclesiology in more communitarian terms, bringing together the concepts of community and ministry, of charism and ministry, and of abandoning the pyramidal concepts of the Church.

In a talk she gave at Rocca di Papa in December 1986, Chiara summed up her vision of the laity, with her usual lucidity and capacity for synthesis. The seventh General Assembly of the Synod of Bishops was imminent, which would address the theme *The Vocation and mission of the laity in the Church and in the world*, which would lead to the publication of John Paul II's apostolic Post-synodal Exhortation, *Christifideles Laici*.

Chiara said:

> *It may sound over-simplistic, but the layperson is a Christian. As such, he or she is a follower of Christ and his Gospel. That*

is why they must live to the full what Jesus wants from them, and work above all to expand the kingdom of God, to build the Church. Since they have the possibility of being in the midst of the world, they will bring the light of the Gospel there, bringing it into everything they know.

In the same talk she then defined the lay vocation within the movement she founded:

> And it is in this type of layperson that all of us, the lay people of the Focolare Movement, find ourselves so well expressed. Our Movement has on the one side a more spiritual aspect, if one can say so, where we work to let Christ grow in us, among us and among many, and this means building up the Church; and on the other a more human, more concrete aspect, where we work to infuse the spirit of Christ into the various expressions of the world. We recognize ourselves in this kind of layperson, and we feel that we are very much in tune with what the Second Vatican Council has said in this regard.

With regard to the attitude and commitment to live the Gospel by putting it into practice, she referred to the Word of Life of that month, taken from the Letter to the Romans (15: 7): "Welcome one another, therefore, just as Christ has welcomed you, for the glory of God.," and she said to the focolarini:

> By implementing this Word among us we will maintain the foundation, on which our Work, which is Church, is built. By living these Words in the world of the family, and in the various areas of society, we will lay the most important foundation for the Christian renewal of laws and structures. . . . Let us welcome every brother and sister as Christ welcomed us. He has welcomed us and welcomes us every day, whoever we are, sinners or saints, young or old, beautiful or ugly, healthy or sick, he always welcomes all of us.

The Woman Mary

On October 22, 1963, in his address to the Council Fathers Cardinal Léon Suenens, Archbishop of Brussels, asked the assembly: "But where is the other half of humanity?"

A question as trivial as it is provocative could shake a theological approach that had lasted almost two millennia to its foundations, but it also highlighted a reality that exists and is consistently recognized so little inside the Church: namely the portion of God's people who are female. It is a situation that the Council acknowledged with the presence, albeit numerically symbolic, of twenty-three women in the auditorium, both religious and lay. This presence represented a first attempt to break away from the Pauline declaration that women should be silent in the church (see 1 Cor. 14: 34), preferring the clearly important role of women in the first Christian communities, as described elsewhere in the letters of St. Paul (especially Romans and Philippians).

Such roles were prominent in the Byzantine world and the Western Middle in the form of monasticism that included extensive ministry to female communities. This situation was also predominant even in modern times alongside the development of female third orders which continued into the nineteenth century with female congregations going out as missionaries, to teach, provide support and care for the sick. Everything changed in the twentieth century, which we have spoken about in some detail in previous chapters. The presence of women in ecclesial circles has been, and still is, limited by tradition, culture, mentalities, organizational and religious styles, the transmission of texts, moral norms, ways of thinking and believing, even the image of God, who was always represented as a male figure.

It is perhaps no coincidence that the first official recognition of the Focolare Movement in 1962 was reserved to the rule of the men's Pious Association of the "Work of Mary." The statutes for the women's branch were not approved until the following year. In the audience Chiara had with Pope Paul VI on October 31, 1964, he addressed her with great affection, asking her about the Movement and if there were any requests regarding its development and definition, adding the phrase: "The strangest things are possible..." and indeed, it became possible for the head of the Movement to be a lay woman, with a priest as her assistant and a coordinating council as the bond of unity between the various expressions of the Work of Mary.

Chiara felt that the Holy Father recognized her because of the charism she had been given: "I feel like a daughter of the pope. Not any kind of daughter, but, precisely because there is a charism, the daughter of another charism which is that of the Church." Shortly afterwards she would assume the role of president of the Movement, after a long and painful period of (formal) estrangement from the Focolare leadership imposed by the canonical investigations in 1952.

It was a role she held for the rest of her life and which once again marked out the feminine inspiration and the fullness of maternal love present in the Work of Mary. Pope John Paul II repeatedly emphasized the strongly Marian characteristics of the Movement. It is symbolic that Chiara herself recalled a conversation that dated back to the late 1980s when her collaboration with Pope Wojtyla was very close: 'One day I had the courage to ask him confidentially if he thought it possible to stipulate in our statutes that the president of the Movement should always be a woman. The pope responded immediately: 'And why not? If only...!'" The statutes approved by the Holy See in 1990 contain this norm which is something new in ecclesial movements and offers a glimpse of new horizons for the role of women in the Church.

In 1988 Pope John Paul II dedicated the Apostolic Letter *Mulieris dignitatem*[126] to women, a document to which Chiara had also contributed as consultant. The basis of all Christian anthropology was the truth revealed about the human person, created in the image and likeness of God. In addition, women have a specific vocation and dignity deriving from the concept of "woman-mother of God." Chiara commented on the letter with the following words:

> *Jesus gave all women an incomparable model which every great Christian woman in history has looked up to – Mary, his mother. Every woman who truly wishes to serve the Church can recognize her true self in her.*

All those who see themselves as followers of Jesus are called to live love, placing themselves in a filial relationship with the Father and in a fraternal relationship with all people. Alba Sgariglia expressed this very well:

> *The new way of life deriving from the charism finds a model to be imitated in Mary, the mother and first disciple of Jesus. In her extraordinary life, she experienced God's love in a unique way and left an equally unique testimony of love for all people, marking out for every Christian a true path towards holiness, a luminous way of love.*

With respect to a female charism, referring to the thought of von Balthasar, Chiara pointed out:

> *Mary is Queen of the Apostles without claiming apostolic powers for herself. She has something else and much more. . . . So woman, living her vocation to the full, with faith, nobility and love of Mary, can be the revelation for the Church of the Marian dimension of the life of Christ's disciples and contrib-*

---

126. *Mulieris dignitatem (the dignity of a woman) is an apostolic letter by Pope John Paul II on the dignity of women, published on August 15, 1988.*

ute to keeping alive and manifesting the Marian profile which is essential to the Church.

Chiara's example and experience have also helped encourage the Church to move from the idealization of female role models to concrete reality, that is, to women as flesh and bone, lay and religious women, mothers, wives, female workers... all part of God's people. The spirituality of unity represented a new contribution in liberating the relationship between woman and Church from all abstractness and rhetoric, to purify attitudes and mentalities encrusted in history and to stir up heathier patterns of reality and lay involvement. In this way there would no longer be a need for encyclicals on the role of women in the Church, just as there had never been any thought of writing an official document on the role of man... and one might envisage a synod on God's people, attended by representatives of both halves of the human race.

In an article dedicated to Chiara Lubich that appeared in *L'Osservatore Romano* on March 25, 2011, the historian Lucetta Scaraffia highlighted how:

> *The greatest novelty marking her story is precisely her being a woman... Chiara – who speaks to assemblies of bishops, is heard by popes, welcomed with the same respect as a head of state in the countries she visits – realizes what current times demand of the Church: she recognizes the importance of the role of women. Yet she does so without claiming any rights, without any harshness, rather by demonstrating that she merits the authority with which she is recognized, as it was for the great saints in the history of the Church. Her importance in twentieth-century Catholicism is also proof of a feminine revolution accomplished in silence and modesty. What remains is to take note of it.*

Shalom – Peace

This typically Hebrew greeting literally means "peace" but the biblical concept concentrated in the term *shalom* evokes complex meanings and absolute values, such as fullness of life, physical and spiritual health, blessing and union with God, sincere relationships with the divine and with fellow human beings. Following the proclamation of the new commandment of Jesus, Christians should be the pledge and prophetic anticipation of this peace, a mirror of the kingdom of God brought into the world.

The theme of the summer Mariapolis held at Fiera di Primiero in 1959, was "Mary Mother and Queen of the World." Chiara explained the theme with a talk showing the impact of the ideal of unity in the world with a strong political connotation, reminding all of the social awareness of Christianity and the absolute need for peace between the nations and fellowship among all peoples.

The world then was divided into opposing blocs and "frozen" by the logic of the Cold War where peace existed only because the contenders feared global destruction. This condition was summarized in Pius XII's Christmas radio message in 1954, which defined "cold peace" as merely a temporary calm whose "duration is conditioned by the ever-changing sensation of fear." Four years later, Pope John XXIII in his encyclical *Pacem in terris* would trace the paths to peace for humanity by looking at a world without borders, let alone walls or curtains, between West and East.

On August 22, 1959, the participants of the Mariapolis in Primiero, who came from twenty-seven different countries, decided to consecrate themselves and their nations to Mary. The words of the consecration were read in nine languages, making it clear that the life of unity (and with it, peace) which they had discovered and experienced at the Mariapolis could spread throughout the world. In Chiara's own words:

> *If one day humanity, not as individuals but as peoples, if one day all the peoples were able to put themselves aside, put aside the idea of their homeland, their kingdoms, offering these instead as incense to the Lord, king of a kingdom which is not of this world and who guides history, and if they do so out of mutual love between their nations, in the same way as God is asking mutual love from us between brothers and sisters, that day will be the start of a new era because then, just as the presence of Jesus is alive between two or more who love one another in Christ, Jesus will be alive and present among peoples. He will then finally be in his true place as the only king, not only of our hearts but of our nations. He will be Christ the King. Christian peoples or their representatives need to know how to sacrifice their "collective" I. This is the cost and no less is asked of each one of us for our souls to be consumed in unity. These are times when the peoples should go and look beyond their own borders. The time has come to love the other countries as our own, when our eye needs to acquire a new purity. Being detached from ourselves is not enough in order to be a Christian. Today's times demand something more of the follower of Christ. It demands a social awareness of Christianity which does not only build up one's own country according to the law of Christ but helps to build the countries of others with the universal gesture of the Church, with an eye that looks beyond the material world and that has been given to us by God the Father who from heaven sees things very differently from us. The mystical body of Christ needs to be lived in such an excellent way that it can be transformed into the mystical body of society.*

The Focolare Movement, which came to life amidst Second World War bombs, would always consider the theme of peace as the cornerstone of its spirituality, apostolic activity, and social commitment. It was a concept expressed in a universal perspective, anchored in the principles of the Gospel and the model of trinitarian love and interpreted dynamically according to the evolution of history and the ever-new challenges facing humanity. In the years that followed, the Movement recognized and identified itself in the model of the Church that emerged from the Council, at the service of humanity and in solidarity with people's problems, first and foremost the poorest, and sought to incarnate its spirit in each of its activities. The Church's reflection and teachings on peace proved prophetic with respect to the characteristics that human civilization was moving towards in the final passage of the second millennium.

On March 26, 1967, Easter Sunday, Pope Paul VI announced the publication of the encyclical *Populorum progressio*.[127] It was the fruit of long preparations and an unprecedented collaboration with lay intellectuals and brilliant theologians and gave voice to the pontiff's hopes for social justice and development in solidarity, in search of a true planetary humanism within a framework of the "civilization of love." Around the world events of epochal importance were taking place that were destined to have a dramatic influence on humanity's destiny. For example, the war the United States was fighting in Vietnam; the new awareness of intolerable inequalities caused by a worldwide economic system based on injustice and exploitation; the cultural revolution in China and the growing social malaise that led to the 1968 protests...

"The social question ties all men together, in every part of the world." This sentence from the encyclical summarized the perspective assumed by the Magisterium regarding the great problems facing humanity. In a political climate based on fear and the balance of power, it was the first time that a solemn affirmation had been made that the world was not so much divided between East and West but that the real Iron Curtain was between North and South, dividing "the rich" from "the poor."

---

127. *Populorum progressio (the development of peoples)* is the encyclical of Pope Paul VI that focussed on social justice in the world economy. It was released on March 26, 1967.

In the context of the 1960s, a period marked by the myth of unlimited progress and the conquest of space, this document offered, from a socio-cultural and doctrinal perspective, a reflection on the theme of development at the highest level. In the wake of his talk to the United Nations (the first time for a pontiff) and his vibrant appeal that "humanity must end war, or war will end humanity," Pope Paul VI spoke directly about promoting the rights of all underdeveloped nations and the lack of solidarity with the Third World, repeating forcefully that "development is the new name for peace." Development represented the encyclical's most important theme, and numerous adjectives were used to specify its content: it had to be true, comprehensive, holistic, and inclusive. It went far beyond economic growth alone whose fruits should be shared fairly among peoples, important though this was, but the deepest intention was the development of every person, their "being" much more than their "having."

In this way, the world was beating a path towards a humanism that was more open and sensitive to spiritual values and to God, with the integral development of the person at its center, with fraternity between the peoples and solidarity between the nations, with global responsibility and interdependence, and the primacy of politics over economics. The encyclical was harshly criticized in many circles. In Western conservative circles and the secular cathedrals of capitalism around the world, as well as in many ecclesial environments, Pope Montini was called a seductive demon of Marxist thought and his Church was accused of involving itself in politics instead of dealing with spiritual and moral issues. This ignored the fact that the principles of *Populorum progressio* were based on the Gospel and the traditional teachings of the Church. The theme of the universal destination of goods, in fact, originates from the very first pages of the Bible and continues with the reflections of the Fathers, from Ambrose to Thomas Aquinas.

Chiara's thought and action on the themes of peace always reflected the need for encounter and dialogue between religions. Their role becomes essential to the extent that they show they are capable of walking together. This was the meaning of the international recognition conferred on her in 1977 in London – the prestigious Templeton Prize for Progress in Religion. At the presentation ceremony, Chiara described her own experience of faith and the Movement's contacts with Jews, Muslims, and Buddhists, citing great mystics of major religions who exalt love as the essence of all things. This was to be followed by a commitment with the World Conference on Religion and Peace (WCRP), an international organization that brings together believers of all faiths to work for peace and justice among all peoples. Chiara's interventions and the activity of the Focolare Movement in the assemblies in Nairobi in 1984, Melbourne in 1989, and Riva del Garda in 1994 always insisted on the spiritual dimension of the commitment to peace building. This objective, like other great problems of humanity, is resolved by starting with small groups where believers of different religions can find themselves working, reflecting, or praying together, in fraternity and joy.

The period marked by the fall of the Berlin wall and the end of the Cold War coincided with a profound change of heart worldwide regarding the environment. It set new challenges in the pursuit of peace. Humanity's unstoppable technological progress started to be perceived as a threat. It had indeed reached a point where it threatened the equilibrium of the biological and physical world to such an extent that it should become subject to effective political control, obviously on a global level. There was a heightened awareness of the growing interdependence of all human activity on the planet, of the common destiny of humanity and the need for global solutions to world problems. Such new international scenarios did not prevent the outbreak of new wars. The early 1990s saw the outbreak of the Gulf War which set Iraq against a coalition of thirty-five states formed under the aegis of the United Nations and led by the United States. This conflict was destined to redefine many of the concepts and models of twentieth century wars. Another conflict arose in the Balkan region. As a legacy of colonialism other wars erupted in several African countries, resulting in tremendous ethnic massacres. Pacifism, in its broadest sense as a non-violent method of political action, was progressively growing, becoming an essential component of the vast and varied movement of transnational opposition to economic and liberalist globalization that developed in the final decades of the twentieth century.

On December 17, 1996 in Paris, Chiara was awarded the UNESCO Prize for Peace Education. In her address when she received this important award, she described her own concept of peace and the "recipe" for its pursuit. This speech, although delivered in a totally secular institutional and cultural context, proposed Christ as the model to achieve peace:

> The secret lies in a new way of life, in a new way of doing things embraced by millions of people inspired by fundamentally Christian principles. Without overlooking parallel values present in other faiths and different cultures, but in fact embracing them, it has brought peace and unity to a world in great need of rediscovering and re-establishing peace.
>
> The spirituality of unity presupposes in its members a profound awareness of God for what he is. He is Love, he is Father.... And we know that the will of a father is primarily that his children treat each other as brothers and sisters, by concerning themselves for each other's welfare and loving one another. They must understand and practice what can be called the art of loving. This means we must be the first to love without waiting for the other to love us. It means loving the other as oneself, because "You and I,'" Gandhi says, "are but one. I cannot injure you without harming myself.

> ... Christ, the "Son" par excellence of the Father, the brother of us all, has left us this universal norm: mutual love. He knew it was essential if there were to be peace and unity in the world and all become a single family.
>
> ...It is not easy to commit yourself to furthering peace! It demands courage and much suffering. But if more people would accept suffering out of love, with the suffering that love requires, it could become the most powerful weapon for bringing humanity to its highest dignity. The human race would not just be a collection of peoples, one next to the other and often in conflict, but would become a single people, a family.

With ever greater intensity Chiara continued to call for peace: she spoke about it at the UN headquarters in New York in 1997, at the symposium organized by the WCRP, and in Strasbourg in 1998, where she received the European prize for Human Rights from the Council of Europe.

The new millennium was accompanied by a further sharp deviation from the traditional concept of war with the attack on the Twin Towers in New York with its impact on the political equilibrium and the world markets and new scenarios punctuated by the fight against international terrorism.

Chiara, echoing Pope John Paul II, warned that "the planet is at a crossroads" and that "it depends on us whether the civilization of love or the uncivilization of systematically erected selfishness would impose itself on the future." In Stuttgart, in 2004, when ten Eastern European countries joined the European Union, she proposed peace and mutual love between nations as a condition for Europe to become a family of nations.

To new questions and problems arising from a multicultural society, Chiara Lubich responded with the proposal of an intercultural society marked by dialogue and mutual love between different cultures. Emblematic in this sense was her talk on

June 19, 2004, at Westminster Central Hall in London before representatives of many different religions. She identified the elements of epochal changes the world was going through due to vast migrations all across the world, global economic and financial crisis (which would begin four years later), deepening social inequalities and a denial of the dignity of the person. She defined those times as a "collective and cultural dark night" that would generate frustration, a sense of failure, suffering, anger, violence, and conflict in people, in relationships, in social relations and between nations. Referring to St. Augustine's sermon about the collapse of the Roman Empire due to the pressure of people migrating from the north and east, she argued that it didn't signify the end of the world but the birth of a new world. Her vision came from the faith and conviction that God was not absent from history; he knows how to direct everything to good. This faith was not only the profession of a religious belief but also an existential orientation, a positive attitude of hope in life, a sharing of deep human values such as justice and peace, creating one single family of all peoples, believers or not, as brothers and sisters. It was a vision based on relationship, with fraternity forming the foundations of existence:

> *Before faith, what counts is what "spirituality" I live, what spirit animates and guides my way of feeling, thinking, wanting, deciding, in a word, of living. . . .*
>
> *How could we consider unity and fraternity in society and in the world without a vision of all humanity as one family? And how can we understand this, unless there is one Father of all? . . . The gospel says that he counts even the hairs of our head (see Lk. 12: 7), and the Qur'an says: "We [God] are closer to him [man] than his jugular vein" (Sura 50: 16).*

The synthesis of Chiara's message on peace can be found, once again, in Jesus' words, when he says that those who live in his love do not lack peace ("Peace I leave with you; my peace I give you. I do not give to you as the world gives," [Jn 14: 27]). Peace is the condition of those who have found the way, who know where they are going and know they are not alone on the journey. Jesus leaves humanity his peace, the peace that only he can give. In the Gospel texts there are no other explicit references to peace. It has no abstract characteristics. It is not the fruit of any human initiative. Nor is it a moral or social attitude. It comes rather from the experience of dwelling in the love of Christ ("Abide in my love," [Jn 15: 9]). These references do not mean that we should not be concerned about peace; they are an invitation to build it from the experience of Easter, where everything, including our betrayals, is taken up into the heart of Love that saves.

New generations

In the latter half of the 1960s, young people across the Western world were in deep turmoil, manifesting their unease with forms of protest that exploded in American and European student and university circles, leading in turn to a wider movement of dissent that eventually culminated in the so-called 1968 riots. Through an awareness dating back to 1949 which could be summarized by the maxim "my I is humanity,"[128] Chiara understood the sense of disillusion felt by the younger generations in the 1960s. Her intuition to invest in them dates to 1962.

Appreciating young people's desire to be heard, interpreting their profound search for authenticity and the meaning of life, understanding their need for being protagonists, foreseeing the imminent manifestation of largescale youth protests and con-

---

128. Paradise '49:, 582 (unpublished).

flicts between the generations, Chiara called together numerous young people who shared the spirituality of unity. She entrusted them with the task of launching a peaceful revolution in the world, based on Gospel love and the slogan – which sympathetically paraphrased the appeal made in the closing paragraphs of the *Communist Party Manifesto* of Marx and Engels of 1848 – "Young people of the whole world, unite!" In the spring of 1967, the Gen (New Generation) Movement was born and its first international meeting was celebrated with the symbolic gesture of passing a flag from the first to the second generation of the Movement. On either side of that flag were printed the same program and secret for making unity a reality. On one side: "That they may all be one" (John 17: 21); and on the other: "My God, my God, why have you forsaken me" (Mt. 27: 46).

Rather than forming the Gen according to the traditional methods of Catholic catechetics and pedagogy, Chiara entrusted them with the world and its mission.

On April 1, 1969, at an audience with Pope Paul VI, Chiara presented the Gen to the pope as the new generation of the Movement, describing them with the following words: "They are thirsty..." —a thirst that the pope, speaking to twenty thousand young people gathered in St. Peter's on March 2, 1975, for the first Genfest,[129] sought to quench by inviting them to follow Jesus the Master, as the "light of thought and the lamp of life," and to build "a new world, the Christian world of faith and charity." The Genfest would be repeated every five years, where signs of the times could be scrutinized from the young people's perspective, where the Movement's focus could be updated with respect to the

---

129. A Genfest is an international festival of the youth of the Focolare Movement (the Gen) who want to show the world that universal fraternity, a united world, is an Ideal worth living for. They have been held more or less every five years from 1975 onwards.

course of history, where the fruits of the charism could ripen, and where initiatives promoting unity at every level through actions, projects, debates, and cultural and spiritual manifestations would be highlighted.

The Gen Movement proposed a vision of God's love known as the "rainbow revolution," referring to the image of light refracted into seven colors signifying how love can be applied to different aspects of daily life: red, communion (of goods and experiences) and work; orange, spreading the ideal that animates people; yellow, the relationship with God; green, care and relationship with body and soul, nature and ecology; blue, order, harmony, protection of the environment and the body; indigo, wisdom and study; violet, means of communication.

The Gen expressed a living, creative, and universal Church, keen to share the light of the Gospel with their peers and adults, bearing witness to the love of Jesus, welcoming and reaching out to those who are far from God. Theirs was a Church asking young people to be an example of unity in a divided world and a light for all Christians, the faithful of other religions and those who did not have a religious reference point. Youthfulness was primarily a condition of the soul, an energy that comes from within, a desire to change and bring fire into the world. Faced with the challenges of a multicultural, multi-religious, and multi-ethnic society that had been growing since the early 1970s, Chiara offered young people the vision of the "world person" who knows how to go beyond the limits of their own culture to open up and love another's country, culture and religion as their own. By tackling prejudice and conflict, a new planetary civilization could be prepared. In this project, young people were called to "give an indispensable and decisive response to the turning point facing humanity, granting it the highest dignity: that of feeling themselves not to be just a gathering of peoples, often in conflict with each other, but one single people."

Chiara, who understood like no other how time passes and how nothing ages more quickly than the concept of "new," divided the Gen Movement into various branches. Each branch included a specific age group with specific objectives and methods of formation. The Gen-2 are the young adults, committed to discerning their own vocation and to works of service aimed at building unity among all peoples. The Gen-3 are boys and girls aged nine to eighteen, dedicated to going into depth with their spiritual life and sharing group experiences. This is how Chiara described them:

> The Gen-3 aim high. They have understood that the saints count amongst those who have had the most profound impact in the world, in history: they have dragged the masses to God, brought so many people to God, changed society ... They wish to be – and don't be surprised at this – a generation of saints.

Large numbers of young people eager to share their way of life gathered around them to form the Youth for Unity Movement, committed to walking what they called "paths to unity," namely local and international initiatives to build a united world.

Then the Gen-4 were born, children taught how to "live the art of loving" and understand what a united world means; and the Gen-5, children aged 2 to 4 who are taught to interact with others through games created specially to form a sense of unity. Following the evolutionary dynamics of the Movement, Youth for a United World was born in 1985, young people committed to spreading the life of the Gospel among young Christians, the "golden rule" among those belonging to other religions and the idea of universal brotherhood among those not professing a religious faith.

Music, a universal language, became the preferred means of expression during the student protests, conveying personal and collective ideas and moods, like no other. In ecclesial circles it became a formidable instrument for bringing young people together, supporting catechesis and bible teaching, animating the liturgy, which experienced a period of unparalleled vitality following the reform of the Council. From the Gen who played music in local groups and at meetings of various kinds emerged the international music groups Gen Rosso and Gen Verde, based in the town of Loppiano. Their repertoire, inspired by the spirituality of the Focolare Movement, accompanied generations of young people, believers and non-believers, also beyond the confines and activities of the Movement, in parishes, chapels, and campsites, diocesan assemblies and World Youth Days, leaving a melody, chord, verse, concept, or fragment of emotion that recalled the culture and message of unity imprinted in their minds.

Chiara could listen to humanity and the Church, read its history in depth and foresee its future, anticipating and developing the works and evolutionary processes with her suffering, made up of nights of the spirit, pains, sicknesses and the lack of recognition. From her intuitions blossomed the various branches of the Movement.

The commitment to renew society that had marked the activities of the Focolare Movement since the early years gave rise to specific centers dedicated to developing the charism with respect to economics, politics, education, social sciences, art, and medicine. In the turmoil of the late 1960s, Chiara saw the need to integrate the various themes into a movement that, in 1968, would take the name of "Toward a New Society," and later, "New Humanity."

Profound socio-cultural upheavals during those years had shattered the foundations of human reality and legal structures, including the family, which until then had not been under question. On July 19, 1967 Chiara founded the "New Families Movement" which aimed, in the name of unity, to help families that had been divided, "empty the orphanages," develop a new culture of education and solidarity, follow separated couples and those in difficulty, take care of foster care and adoption. On December 25, 1973, in an address given to the focolarini, she said:

> *The family:* a word which is immensely significant for us, rich, profound, sublime and simple, above all real. A family atmosphere is an atmosphere of comprehension, of serene relaxation, an atmosphere of security, unity, mutual love, peace, which welcomes its members in all their divine and human being. Starting from a more than natural way of looking at each other, seeing Jesus in one another, the members of a family arrive at the most concrete, simple, characteristic expressions of a family. In synthesis, a family where the siblings do not have a heart of stone but a heart of flesh, like Jesus, Mary, and Joseph. If I were to leave this earth today and were asked for a final word that speaks of our ideal, I would say to you, certain of being completely understood: be a family.

Even the most inner circles of the Church, those who lived a consecrated life, during those years found a place in the Focolare's organizational model, with branches that received canonical approval at different times and in different ways, some sooner and some later.

The spirituality of unity and the affirmation of Church-communion as a concept had also inspired priests, members of religious families, and even bishops who, experiencing a new evangelical vitality, rediscovered the roots and an enthusiasm for their own vocations and their own personal and communitarian charisms. Besides the section of the Movement dedicated to priests and members of institutions of consecrated life, which had existed since the 1950s, in 1967 the Parish and Diocesan Movement was born and in 1968 the branch of the Gens (Gen seminarians).

In 1976 a series of international meetings of bishop-friends of the Focolare Movement, promoted by Klaus Hemmerle, Bishop of Aachen, was inaugurated to develop the spirituality of unity and live an experience of "effective and affective" collegiality. In 1998 Pope John Paul II gave his approval also for bishops to be officially included as "friends" within the Work of Mary.

IN DIALOGUE

THE SOURCES OF THE CHARISM OF UNITY

The cathedral of Trent was one of the churches where the young Chiara Lubich spent many hours of meditation and prayer, and one of the places where her spiritual formation took place.

The cathedral's architecture is in a late thirteenth-century Romanesque style, but includes an eighteenth-century marble canopy overlooking the high altar that resembles the one by Bernini in St. Peter's. Its majesty makes it easy to overlook the southern transept, which houses a small apse dedicated to St. Stephen. Since the mid-1860s this altar has contained the relics of the proto-martyrs of the pilgrim church of Trent: the deacon Sisinnius, the lector Martyrius and the doorkeeper Alexander. The cathedral was built on the site of the ancient church-sanctuary, erected at the end of the fourth century for the cult of the martyrs. It owes its origin to the burial of the three missionaries, slaughtered by the pagan populations of the Non Valley (Val di Non) in 397 AD. Their cult was promoted by Bishop Vigilius, evangelizer and patron of the diocese of Trent who, at his death around the year 400, was buried alongside his three young collaborators.

Sisinnius, Martyrius and Alexander came from Cappadocia (now Turkey), a land of great saints and a proud missionary tradition. Figures such as Basil of Caesarea, John Chrysostom, Gregory Nazianzus, and Gregory of Nyssa are among the most distinguished Fathers of the Church; from their authority and example the three drew their commitment to God. They followed St. Basil's model of missionary monasticism and brought from Cappadocia the spirit that shaped and animated their way of evangelization, so giving witness from east to west to the faith of a still united Christianity. Their pilgrimage took them to Milan, where bishop Ambrose presided, undoubtedly attracted by his reputation for holiness. They also wanted to pray at the tomb of the Milanese Bishop Dionysius who was martyred in Cappadocia, where he had been exiled by the philosopher-emperor Constantine II. In Milan they also met Simplician, teacher of Augustine of Hippo and a future Bishop of Milan. At that time, the diocese of Trent was subsidiary to the metropolitan see of Milan under bishop Ambrose.[130] Ambrose sent the three Cappadocian missionaries to bishop Vigilius who, after their martyrdom, wrote letters to Simplician and John Chrysostom, the Archbishop of Constantinople, to inform them of the incident. These letters are of great historical and spiritual value and are a unique and reliable source for the biographical data and activities of the three martyrs.

In the middle of the southern nave of the Cathedral of Trent there is a chapel richly decorated in Baroque style, built in 1682 at the direction of archbishop Francesco Alberti Poja. Inside there is a large crucifix, with Our Lady of Sorrows and St. John on either side, the work of the Nuremberg sculptor Sixtus Frey, dating back to the early 1500s. Prior to its current location, the sculpture hung above the altar of the Holy Cross at the head of the central nave. Between 1545 and 1563 that crucifix witnessed the work of the Council of Trent and at its base the Council Fathers solemnly proclaimed the decrees resulting from their work. There is an inscription saying: *Ecce crucem domini ad cuius sanctissimos pedes in hoc sacrosancto concilio tridentino fidei nostrae decreta iurata et publicata sunt* (Behold the cross of the lord at

---

130. In the next century, it was to be included in the ecclesial province of Aquileia.

whose most sacred feet in this holy Council of Trent the decrees of our faith are witnessed and proclaimed). This refers to the work of the Council and has made the artwork particularly dear to the people of Trent, becoming an object of profound devotion. It is an image of Jesus in his abandonment on the cross, with Mary standing at his feet, depicted in the desolation of that moment, and the beloved disciple, symbol of suffering humanity and recipient of the words of the Lord, pronounced with his last breath: "Woman, here is your son!" (Jn 19: 26). This image may well have been a source of inspiration for the ideal of unity, the center of Chiara Lubich's spirituality.

For centuries, the Council of Trent has been interpreted in the light of the dialectics of the Counter-Reformation—the firm response of the Roman Catholic Church in opposition to the birth of modernity during that period. More recently, reassessments of the historical texts that apply to the Council, in particular by the Italian historian Paolo Prodi, place it in a broader and more challenging perspective.

In addition to its efforts to reform the Church and address the disorders and abuses that had developed over the centuries, the Council of Trent made a significant attempt to face up to modernity and to adapt to its demands. It sought to provide effective answers to problems posed by the new society that was developing both in Europe and in the New World. First, at the individual level, there was a new relationship between conscience and the sacred, which was reflected in the anthropology, ecclesiology, and spirituality of those days.

The Council happened at a moment in the history of the Western world and the Church that saw the development of theological and philosophical thought which focused on God's transcendence in relation to the world. This development gave creation a new autonomy with respect to the sacred sphere. This happened within the process of confrontation and integration of Christian doctrine and classical philosophy as advocated by humanism. It was a time that marked the beginning of secularization, the birth of pluralistic legal systems (political, ecclesial, economic), the recognition of the autonomy of the natural world governed by laws that rational scientific investigation sought to decode, and the civil world whose order could be independent of Church law.

The domain of the sacred was regulated by the profession of faith and by the theological definition and discipline of the sacraments. Different interpretations of these served to distinguish, separate, and divide the Christian Churches. However, throughout the world, there was a growing call for individual conscience in relation to divine grace and to the freedom of the individual. This confrontation with modernity would characterize the history of Christianity and the Churches over the following centuries. It would only reach a new equilibrium, possibly, at the end of the millennium, with the Second Vatican Council and its focus on the "signs of the times" and with its decisive turn towards a spirituality of communion and its acceptance of the charismatic dimension in ecclesiology.

Perhaps this provides the context to understand a comment made by John Paul II on April 30, 1995 when visiting Trent to celebrate the 450th anniversary of the opening of the Council: "Chiara (Lubich) was born here, she comes from Trent. Chiara of Trent ... We could write a treatise: From the Council of Trent to Chiara of Trent. This would be very interesting!"[131]

These references to the first centuries of the Christian era and to one of the key events of Church history can help us grasp some features of the spiritual and ecclesial ground that characterizes the history of Trent and its Church, and to connect some threads that link Chiara Lubich's life and work to her city

---

131. John-Paul II, Pastoral Visit to Trent, April 30, 1995.

of origin, even after her transfer to Rome and the wider world. It is a story and a link that would have further consequences especially when the story of the Church and the human and spiritual story of Chiara met within the grand panorama of unity.

On Sunday March 8, 1964, in St. Peter's Basilica, Paul VI presided over a solemn liturgy for the anniversary of the fourth centenary of the council of Trent. Many pilgrims from across the archdiocese of Trent were present, led by Archbishop Alessandro Maria Gottardi, and most of the clergy and representatives of the civil authorities of both the region and the city. The pope's homily ended with these words:

> *The spirit of the Council of Trent rekindles and revives the spirit of the present (Second) Vatican Council, which is connected to and proceeds from the Council of Trent to face the old and new problems which remain unresolved at this time, or which have arisen as we move into the modern era. And the Council opening, which the Church is commemorating today, puts into stark relief the great and difficult question which gave rise to the Council of Trent but to which it unfortunately failed to find a solution: that of the reunion of all Christians in the same faith and mutual love . . .* [132]

Paul VI was recalling the need to pursue the unity of the Church and unity between Christian denominations, already torn apart in the first millennium and again through the great schisms of the second millennium. At that time his first encyclical, *Ecclesiam Suam* (promulgated on August 6, 1964), was almost ready for printing.[133] The document set out a program for his pontificate which was complementary to the guidelines and decisions that would result from the work of the Council. It was an encyclical that decreed a new approach by the Church both towards the world and towards other religious realities, revealing

---

132. Paul VI, homily Vatican Basilica, 8March, 8 1964.
133. Paul VI, *Ecclesiam Suam*, encyclical letter, 6 August 6, 1995.

the desire to relate to modernity and to dedicate the Church's attention to ecumenism. In this regard, the third chapter was titled and dedicated to the theme of dialogue and to the way in which the Church should proceed in its evangelizing mission in the contemporary world and how the Church should conceive her own ministerial activity and apostolic mission.

On November 21, 1964, the Council assembly approved the decree on ecumenism, *Unitatis Redintegratio*. It acknowledged that a communion of the faithful of the various separate communities is already established through baptism, and this makes it possible for their adherents to achieve salvation.[134] It defined the ultimate objective of a binding ecclesial communion and visible unity in faith and sacraments. This search for unity was proclaimed to be a duty for all the faithful, to be accomplished through mutual knowledge of and respect for each other's traditions, living in accordance with the Gospel and practicing prayer in common.

Paul VI's speech on the anniversary of the Council of Trent ended with a solemn mandate entrusted to the city of Trent which, in the light of the documents just mentioned, was a challenging program of life:

> *The city of Trent had been chosen to facilitate the meeting [of people of diverse denominations], to act as a bridge, to offer the embrace of reconciliation and friendship. Trent did not previously have this joy and glory. Like us, like the whole Catholic world, it must henceforth have this desire. It will have to rise as a symbol of this desire, especially today, today more than ever, alive, imploring, patient, praying. With the firmness of her Catholic faith, she must not constitute a barrier, but open a door; not closed to dialogue, but ever open; not blaming mistakes,*

---

134. This is a reference to and a clarification of the often-misinterpreted teaching that "there is no salvation outside the (Catholic) Church" (Latin: *extra Ecclesiam nulla salus*).

but seeking virtue; not waiting for those who have not come for four centuries, but fraternally seeking them. It is what the new Council, in continuity with the old, with the help of God, wants us to do; and it is what you, more than any other, in the Church of God, must understand, and, as Providence suggests, pursue.[135]

These words formally mark the beginning of an ecumenical commitment for the city of Trent which, due to its geographical position has always constituted a natural bridge between the cultural and spiritual basins of central Europe and the Mediterranean world, between east and west.

On October 7, 1984, at the foot of the Crucifix of the Council in the Cathedral of Trent, a step was taken that demonstrated tangible progress in this regard. On that occasion, for the first time, representatives of the Catholic Church,[136] the Orthodox Churches, and the Reformed Churches gathered in the Cathedral of Trent, around the Crucifix of the historical council, to recite together the Nicene-Constantinopolitan Creed[137] and exchange an embrace of peace.

Vatican II radically changed the relationships between the Catholic Church, the different religious traditions, and the various cultures of the world. Religious pluralism was recognized and accepted, and relationships were built not by ignoring diversity, but by welcoming it. Karl Rahner went so far as to say that "optimism concerning salvation appears to me one of the most noteworthy results [of the Council]."[138] From the Council there

---

135. Paul VI, homily 3 March 8, 1964.
136. Cardinals Marco Cé, then patriarch of Venice and vice-president of the Italian Episcopal Conference and Basil Hume, Archbishop of Westminster.
137. The original Greek version of the Creed from these historic Councils without the contentious "filioque" addition in the Western version.
138. Karl Rahner, "Observations on the Problem of the 'Anonymous Christian" in *Theological Investigations*, tr. David Bourke. New York: Seabury Press, 1976, 238.

emerged an awareness that all people are one family in God; that there is a universal awareness of the existence of God. It recognized the fraternal relationship of all men and women, emphasizing the fundamental importance of the commandment of love and proposing respect for all religions.

The strategic objective of Paul VI and his encyclical *Ecclesiam Suam* was to open the boundaries of the Church, with his famous image of the three "concentric circles in which God has placed us" (ES 96).

The first circle, whose "limits stretch beyond our sight and merge with the horizon" (ES 97), represents the whole of humanity and all that is human. In this circle there are those who do not profess any religion and who call themselves atheists. To these the pontiff recommended we turn with care and attention, to grasp their most intimate spirit, their anxieties, their yearnings "fired with enthusiasm and idealism, dreaming of justice and progress and striving for a social order which they conceive of as the ultimate of perfection, all but divine and which, for them, is the Absolute and the Necessary. This proves that nothing can tear from their hearts their yearning for God" (ES 104). We need a prophetic language that seeks, in the folds of modernity, fraternal contact with those most distant, whom previously we regarded with denial and condemnation.

This tension towards the unity of humanity led Paul VI to define the boundaries of the second circle, the perimeter of interreligious dialogue which is "vast in extent, yet not so far away from us [comprising] all those who worship the one supreme God, whom we also worship" (ES 107). The third circle, that of ecumenism, was considered "nearest to us, and ... comprises all those who take their name from Christ" (ES 109).

The path of dialogue Pope Paul mapped out represented a "point of no return." It was up to the goodwill of the people of God to follow it with evangelical foresight and loving endorsement.

The Focolare Movement had already started walking this route, often with original and innovative approaches, choosing on the world map the routes that the breath of the Spirit suggested to them. The compass for these journeys was described by Chiara with her usual capacity for synthesis: "Remember that, for us, dialogue means loving, it does not mean speaking; because by loving we already establish a relationship."

Unity among Christians

The Council "Decree on Ecumenism," *Unitatis Redintegratio*, was the fruit of the patient and sincere work of the ecumenical movement which, throughout the twentieth century both inside and outside the Catholic Church, engaged many hearts that were animated by the search for Christian Unity. In Catholic theology, as early as the nineteenth century, pioneers of this search included Johann Adam Möhler and John Henry Newman. After them, there was a long history of reflection and ecumenical maturation leading to the current awareness of the urgent need to promote dialogue and achieve unity among those who profess a common faith in Christ. This prompted a decisive return to the biblical and patristic tradition which brought about a new and clearer understanding of the nature of the Church. The Council redefined the eschatological dimension of the Church, emphasizing that it is not a static but a dynamic reality, where the people of God are in constant pilgrimage between the "here and now" and the "not yet." Ecumenism thus became the way of the Church, an integral and organic part of her life and pastoral activity.

In Chiara Lubich's formative journey of spiritual growth, in her mystical experience of 1949 and especially in the ecclesial contexts in which she lived, neither the term "dialogue" nor an ecumenical perspective were directly present. However, a trinitarian focus, the "transcendent origin" (Paul VI's expression) of dialogue itself, was clearly there. It was Igino Giordani, from the outset an attentive and active observer of the ecumenical movement, who helped Chiara recognize that the vocation of pursuing Christian unity was inherent in her charism. As early as the mid-1950s, with its first contacts with Eastern Europe, the story of Chiara and the Focolare Movement was confronted with the tension towards the full unity of the disciples of Christ. Chiara's trip to the Holy Land in 1956 and the sight of the Holy Sepulcher in Jerusalem divided and disputed between the various Churches deeply affected her. This experience prompted Chiara to reorient her work decisively towards the renewal of the mystical body of Christ, torn and separated over the centuries by human disputes.

In the early 1960s, the first contacts took place with the evangelical world in Germany, with a meeting between Chiara, the Marienschwestern (Lutheran sisters of Mary) and the Lutheran pastors Klaus Hess, Dieter Fürst and Ernst Gleede. The Reformation of the sixteenth century had been a complex and multi-faceted phenomenon, as much historical-cultural as doctrinal in nature. The evangelical communities continued to share many ecclesial elements with the other Christian denominations, particularly baptism and the proclamation of the Gospel. On these foundations a path towards unity could be set without imposing any burdens apart from the essentials (Acts 15: 28) and considering full communion not as uniformity, but as unity in diversity and diversity in unity.

At the height of the preparations for Vatican II, Cardinal Bea[139] involved Chiara and encouraged her to undertake her

---

139. Cardinal Bea was a German Jesuit who served as the first president of the Secretariat for Promoting Christian Unity from 1960 until his death in 1968

commitment to the ecumenical front with determination. In April 1961, the archbishops of Canterbury and York sent canon Bernard Pawley to Rome as an (unofficial) observer representing the Church of England. On May 19, 1961 Chiara had her first meeting with the English theologian and his wife Margaret. A few days later the ecumenical secretariat of the Focolare Movement, *Centro Uno*, was founded. On that occasion Chiara said:

> *The will of God is mutual love. Therefore, to stitch up the breaks of division, it is necessary to love one another ... It is necessary, while the Council is being prepared, to stir things up in order to keep alive the question of unity among all Christians. We do not know when there will be another Council therefore it is necessary to do this work now.*

Centro Uno was directed by Igino Giordani, with the assistance of various members of the Focolare: Gis Calliari, Bruna Tomasi, Giosi Guella, Dori Zamboni, Aldo Stedile, Enzo Fondi, Iolanda Calderari, and Fabio Grazzadei. To maintain and develop contacts between Christian denominations, "ecumenical weeks" were started in 1962. In a short time, dialogue, based on the foundations of the spirituality of unity, began to bear fruit. It was welcomed in the Anglican Church, among the Reformed Communities of Switzerland, Holland, and Hungary, and in some Orthodox Churches in Eastern Europe and in the Middle East. Contacts and collaboration began with the World Council of Churches in Geneva which were quickly consolidated on the basis of sincere friendship and mutual trust. *Centro Uno* became a sort of outpost through which to experiment with various forms of meetings and dialogue. On several occasions these received praise from Paul VI who Chiara continually updated about every initiative. They foreshadowed official acts of unity and reconciliation among the Churches.

The Focolare approach was always to cultivate "basic" fraternity – often much more real and concrete than what might be built at the theological and institutional level – in the awareness that dialogue is a constitutive element of faith because it is constitutive of the relationship of God with humanity and of persons with one another. Chiara understood that, before contacts between the official representatives of the Churches, ecumenism depended decisively on the more or less informal encounters between Christians living in separate ecclesial communities, who wanted to understand the different viewpoints and attitudes of others, and through that to enrich one another.

Where there were as yet no theological and political conditions for dialogue, people began to get to know each other, to live together, to create places where their respective identities and stories were shared, speaking the language of the heart and of friendship, which is always understandable.

This approach has its roots in the invitation of St. Augustine who, recalling the prophet Isaiah, said: "To those who say to you: you are not our brothers, answer: you are our brothers,"[140] and referring to the Gospel of Matthew, Augustine said: "They will cease to be our brothers, when they no longer say 'Our Father.'"[141] When we say "Our Father" not only does our "sonship" resound within us, but also the fact of being brothers and sisters. In this way we become aware that the true oxygen of ecumenism can be found in prayer, which sustains communion and allows the wind of the Holy Spirit to take it ahead. In this way, we can also go beyond certain expressions used in official documents and in theological and juridical texts, however advanced they might have seemed in comparison with the not too distant past, like "separated brethren." Catholics, Orthodox, Anglicans, Lutherans, Copts, Waldensians, Methodists and so forth are first of all the faithful in Christ and bearers of an enormous wealth

---

140. Augustine, Sermon on Psalm 32 (CCL 38, 272-273).
141. Ibid.

of faith, spirituality, holiness and theological and liturgical traditions, to be recognized as such and to be looked at within the hopeful expectation of full communion.

In a private audience granted to Chiara by Paul VI on October 31, 1964, the relationship with the Lutherans was discussed with an explicit invitation from the pope to cultivate the dialogue: "Go, continue, try to understand them, put yourselves in their shoes in order to understand them." The following June 9 a group of German Lutheran Christians, in Rome for an inter-denominational conference, participated in the general audience of the pope and for the first time they were publicly acknowledged.

The work of the Focolare continued in the following years, creating in Ottmaring, near Augsburg, a "meeting center for life," inaugurated in 1968 with the blessing of the local Catholic and Lutheran authorities. This "little town" in Bavaria would soon become a center of ecumenical activities and a witness for all Christians united within their own Churches, to be a leaven and to create communion among all Christians.

Around the same time, in Rome, Chiara met with brother Roger Schütz, founder of the ecumenical community of Taizé, which was the start of a deep and lasting friendship. The French inter-denominational monastic experience of Taizé was born during the turbulent years of the 1960's which were characterized by social upheaval and student protest. As with the Focolare Movement, born in the devastation of the Second World War, it made listening to and dialogue with the younger generations a distinctive trait. It had become a point of reference for the world of young people who were searching for meaning. It offered its own message of profound spirituality that recalled the ancient models of monasticism, the basic simplicity of community life, a humanitarian commitment, and a constant tension towards Christian unity.

Equally fruitful was the dialogue with the Anglicans. During the week of prayer for Christian unity in 1967 Chiara was invited to speak at Canterbury Cathedral.[142] In the following years the ecumenical commitment of the Focolare in Britain and Ireland received the praise of both local authorities and the pope. The joint declarations signed by the representatives of the two confessions between 1966 and 1977 marked a decisive progress in relations at the theological level, but they also represented the fruit of the various forms of cooperation between the respective communities, of which the Focolare Movement was always a promoter and co-protagonist.

One of the most significant and prophetic ecumenical gestures of Pope Paul VI was the embrace of the Orthodox Patriarch of Constantinople Athenagoras on January 5, 1964 in Jerusalem. This was a historic meeting, which led to the joint declaration that revoked the mutual excommunications, dating back almost a thousand years, which had precipitated the great schism[143] between the Churches of the East and West. East and West accepted the same Gospel differently and had developed different forms of spirituality and ecclesial organization. Nevertheless, they still agreed on the communion of faith and on the fundamental structures of Eucharistic sacrifice and the episcopacy. With this in mind, the pope's first words were: "I want to express to you all my joy, my excitement. Truly I think that this is a moment we are living in the presence of God." To which the Ecumenical Patriarch responded: "In the presence of God. We have the same desire." Then followed the pope's reply:

---

142. Mother Church of the worldwide Anglican Communion and seat of the Archbishop of Canterbury.
143. The Great Schism, also called the East-West Schism or the Schism of 1054, is the event that precipitated the final separation between the Eastern Christian Churches (led by the Patriarch of Constantinople, Michael Cerularius) and the Western Church (led by Pope Leo IX).

"We will discuss, we will seek to find the truth." In total harmony Athenagoras replied: "The same from our side and I am sure that we will always be together."[144] Their exchange of messages, based on an infinite love for unity, came to be called the *Tomos Agapis* (Volume of Charity).

The desire to recompose full unity and communion in the mystical body of Christ, agreed at that meeting, resulted, over the following years, in a great ferment of dialogue between the two confessions, carried out at multiple levels and with different degrees of officialdom. Chiara Lubich became one of the contacts between these representatives of the Roman Catholic and the Orthodox Constantinopolitan Churches. In 1967, Fr. Angelo Beghetto, a prime mover of the ecumenical activities of the Focolare Movement with the Orthodox since the early 1950s, was rector of the church of St. Anthony in Istanbul. In a meeting with the Orthodox patriarch, he got to talk about the spirituality of unity and Chiara Lubich. Athenagoras invited Chiara to the Ecumenical Patriarchate. Their common understanding that the divisions between Christians were a face of Jesus "crucified and forsaken," gave birth to a profound spiritual meeting of minds which aroused the same urgency, expressed previously by Pope Paul VI, to bring about the fulfillment of the commandment of Christ, of love in unity.

On July 13, 1967, the pope (shortly before his apostolic visit to Istanbul where he would again meet with the Patriarch) received Chiara in a private audience and entrusted her with the mandate to cultivate relations with the Orthodox Churches. From that moment Chiara became the "unofficial" ambassador between the two religious leaders. In the period up to April 1972 (Athenagoras was to die the following July 7) Chiara made eight

---

144. Catholic News Agency, *Interview and Joint Declaration of the Pope Paul VI and the Patriarch of Constantinople Atenágoras I, January 5, 1964*.

trips to the Fanar district, home of the Patriarchate and the cathedral of St. George, and was received in audience twenty-five times. Their dialogue kept alive and nourished that hitherto rarely experienced climate of mutual trust between Catholics and Orthodox. It erased ancient divisions and put into proper perspective the differences of a theological, liturgical, disciplinary, and institutional nature. The prospect of that work is reflected in the prophecy of Athenagoras, reported by Chiara: "The day will come... the sun will rise high, the angels will sing and dance and all of us, bishops and patriarchs, gathered around the pope, will celebrate with the one chalice."

The commitment and fraternal dialogue of Chiara and the Focolare Movement with the Orthodox Church of Constantinople would continue after the death of Patriarch Athenagoras, with his successor Demetrios I and subsequently with Bartholomew I. The latter, remembering Chiara after her death in 2008, expressed his admiration for her "monumental work in promoting ecumenical relationships through the 'dialogue of love,'" a work that – in the words of Paul VI – was following the path of "an authentic rapprochement, starting from respectful listening, fraternal dialogue, prayer in common and from a reciprocal service for one's neighbor."

The work of the Focolare includes renewal and conversion, without which there can be no ecumenism, and an intense dialogue, seen more as an exchange of gifts than as an exchange of ideas. For as far that we are united to Christ, we will be united to one another and we will concretely and fully bring about the real catholicity of the Church. The years of Paul VI's pontificate saw the maturation of the Church's awareness of the ecumenical journey, made together in truth and charity towards full visible communion, passing through the sharing of real spiritual and human relationships, without denying the difficulties and without indulging in enthusiasm and sentimentality, but letting the Holy Spirit work, trusting in the presence of Jesus in the midst. Chiara's dialogue was built on walking together "with sensitivity," based on the method of the "dialogue of life" and the "way of love" and lived in the light of the passage of Revelation (3: 20): "Listen! I am standing at the door, knocking; if you hear my voice and open the door, I will come in to you and eat with you, and you with me." The door had been opened, and all that remained was to enter.

In 1978, Paul VI died and the long pontificate of Karol Wojtyla began. The aspiration of the Church to be "one" always accompanied the pontificate of John Paul II. The ecumenical commitment of the Polish pope was described by Cardinal Walter Kasper with the adjectives "human, charismatic, spiritual," rich in gestures, meetings, journeys and encyclicals, and accompanied by a constant aspiration to build a united Church, based on Christ's will for unity and the plan of God.

If the relationship between Chiara Lubich and Paul VI can be compared to that of daughter and father, her relationship with John Paul II – whom she knew well from the time of his episcopate in Krakow where he had made much use of the support of the Focolare Movement – can be considered deeply fraternal. Many key aspects of his pontificate saw the discreet but intense collaboration of Chiara and the Movement, especially on the themes of ecumenism, inter-religious dialogue, and the promotion of peace.

In 1981, the Movement organized "schools of ecumenism" in Germany, Great Britain, Switzerland, Brazil, Argentina, and the USA. In Castel Gandolfo there were "international schools" dedicated to the deepening of ecumenical thought, with teachers of various confessions. From the Orthodox there were the metropolitans Bartholomew (future patriarch of Constantinople) and Gennadios Zervós (future metropolitan bishop of the Greek Orthodox archdiocese of Italy); others included Archpriest Traian Valdman of the Romanian Church, Fr. Sarkis Sarkissian of the Armenian Church, and the Anglican bishop John Dennis from England. On the Catholic side there were the bishops Walter

Kasper and Eleuterio Fortino (of the Pontifical Council for the Promotion of Christian Unity), Bishop Martin Molyneux of the Beda College and Albert Rauch (then rector of the Institute of Eastern Churches at Regensburg University).

From the early 1990s the Focolare's "Abba School," initiated by Chiara to deepen the spirituality of unity in the light of her mystical experience lived in 1949, dedicated a great deal of its reflections to the ecumenical issues.

The pope who came from Eastern Europe looked with particular love and hope to the Eastern Orthodox Churches. In 1985 he dedicated the encyclical *Slavorum Apostoli* (Apostles of the Slavic Peoples) to Sts. Cyril and Methodius, the evangelizers of Eastern Europe. He called the East and the West, with their respective cultural and spiritual traditions, the "two lungs" with which the Church and the continent had to breathe again. Immediately after the fall of the Berlin Wall, he convened a special synod for Europe, fraternally welcoming the delegates of the other Churches. In 1995, he dedicated the encyclical *Ut Unum Sint* (That they may be one) to ecumenical commitment. In it one can read (n. 95): "the full and visible communion of all the communities, in which by virtue of the fidelity of God his Spirit dwells, is the ardent desire of Christ." In 1999, the Joint Declaration on the Doctrine of Justification, signed in Augsburg by the Catholic Church and the World Lutheran Federation, contributed to the healing of a wound that had torn apart the civil, cultural and spiritual fabric of Europe since the sixteenth century.

Two gestures opened the great jubilee of the year 2000 and announced the dawn of the second millennium in the sign of dialog and unity. On January 18, the holy door in the Roman Basilica of St. Paul Outside the Walls was opened by the pope together with Metropolitan Athanasios of Helioúpolis and Theira and the Archbishop of Canterbury, George Carey, in the presence of twenty-two delegations of Christian Churches. On the following

March 12 the Jubilee Day of Forgiveness was celebrated, where John Paul II recalled the divisions that have occurred among Christians throughout history and which are associated with the modern evils of atheism, religious indifference, secularism, ethical relativism, and violations of human rights.

In 2004 the paths of dialogue with the Orthodox world were reopened, with the visit of the Ecumenical Patriarch Bartholomew I to the Vatican and the return of the icon of the Mother of God of Kazan to Alexis II, Patriarch of all Russia and of the "third Rome"[145] (a title of Moscow since the fall of the Byzantine Empire).

These symbolic gestures, which characterized the institutional dimension of the Churches, were also the result of and mirror for the great work of the charismatic dimension of the Churches and of spiritual ecumenism, an ecumenism based on internal conversion, renewal in the Spirit, mutual charity, humility, patience, and prayer. All are concepts dear to the spirituality of unity, which make ecumenism an adventure of the Spirit. Chiara was invited to present the spirituality of unity at the opening of the Second Ecumenical Assembly of the Christians of Europe in Graz (1997), at the World Council of Churches in Geneva in 2002, and in various other historical venues and in front of numerous leaders of the Christian Churches.

---

145. Moscow as "the third Rome" is a theological and political concept asserting that Moscow is the successor of the Roman Empire, representing a "third Rome" in succession to the first Rome (Rome itself, capital of the ancient and Western "Roman" Empire) and the second Rome (Constantinople, capital of the Eastern "Byzantine" Empire).

Dialogue between religions

The Council decree *Nostra Aetate* solemnly affirms that "the Catholic Church rejects nothing that is true and holy in all religions" and "regards with sincere reverence those ways of conduct and of life, those precepts and teachings which, though differing in many aspects from the ones she holds and sets forth, nonetheless often reflect a ray of that Truth which enlightens all men" (NA 2). Moreover, the Council affirmed its deep esteem for all great spiritual values and for the primacy of what is spiritual and finds its expression in the life of humanity in religion, morality, and culture.

Chiara always pursued relationships with representatives of other religions according to these principles for inter-religious dialogue and the key elements of the spirituality of unity. Such dialogue started from walking side by side with people, communities and faiths, as an expression of universal fraternity and on the basis of the "golden rule" which is present in all religions and which is the foundation of relationships between the faithful of every creed.

Authentic dialogue presupposes a plurality of participants who are open to a reciprocal exchange of views, who are mutually tolerant and open to the possible growth in knowledge that can come to light through dialogue. A dialogue between people is based on practical things, starting with their respective identities. It should be based on a search for what they have in common, avoiding any masking of their differences. It should be based on the willingness to listen, to enrich each other, and to accept unity in diversity. Reciprocity is the attribute associated with every action linked to dialogue between believers of different religions. It expresses itself through "mutual trust," "mutual esteem," "mutual knowledge and understanding," "mutual acceptance"…

It rejects and challenges all egoism and self-centeredness and avoids any kind of conflict.

Chiara went even further, offering to engage in dialogue on her own perspective of faith through a particular form of communication. If dialogue starts from what is common, and seeks further harmony, if it acts on issues where collaboration is possible (such as peace, solidarity, justice), then "proclamation" is the simple and uncomplicated offering of what is dearest to one's heart and from which one would like everyone to draw for their joy. For the Christian, this treasure is represented by the cross, the mystery of God who gives himself in his Son to the point of taking upon himself our evil and that of the world. Chiara never avoided affirming this, adapting her approach and language to contexts and situations:

> *Jesus forsaken is the model which teaches us to be "nothing" in front of people of other religions, to be a "nothingness of love," to be able to "enter" in them, because we must "know how to get into the other's skin," to the point of understanding what it means for them to be Buddhists, Muslims, or Hindus. But we can enter in others if we are nothing.*[146]

Enzo Maria Fondi, who, with Natalia Dallapiccola, for many years was in charge of the Focolare Movement's Relations with the Great Religions, identified the Templeton Prize for the Progress of Religion, received by Chiara Lubich in 1977, as the pivotal experience of interreligious dialogue for the Work of Mary. In the Guildhall, in the City of London, where Chiara was invited to speak about her spiritual experience, there was a lively interest expressed by representatives of Judaism and Islam, Buddhists, Hindus, and Sikhs. This made her recognize the fundamental connection between interreligious dialogue and her charism.

---

146. Chiara Lubich, audience with the Archbishop of Canterbury, Most Rev. Rowan Williams, June 25, 2004.

Commenting on the reaction of the representatives of non-Christian religions to her words and to the perception of a "new current of love that was flowing through the world" Chiara said:

> I had the impression that all of us present were one, even though we were of different religions, almost as if Jesus' ut unum sint *had been brought to fulfilment in that room.... This encounter with people of other religions, with whom I immediately felt like a sister, was a sign that opened me to God's will for us in that moment, that from now on we should not only try to bring this spirit, our love, our life to other Christian Churches and ecclesial communities, but that, letting ourselves be guided by the Holy Spirit, we should resolutely take the path towards our brothers and sisters of other faiths.*

In 1979, there was an important encounter for the development of interreligious dialogue. It was the meeting between Chiara and Nikkyō Niwano, the president and founder of the Risshō Kōsei-kai, a secular Japanese Buddhist movement with over six million members. He is also the co-founder of the World Conference of Religions for Peace (WCRP).

Two years later he invited Chiara to Tokyo to speak about her Christian faith in a Buddhist temple in front of 12,000 people. As they got to know each other better, they began to collaborate in the humanitarian field and in the promotion of peace. Faced with a planetary situation in constant and rapid change, threatened by clashes of civilizations and in which religions are often perceived as a factor of division and conflict, religious leaders felt the need for reflection on themes of nonviolence and compassion which are present in the various spiritual traditions.

Buddhist spirituality and its doctrine of interior peace immediately attracted Chiara's interest. By denying selfishness, Buddhist sages achieve emptiness of self; they can achieve an inner peace without carnal desire and exhibit a particular benevolence towards all that exists in the world. Chiara considered these elements outside of all dogmatism, viewing them in terms of one's interior life and individual and social ethics, as a way to be sensitive to suffering and as a means of self-transformation and healing. She compared them with the Gospel's *Sermon on the Mount*. In Buddhism she recognized the goodness of a sensitivity to suffering caused by the destruction of life, which commits us to cultivate compassion; to suffering caused by exploitation, social injustice, or oppression, which urges us to cultivate loving kindness towards others; to suffering caused by the inability to listen to others, which requires us to cultivate communication based on profound detachment and the sharing of joys and sorrows; and a sensitivity towards the need for an individual and collective healthy consumption. She found points of comparison on the question of salvation, which in Buddhism depends on refuge into the so-called *Three Jewels:* the Buddha, the Dharma (the doctrine) and the Sangha (the monastic community). She drew a comparison with the affirmation that Christians are saved in Jesus Christ, collaborate actively in their own salvation by living as he lived, making Jesus their road to salvation.

On May 18, 1997, Chiara, her head covered by a hijab, entered the mosque of the American Muslim Mission in Harlem, New York. Chiara had been invited by Imam Warith Deen Mohammed to speak in the Malcolm X Mosque, named after the African American Muslim civil rights leader murdered in 1965. Over three thousand people listened to her. The words of the first Christian woman to speak in the mosque were dedicated to the urgency of creating a new universal fraternity and to an invitation for Christians and Muslims to work together for the good of humanity. At the end of the speech the Imam commented: "Today in Harlem a page of history has been written. As God is my witness, you are my sister. I am your friend and will always help you."

This was a meeting and a spirit that recalls that of 1219, at the height of the Fifth Crusade, when Francis travelled from Assisi to the port of Acre in northern Palestine and visited the Sultan of Egypt al-Malik al-Kamil to speak of peace. This encounter had deep roots in Sacred Scripture: just as God promised that Isaac, son of Abraham, would become father of the Jewish people, so God reserved particular blessings for Ishmael, son of the patriarch and the slave-girl Hagar. God promised Abraham that he would also make Ishmael father of a great nation (Gen. 21: 13-20). Many centuries later Muhammad, the prophet of Islam, would be born from those tribes. From that blessing and from the common sonship attested by the Bible was born the spirit of dialogue. This approach was affirmed by the Council in *Lumen Gentium*: "the plan of salvation also includes those who acknowledge the creator. In the first place amongst these there are the Muslims, who, professing to hold the faith of Abraham, along with us adore the one and merciful God, who on the last day will judge mankind" (LG 16).

John Paul II strongly promoted a meeting at Assisi on October 27, 1986 between representatives of world religions where the relationship between interreligious dialogue and peace appeared in all its clarity, committing religions for the future of the world. Every year since then, the St. Egidio Community honor their commitment to keep the "spirit of Assisi" alive. Recognizing that in all religions, in some way, the Holy Spirit is present and active, Chiara and the Focolare Movement made the strong commitment to this same spirit "so that the religious pluralism of humanity may be cleansed more and more of any negative values or source of divisions and wars, and rise to the challenge to recompose unity among the human family."

Chiara strengthened relations with Mahayana Buddhists in Japan, with Theravada Buddhists in Thailand and with the Gandhian-inspired Hindu communities of the Indian Swadhyaya

Movement, each of which demonstrated features of surprising spiritual congruence with the Focolare Movement. Their spiritual experiences were marked by a strong disposition towards community and social engagement, personal development, education, and commitment to peace. These experiences are inscribed in the ancient Eastern religious traditions, with perspectives of faith centered on an inner reality of the human person that transcends the material, and that aims at the elevation of the person in themselves and in their relationship with others.

The encounter with people of the Jewish faith, which took place through the Jewish community of Buenos Aires, Argentina, in April 1998, was particularly special. This dialogue is in line with the Vatican Council's declaration *Nostra Aetate*, which emphasized the enduring validity of the promise made by God to the chosen people (NA 4), and was reiterated by John Paul II during his visit to the synagogue in Rome on April 13, 1986, where he affirmed that the Jewish religion "is 'intrinsic" to our own religion" and declared "You are our dearly beloved brothers, and in a certain way, it could be said that you are our elder brothers."[147] Such dialogue utterly rejected the centuries of prejudices whereby Christians had considered the Jewish people responsible for the death of Jesus – and therefore of deicide – and which then fed the anti-Semitic sentiments that exploded in Europe in the first half of the twentieth century. Instead it acknowledged Jewish people to be the people of God's covenant, the guardians of Sacred Scripture and the "holy root" from which the Church grew.[148]

Chiara, well aware that formal unity between the two religions must be seen in an eschatological perspective, to be

---

147. New York Times April 14, 1986, Section A, P. 4: Pope John Paul II's speech at Rome Synagogue, April 13, 1986.
148. See Pontifical Biblical Commission, *The Jewish people and their Sacred Scriptures in the Christian Bible*, Libreria Editrice Vaticana, Vatican City, 2002. N.!.

achieved at the end of time,[149] drew a parallel between key teachings of the two religions, between the Gospel verse: "For where two or three are gathered in my name, I am there among them,"[150] and the Jewish Midrash, where it is stated: "But two who are sitting together and there are words of Torah [spoken] between them, the Divine Presence [*Shekinah*] rests with them."[151] She then recalled the Old Testament root of the mystery of Jesus on the cross who cries out, using the words of Psalm 22: "My God, my God, why have you also forsaken me?" The suffering of the apparent abandonment by the Father, experienced also by the Jewish people, is, however, aimed at recomposing the unity of humanity with God and among themselves, healing the separation caused by sin.

Christians, in order to understand themselves, cannot fail to refer to the Jewish roots that speak of the "God of the not yet," and experience his true yet imperfect presence, jealously guarded by the Bible and cultivated with faith even after the destruction of the Temple. At the same time, the Church, while professing salvation through faith in Christ, recognizes the irrevocability of the Old Covenant and God's constant and faithful love for Israel.

With the approach of the new millennium, with the evolution of international scenarios and with the great cultural changes taking place, new frontiers and ever more demanding prospects for interreligious dialogue were opening up, which no longer stopped at the theological sphere and cooperation for peace, but embraced new dimensions of worldwide humanism, such as the promotion of freedom of conscience, thought and religion, or

---

149. See *Nostra Aetate*, sec. 4, "the Church awaits that day, known to God alone, on which all peoples will address the Lord in a single voice and 'serve him shoulder to shoulder.'"
150. Mt. 18:20.
151. Mishnah tractate Avot (3:2).

the duty to provide the new generations with an education that responds to the great ideals to which humanity must look. If in modern times these themes had been absorbed and (partially) resolved by the juridical and civil spheres, by states and laws, with post-modernity there remains also the direct and common commitment of religions in these fields, a common goal to be achieved in places and contexts where each religion exists and acts.

Chiara had understood the urgency of defining an ontological and non-transient foundation for humanity, and a vision of law based on the dignity of the person and of peoples, which is valid at all times and in all places. Towards this end, too, the dialogue between religions had to be directed.

DIALOGUE WITH HUMANISTS

Jürgen Moltmann, one of the greatest theologians of the twentieth century, published *Theology of Hope* in 1964. This book was seen as a putting into question *The Principle of Hope*, written by the Marxist philosopher Ernst Bloch. Moltmann based his work on the power and capacity of "being" and its openness to change in contrast to the ideology of the "end of history," nihilism and anguish. Moltmann's image of God, freed from the constraints of the metaphysical tradition and anchored in Scripture, emerged as a personal, living God, capable of death and glory. He sees human persons, even though they die, as capable of experiencing eternal life. For him the fullness of life passes from freedom to love, from hoping to thinking, from suffering to happiness, from the toil of earthly existence to the horizon of eternal life. Moltmann's work engendered a perception of the need for dialogue with the currents of secular thought, which resonated with the post-Conciliar climate and more open circles of Christian culture.

In 1965 the Catholic Church established the *Pontifical Council for Dialogue with Non-Believers,* presided over by the Cardinal Archbishop of Vienna Franz König, to show pastoral concern for those who do not believe in God and do not profess any religion, and to establish dialogue with those who are open to sincere collaboration on all possible avenues of encounter that express faith in humanity.

The crisis of ideologies and the advance of postmodernity highlighted the lack of a common horizon, of a shared ethos, of a foundation that guided living and acting. This vulnerability could stimulate dialogue between believers and non-believers on our common destiny, on the historical crisis and existential confusion of our era.

When people ponder life's meaning they recognize that there are conditions common to contemporary humanity: we have an uneasy tension between faith and reason. In searching and confronting these issues we recognize both a sense of otherness and the need for others; we develop compassion, the desire for sharing, and the need for the transcendental. These deep tensions stir our conscience in search of integrity and honesty. They make us recognize others whom we encounter to be a gift and emphasize our need to be in harmony with them, whether believers or not. They push us towards developing a common mindset: men and women who strive to go forward, to seek, to believe, hope and love, always infused with the desire for an ultimate goal and an aspiration to investigate the mystery of existence. The result is a mature existence, an other-oriented lifestyle that can generate the positive suspicion that there is a mysterious and sovereign "Other."

For Chiara, animated by the charism of unity, there were no boundaries to dialogue. Even as a child she had been used to confronting her father Luigi and brother Gino who, in addition to their militant socialist and communist political ideals, always had more doubts about religious matters than she did... She admired their honest commitment to social justice, even at the cost of enormous sacrifices.

The Focolare Movement's activity and contacts in socialist Eastern Europe had sensitized it to respect the universal heritage represented by human freedom and human rights. Chiara recognized the historical significance of the fall of the Berlin Wall and the beginning of the dissolution of the communist regimes in 1989. She also recognized the suffering experienced by so many people of good will who had honestly believed in the humanitarian and egalitarian ideals at the basis of communist thought. She commented:

> *There should be neither winners nor losers. We must love one another. We must love the others who had believed in the values of solidarity, peace, unity, human rights, and justice. These values must be re-proposed and revitalized by new ideals.*

Among the various tasks he entrusted to the Movement, Paul VI gave Chiara the mandate to pursue a dialogue with non-believers. An initiative in 1978 saw the inauguration of a "Focolare Centre for Dialogue with People without Religious Convictions." The approach was the same as that adopted with Christians of other denominations or with believers of other religions. One had to dare to enter a relationship with people – one did not meet "Muslims" or "Jews," but people who lived their Muslim or Jewish faith. It was the same with those who did not live within the horizon of faith, but with whom it was still possible to enter a relationship, to walk a stretch of the road together. Human identity, shaped by a specific culture, is still discernible by those who belong to another culture. Dialogue is a mutual enrichment, a feeling of being brothers and sisters, a creation of a universal fraternity already on this earth, with sincere love for humanity and without selfishness:

> *Dialogue means loving, giving what is in us out love for the other, and also receiving and being enriched. It means becoming*

"world people" who have the others within themselves and have been able to give to others what is theirs.[152]

Dialogue, as understood by the Focolare, is a new approach, devoid of dogmatic and ideological prejudices, for which the Christian faith represents a stimulus and an imperative, which first generates friendship, then conversation, then communion. It is Jesus who urges us to a love that is capable of dialogue, without closing ourselves in our own space, but opening ourselves to all and collaborating with all people of good will in order to build peace and unity in the world.

> *The crucifix that will convert them will not be the one presented to the Jews or Gentiles in the first centuries, because these brothers of ours do not necessarily care about salvation, the resurrection, or life after death. Rather, we need to present a crucifix in which Christ seems to be only human. We need to present Christians who love other people so much that they, like Jesus forsaken, are able to experience losing God for them. In other words, Christians who know how to become "as one without the law'"(1 Cor. 9: 21), in order to save their brothers and sisters who are– as Paul says – living crucifixes.*

---

152. Chiara Lubich, *Essential Writings*, New City, New York, 2007, 356.

WITHOUT BORDERS
THE GLOBALIZATION OF LOVE

The city-world

Among the oldest documents ever written and surviving till today, there is an Egyptian ideogram symbolizing a town or city. It is made up of a circle with a cross inside. This represents the convergence of access roads to a city center for the movement of people, goods, and ideas. The circle represents the walls of the city, independently from the fact of whether they are materially erected or not. The important thing is what they represent, keeping the citizens together, aware of belonging to a homogeneous group, proud to be so and all connected with one another.

From the origins of great civilizations – in Egypt, more so than in Mesopotamia or China – the city has been the primary model of organized coexistence. It was usually founded at a place where important roads and waterways met and formed the basis of the social and economic organization, developing an administrative culture, legal order, division of labor, management and redistribution of surplus goods, stimulating the art of writing and accounts. It was a place created by a community for the activities that could not be done by individuals or a small group.

More than half of the world population now lives in cities. From the start, Chiara and the community around her were aware of the problems of their city and its inhabitants. The solution to the social problems of war-torn Trent occupied much of their attention and activities. The linguistic root of both "city" and "civilization" points to an animating principle and a culture in continuous evolution, capable of overcoming traditional forms of life, of making up and experiencing new ones within a community respectful of its fundamental institutions and the ethical and political ideas that inspired them.

One of Chiara Lubich's most famous writings, entitled "The Resurrection of Rome"(*Essential Writings*, 173-76), dates from 1949 and was published by Igino Giordani in *La Via*. It was a special period in Chiara's spiritual life, rich with illuminations and mystical experiences, in which she was given to contemplate the reality of God and to see clearly the path on which to set out and direct the development of the Movement.

After that period, Chiara continued to look at the world in the light of those illuminations, recognizing the divine design on the city, with Rome as a sort of archetype, as the meeting place of the light that dwells in each of us, identifying it with the risen Jesus, where everything can be reborn. From "the Resurrection of Rome" we can recognize the main lines of Chiara's perspective and thought and the directions in which her actions unfolded. It is a vision of humanity rooted in relationships with a strong trinitarian imprint. It is fully expressed in Jesus, in whom the mystery of God and his plan for humanity come together and is brought to completion through the love conveyed by the Holy Spirit. In this way God's plan for humanity is revealed, giving meaning to its existence and its vocation, and discovering our identity as persons fully realized in love. The writing is the fruit of her first experience in the city of Rome, coming from a provincial place like Trent, in the chaotic period of post-war reconstruction. Rome is a city that, also because of its 2,500-year history and its civil and spiritual role, becomes a symbol for every city. It is a short and dense text, an authentic "manifesto" for understanding the urban phenomenon (as well as of other forms of aggregation). It is also an active immersion in the city, in order to assume its problems and aspirations, accompanying humanity to its full realization, up to a fraternity that opens up to the unity between heaven and earth.

The text describes the charism of unity and gives us a program for the renewal of society. It can be read as a provocation against one of the core principles of society today, namely the distinction between the sacred and the secular, between religion and social life. But it is a provocation that does not idealize medieval legacies, neither does it abolish the distinctions that have been the conquests of our civilization and of secularism. It wants to overcome what has become a separation, developing a humanism with deep roots, with an integral (non-integralist) vision on and of the human condition. Starting from the Gospel it shows how the human dimension is not diminished but empowered by it, and how society can receive light, life, and inspiration from it.

Chiara concludes:

> *Jesus must be resurrected in the Eternal City and placed everywhere. He is life and life to the full. It's not something religious... This separating him from all life is a modern heretical practice, enslaving us to something less than human and separates God, who is Father, from his children. No, Jesus is man, the perfect man, who sums up in himself all of us and every truth and motivation we can feel to take ourselves up to our proper place. And those who have found him have found the solution to every problem, both human and divine. As long as you love him.*

Something similar can be found in chapter XIV of St. Augustine's "City of God," when he speaks of the characteristics of the city of God and the city of man:

> *Two loves therefore gave rise to two cities; the earthly love of self to the point of indifference to God, and the heavenly love of God to the point of indifference to oneself... In that city the passion for control dominates in its leaders over the peoples that*

> *it subjugates, ... in this one they exchange services in charity, the leader's deliberation and the subject's obedience . . . . In the heavenly city the only philosophy is the religion with which God is fittingly worshipped, because it awaits the prize in the company of the chosen ones, not only men but also angels, so that God may be all in all.*

During the years Chiara was formulating and communicating her ideas on the city, another protagonist of the Italian Catholic world, Giorgio La Pira, dedicated a significant portion of his cultural and spiritual reflection on the same subject. He was a jurist, university lecturer, member of parliament, undersecretary during the time of the first De Gasperi government. In 1951 La Pira became mayor of Florence. He immediately characterized his political and administrative activity by placing the city at the center of his vision. He considered it as the ideal place from which to develop the unity of the human race and to overcome the state of poverty most people found themselves in. At a time when the threat of a nuclear apocalypse loomed, he gave the city a political and moral role. For him the city was the heritage of humanity that existed before the states and the blocs into which the world was now divided. It formed the cradle of the history and civilization of peoples, which needed to be passed on to future generations. In 1954, in a famous speech to the Red Cross headquarters in Geneva, he said that the world was living "the historical time of the cities." For him the city had become "the new center of orientation for all that concerns humanity," an inexhaustible asset, embodying the "right of existence within one's own historical, artistic, cultural and religious values." He was a layman (for whom the Church initiated the process of beatification) with a very deep spirituality. He had an innate capacity to draw on the wisdom of biblical and patristic texts, and possessed a particular prophetic vein that led him to develop a theology of history that unfolded along the "path of Isaiah" and that, with the power of

Grace, had as its aim peace and the unity of all peoples. He found an unshakable hope in both the Old and the New Testament, as well as in the Qur'an: from Abraham, with the history of Israel and Ishmael, through the patriarchs, Moses and the prophets up to the risen Jesus. From the common seed of the three great Abrahamic religions – Judaism, Christianity, and Islam – he saw this hope spreading to all the peoples of the Mediterranean and to all other civilizations.

In both Chiara Lubich's and Giorgio La Pira's thoughts, the city is the center and meeting place for all human history and action. In the midst of the crisis of the individualistic philosophies that characterize our time, the truth – as summarized by Augustine – remains standing: "that nature is subordinated to grace, time to eternity, and the earthly city to the celestial city."

Chiara's intuition of building model cities as expressions of her ideal dates back a long way, to the time of the first summer Mariapolis. Those first moments of living together in the mountains – born with the aim of spending the holidays living the Gospel, especially Jesus' commandment – were in some way building a small model or "new" city, where people of different cultures, social backgrounds, and ages tried to live together, with a single law, that of mutual love. From there came the desire to make this experience permanent.

Pasquale Foresi, considered by Chiara to be a co-founder of the Movement, worked out many of the principles and cultural initiatives of the Focolare Movement and was prominent in the theological reflection on the spirituality of unity. He was the main protagonist behind the birth of the first little town of Loppiano. It was an estate of eighty hectares in Valdarno[153] that had been inherited by Vincenzo Folonari ("Eletto"), a focolarino, together with

---

153. The valley of the Arno River. Loppiano is about two kilometers from the town of Incisa Valdarno, some thirty kilometers from Florence.

his sisters Giulia and Camilla. On July 12, 1964, subsequent to his accidental death on Lake Bracciano at only thirty-four years of age, he property came into possession of the Movement. At that time, the Focolare Movement was actively building the first Mariapolis Center in Rocca di Papa, intended to welcome and prepare people who wished to deepen the spirituality of unity. A buyer came forward to purchase the land in Valdarno, Tuscany, a few miles south of Florence. Pasquale went to Tuscany to see the place for himself and came to the conclusion that it had all the ideal characteristics to make it a center of formation for focolarine and focolarini, which at that time was done in Grottaferrata, near Rome.

So the first permanent Mariapolis was born, something Chiara had dreamed of ever since their first meetings were held during the summer in the shadow of the Dolomite peaks. The idea of founding a little town gradually took shape. In the history of the Church there were examples of monastic strongholds, born from the inspiration of St. Benedict. Monasteries and abbeys, which often became the center of villages, Christianized the people, and cared for the territories, and so preserved and spread their traditions around. Thanks to Chiara's intuition during the summer Mariapolis of 1956, which was further developed in 1962 while visiting the Swiss Benedictine abbey of Einsiedeln, Loppiano was born in the form of a little town. It is a miniature society with all the various religious and civil vocations, creating an example of what humanity can become when it is imbued with the Gospel.

Its development was neither planned nor anticipated by its founders. Loppiano became a model and was replicated in many other parts of the world, taking on different and peculiar characteristics, depending on the areas in which they developed.

The only essential element that defines the necessity and the forms of such places is relationship. City, home, workplace, are all understood as a human environment in which to live. The living-city is a pulsating body because its very existence is a consequence of the life that generates it. The design of every space is never indifferent to those who live in it. The city is the city of people and for the people. The little towns are, first of all, conceived as a school of life, where the whole day has a formative value which is directed towards the human person seen in all its aspects.

The Benedictine influence can also be seen in the threefold division of time and activities, which are essentially carried out between work, study, and prayer. This gives value to the different aspects of life as emphasized by the Focolare and Loppiano. Among the main infrastructures there is the Lionello Bonfanti business center, inaugurated in 2006, and currently home to companies that operate according to the principles of the Economy of Communion. The study dimension has always been carefully cultivated: first as the Mystici Corporis Institute, dedicated to those who wished to be formed according to the life and spirituality of Chiara's charism; and now as the Sophia University Institute, founded in 2008.

The main center for prayer is in the church dedicated to Mary *Theotókos*, the Mother of God. Located on a small hill, it is visible from many parts of the little town, and for most of the day is illuminated by sunlight. The large paved stone churchyard functions as the meeting place of Loppiano. The dominating feature of the sanctuary is its sloping copper roof, which soars upwards from the ground, culminating in a golden triangular bell tower as a symbol of the Trinity. It was designed as a collective enterprise by *Centro Ave Arte*: a team of artists, architects and designers who give expression to the spirituality of unity in the buildings and spaces they create, and inaugurated on October 30, 2004.

The most striking features of the building are certainly the large stained-glass windows that blend in with the architecture of the church. The central one, by the Portuguese painter Dina Figueiredo, depicts the Mother of God as a great blue sky containing the sun, the emblem of the Lord. The stained-glass window on the left is an invitation to meditate on the mystery of the Passion: from Holy Thursday, when Jesus says his prayer to the Father for unity, it reaches the moment of the crucifixion and abandonment. Here the colors of martyrdom – purple pinks, scarlet red, purple and dark blue – convey the intensity and the cruelty of the cross. This then is followed by the irruption of colors and light that mark the moment of the resurrection. On the right side, adjacent to the chapel of Our Lady, the stained-glass window represents the stages of Mary's life: the annunciation, the incarnation (in yellow-gold colors) right up to the time of the fire of Pentecost and the fullness of glory. These shapes and colors follow a theology of the icon consistent – as Paul Evdokimov explains – in its intrinsic dynamism, in its energetic presentation of relationships that are not localized or enclosed but radiate around its point of greatest density. It expresses what Chiara wrote in 1957, "that art is knowing how to transform into a painting, a sculpture, a building, a piece of music... something of what never dies in the soul."

Today Loppiano has approximately 800 inhabitants from different parts of the world, representing more than sixty nations. Half of them are people who live there permanently: families who have moved there, focolarini and focolarine who continue to inspire the shapes and forms of this life. Others reside there temporarily, spending periods ranging from six months to a year, to participate in this experience and then return to their own homes, multiplying the experience and lifestyle of Loppiano in the communities in which they live. Other temporary citizens are the students who attend courses at the Sophia University Institute.

Loppiano is not an "island of Utopia," disconnected from any historical context. It is a tangible world, made up of people, houses, schools, construction sites and small businesses. The people there do not only live "on the mountaintop" but are integrated in the social and civil context of Valdarno, and likewise within the whole world. It is a little town founded on a culture of dialogue, open to all people who share the dream that "all may be one." This dream excludes no one. There are people of different backgrounds and faiths and people who do not have a particular religious belief. Young people especially come to Loppiano in search of meaning and with a desire to experience this powerful and demanding way of living which begins with the relationships that are established and the values that are perceived as they are embodied in everyday life. There is a vision and a hope based on a life where relationships are possible and where openness to the other is always understood as an enrichment.

Loppiano has been called a "town without outskirts" and a "prophetic vision that brings about a new civilization by living the Gospel life as a model for all that is good and beautiful in life." These two definitions underline a Christian urban vision, where the city is seen as a reflection of the anthropology that guides its foundation, growth, and evolution, and which leads to the demand for meaning expressed in the relationship with God. We find this vision in Revelation, with the holy city, the new Jerusalem seen "coming down from heaven, from God, ready as a bride adorned for her bridegroom": a perfect city governed by the law of love. It is the exact opposite of the model of a city of our contemporary world, often dehumanized and composed of a magnitude of individual loneliness, made up of immense urban peripheries. Loppiano, like the other twenty-five little towns built by the focolarini in the world, is a model of coexistence made up of "dialogue" and "proximity," of the coming together of differences, of communion in all areas of life, which complement each other. The little towns have a common matrix of ideals, but their style and organization are quite different, in keeping with the characteristics and cultures of the places where they are built. Each one shows that it possesses its own "charism," developed in harmony with the surrounding social environment.

The main European focolare towns, in addition to Loppiano, are: Montet, Switzerland, which is very international and dedicated to education; Ottmaring, near Augsburg in Germany, founded in 1968, which has a purely ecumenical vocation; the same mission is shared with Welwyn Garden City, a famous garden city in the county of Hertfordshire in Great Britain; Rotselaar, near Leuven in Belgium, it is strongly characterized by ecology. Other little towns in Europe are being developed in Poland, Spain, France, Ireland, and Portugal. The Brazilian towns (Mariapolis Santa Maria in Recife, Mariapolis Gloria near Belem in the Amazon, and Mariapolis Ginetta near São Paulo) are particularly concerned with social issues, civil rights, work, and the economy of communion. The little town built in O'Higgins, Argentina, is characterized by the presence of young people and is dedicated to agriculture and livestock farming. In the Philippines, near Manila, in Tagaytay, with a strong commitment to interreligious dialogue, people are working on the cultivation of the seeds of the Word present in the Asian religious traditions and of the common traits with Christianity and the great Western religions. The construction of unity in a multi-ethnic society is the typical mission of Mariapolis Luminosa near New York and the little town of Križevci in Croatia. Inculturation of the Gospel is the characteristic note of the little towns that have sprung up in Africa: from the first one in Fontem, Cameroon, where together with the Bangwa people, the focolarini set out on the path of faith and fraternity to the Mariapolis Piero, in Kenya and the Mariapolis Victoria, in Ivory Coast, which have the same focus.

Other similar developments are happening in other countries world-wide. They are developing centers where differences in religion, culture, and traditions are valued as a great treasure and as a privileged means of meeting one another... according to the prayer of Jesus: "Father, that they may all be one."

In dialogue with culture

The proclamation of the Gospel must be understood within the current cultural context. It needs to be understood as something positive, not divisive, and provide a convincing reference point for life. It needs to make our experiences meaningful and give a framework to our daily living, which enlightens us on what seems meaningless, strengthens us in a crisis, gives us hope and opens us up to the future. But none of this will happen without a profound encounter between the Gospel and the culture that surrounds us.

One of the most relevant theoretical insights of contemporary Catholic thought (recently analyzed by the theologian Duilio Albarello and expressed in the encyclical *Amoris Laetitia*) concerns the fact that there cannot exist a Christian faith without it being manifested in a specific culture, since one cannot access the truth of the Gospel independently from our historical and practical conditions. As early as the mid-twentieth century Emmanuel Mounier denounced the "disembodied color" of so much of Catholicism that believed it possessed a solid doctrine on which to rely, oblivious to the complexity of the culture that surrounded it. One of the great new theological approaches that the Second Vatican Council introduced with respect to tradition was to overcome the dichotomy between faith and culture, between the data of revelation and its inclusion within the framework of the solicitations and challenges of contemporary thought and science. It was a rethinking of the specific status of revelation and of Christian truth, often uncritically defined and recognized through a controversial method, which contrasted with the demands of contemporary thought. In modern times Descartes and Pascal initiated a long, laborious, and sometimes painful process to make reason, though separate from faith, nevertheless "friendly," via a new relationship with the expressions of anthropological and scientific thought. This created the opportunity to establish a new kind of dialogue. Theology, especially with regard to dogmas, as solidly anchored in the scholastic method, now left room for new criteria based on biblical and historical data and became more deeply integrated with the reality of the world and of life in general.

At the beginning of the 1990s, after the approval of the new statutes of the Movement by John Paul II, Chiara began a cultural experiment that was as new as it was consistent with her vision of the world. She collected and put in order all the writings and notes that she had written during her mystical experience known as "Paradise '49" and in the following years. This collection was set up as a working text to be discussed and examined by a group of scholars working in various fields of knowledge and in different cultural, religious, and lay contexts. This "cenacle" (built around the focolare...) received the name – at the same time evocative and programmatic – the "Abba School."

Some of those who were part of that first nucleus were direct witnesses of the "facts" of 1949 and some were scholars who had studied (though not yet systematically) the mystical and theological dimensions of it. They were called to help Chiara read and study her writings of that period in depth. Among them were Pasquale Foresi, Klaus Hemmerle, Marisa Cerini, Giuseppe Maria Zanghí, and Jesús Castellano. The basic text with Chiara's writings was accompanied by a series of notes from the author herself, and by an explanatory appendix written by the various experts, including notes referring to the sources, comprised of quotations from the Scriptures, from patristic writers, from the philosophical and theological tradition and from the Magisterium.

For many years these writings were kept confidential, both because of the spiritual intimacy that linked Chiara to her own experience, and because of the long period of canonical investigations to which she had been subjected. These investigations involved her having to remain silent regarding all of this, which had been very painful for her. This attitude of silence continued in her personal life even after the end of all the proceedings. However, this was not to be seen as a "delay," but as a necessity to understand whether the times were mature enough to make this mystical experience available for scholarly analysis, for its correct interpretation and for an equally necessary sharing of the experience. Those texts, although not explicitly used by the founder, had marked the beginnings and development of the Work of Mary in all its expressions, in all its activities and initiatives. As a vision of God's plan for humanity, embodied in the Gospel, they needed dialogue partners, such as Igino Giordani in 1949. Now the dialogue partner came in the form of the Abba School, which represented humanity, to better understand the charism of unity.

Like every great spiritual movement, the ideal of unity also aimed at a new revolution and cultural synthesis in order to convey the truths included in its teachings and to contribute to the development of an understanding applicable to all areas of knowledge. Chiara always felt the need to place the many intuitions of her illuminative period and those that followed on a secure doctrinal and cultural basis. Hence, after the collaboration with Igino Giordani and Pasquale Foresi, she wanted to hear, in a systematic way, what other scholars thought. In this way she could better get to know created reality, including human intelligence, as a manifestation of God's love. The intellectual experience then simply becomes one of the expressions and effects of love for God and neighbor. A way of thinking was being developed that had its roots in life and nourished it in return. Article 64 of the statutes of the Movement makes explicit reference to the effort to inform the culture with the light of Christ: "The people who are part of the Focolare Movement seek to possess above all Christian wisdom . . . they will seek to be united with one another so that Christ, who is present through mutual love, can inform their thoughts of his light."

When the Franciscan friars went to study at the Sorbonne in Paris during the Middle Ages, the following expression started to circulate among them: "Paris, you are destroying Assisi." Chiara, recalling that saying, once replied: "We are not afraid of Paris, because it will help Assisi. And one day Hollywood will be added to it as well." For her, the academic world was symbolized by Paris, and popular culture by Hollywood. Both needed to be nourished by spirituality (Assisi), in order that the vision "that all may be one" may reach everyone.

Here we find the idea of applying the principle of unity to the modern divisions of the various forms of knowledge, in particular those that distinguish between the so-called exact sciences and the humanities, with their respective rigidities and ideological dogmatisms (especially during the nineteenth and twentieth centuries), such as scientific positivism and Christian absolutism.

This is how Chiara summed up her relationship with human cultures in November 2000, receiving an honorary doctorate at the Catholic University of America in Washington D.C.: "If those who study live the spirituality of unity, then from the presence of the risen one in their midst every discipline will be renewed." Listening to all that is positive in what humanity has produced throughout history, we will be able to grasp what is true, good, and beautiful in the various forms of knowledge.

The charism of unity brought about not only a new kind of spirituality, but it also contributed to the development of various social projects and other concrete contributions of a social and cultural character. This is reflected in the sixteen honorary degrees and doctorates conferred on Chiara by universities throughout the world: in social sciences (Catholic University of Lublin in Poland in 1996); in theology (Pontifical and Royal University of St. Tomas in Manila and Fu Jen University in Taipei in 1997, University of Trnava in Slovakia in 2003, Liverpool Hope University in Great Britain 2008); in social communications (St. John's University in Bangkok in 1997); in humanities (Sacred Heart University in Fairfield, Connecticut, USA, in 1997); in philosophy (S. Juan Bautista de La Salle University in Mexico City in 1997); in dialogue with contemporary culture (State University of Buenos Aires in 1998); in religious sciences (Pontifical Catholic University of Sao Paulo in Brazil in 1998); in economics (Catholic University of Pernambuco in Brazil in 1998 and Catholic University of the Sacred Heart in Milan in 1999); in psychology (University of Malta in 1999); in pedagogy (Catholic University of America of Washington in 2000); in art (Catholic University of Maracaibo in Venezuela in 2003); in theology of consecrated life (Claretianum Institute of the Pontifical Lateran University of Rome in 2004).

Applying the methodology of the Abba School at a university level, a Summer School "Towards a culture of unity," aimed at university students from all over the world, was held from 2001 to 2007 in the little towns of the Movement in Switzerland, Italy, and Germany. It was a preparation for the launch of Chiara's latest project.

In 2008, the Sophia University Institute was inaugurated in Loppiano. It is dedicated to academic research in various disciplines, to comparison with contemporary culture, to collaboration with other research institutes around the world, both ecclesial and secular. Sophia is now organized in three departments (Economics and Management; Social and Political Sciences; Theology, Philosophy and Humanities) and offers master's degrees and doctorates in economic and political sciences, trinitarian ontology, the culture of unity, as well as a master's degree course in social business management.

With its culture of dialogue, its vision of the unity of all forms of knowledge, the Work of Mary has an inborn educational character, because by its very nature it opens up to new horizons and enters into all the complexity of today's world.

In the so-called post-secular and post-Christian era (according to Émile Poulat), religion and belonging to a religion no longer requires the effort of protecting one's territories, of defending one's faith or of claiming the rights of one's community. We say good-bye to the contrast between the secular and the religious, typical of modernity. New and previously unthought of opportunities open up to walk together. Coherence and participation can become the essential supports for Christianity in the times to come, as well as the need to dialogue responsibly with the culture of one's own time.

The Economy of Communion

On May 1, 1991, on the centenary of Leo XIII's encyclical *Rerum Novarum*, which had brought social issues to the center of the Church's attention, Pope John Paul II signed the apostolic letter *Centesimus Annus*.[154] In a global economic, social, and political context that was evolving rapidly and radically, and with very uncertain perspectives, the pontiff had decided to make his voice heard in matters of social doctrine, placing ethics and the human person at the center of every economic theory and activity. This document summed up the tradition of the Church's reflection on the subject and the events of recent history, in particular the recent collapse of communist regimes and the consolidation of democratic and capitalist economic systems in the West. He criticized their social and political shortcomings, developing a deeper understanding of private property and the universal destination

---

154. *Centesimus annus (the hundredth year) is an encyclical on the social doctrine of the Church written by Pope John Paul II in 1991 on the hundredth anniversary of Rerum Novarum.*

of goods, as well as of the nature and function of the state. The encyclical was based on the idea of a Christian anthropology that affirms openness to the transcendent, the dignity of the person and his or her centrality in society, and the integral development of humanity as a goal that cannot be separated from economic progress. The object of the economy is therefore the formation of wealth and its progressive increase, which will acquire a moral value if they are aimed at the global and integral development of the human person and of society.

It was a period in which capitalism was facing globalization and the advent of new technologies. Global political systems and the geography of power were being redefined after the end of the Cold War. Western economic systems were experiencing a heavy public debt with a consequent welfare crisis. New players and new markets with extremely innovative features and new operating logics were emerging. The speed of the evolution of the international economy in a globalizing sense seemed little inclined to consider the importance of ethical references, to accept any form of direction and control by politics, accentuating world imbalances and concentrating wealth in the hands of the few. It developed the uncontrolled diffusion of mainly speculative technical instruments in the financial markets. The economy of the digital era tended to become virtual and to exceed the traditional one in value. The political and legal systems, national and international, were not able to follow and regulate this new dimension adequately, resulting in the birth of monopolies and oligopolies with a global dimension which were hardly controllable.

At that time Chiara went to Brazil, which was going through a period of severe recession. The government had blocked bank deposits to combat inflation, causing a considerable increase in poverty, already widespread in the country. On her way from Sao Paulo airport to the Mariapolis Aracoeli, she crossed the enormous favelas of the suburbs, with the modern city in the background.

That sight caused her enormous suffering, and a profound conviction for the need to rethink the fundamentals of the economy. It needed to be freed from the domination by market forces and to find alternative forms for the use of wealth, for the reorganization of economic theories and practices with production systems that provided possibilities for the communion of goods. Her inspiration came from the desire to imitate the first Christian community in Jerusalem, "There was not a needy person among them" (Acts 4: 34). After a short time, on May 29, she announced the project of the Economy of Communion.

Starting from the communities of Brazil, a new form of communion of goods had to be implemented, first within the two little towns in Brazil, and then expanding wherever possible in the world. The principle consisted in the creation of companies and industries where all interested parties participate, setting up industrial parks where everyone puts their profit in common. The member companies had to commit themselves to divide the profit into three parts: one for the company, for its development and support; another for the formation of "new people" and so spread the "culture of giving" and the principle of reciprocity; a third to set up a solidarity fund to help disadvantaged people. Hope was high that this model would be imitated and multiplied. On the wave of the enthusiasm aroused by Chiara's proposal, several companies were immediately set up for the project. Over time and as the theoretical reflection and the results matured, many others adhered to the idea, transforming themselves into companies of communion. Various industrial parks have developed in different parts of the world: in Brazil, the Spartaco Lucarini business park in Vargem Grande Paulista, near Sao Paolo, and the Ginetta Calliari park in Recife; in Argentina the Solidaridad park in O'Higgins; in Croatia the Faro park in Križevci, the Solidar park in Belgium, the Giosi Guella park in Portugal, and the Lionello Bonfanti park in the little town of Loppiano, Italy. Others are in the process of being established in Brazil, the Philippines, and Germany.

Right from the start, the project was not driven by spontaneity or pure intuition but was characterized as a process in need of extensive research and training. Chiara had put the charism of unity at the service of society and economic research. She sensed the risk that practice, however virtuous, without a theory to support it could be exhausting. She brought together some experts in the field – in Italy academics such as Luigino Bruni and Stefano Zamagni – and invited them to compare existing theories and economic schools in respect to her intuition that, starting from the condition of the poor, communion should become the new way of the economy, for everyone. As in all her spiritual and social adventures, she did not fail to emphasize that there can be no authentically intellectual experience if thought and theory do not become the life of both those who develop them and those who experience them.

New expressions and new concepts such as "relational goods," "gratuitousness," "unconditional reciprocity," "communion," "agape" entered scientific research and vocabulary. It is research aimed at discovering the profound meaning of wealth, poverty, work, reread in the light of the relationship with God and with people, and of mutual love that brings about the presence of Jesus in the midst. Through reciprocity, goods acquire their real value and mutual love leaves no one destitute. Communion and mutual gift create happiness, a vital element totally absent from the traditional logic of market forces.

All this is also a development of some long-standing traditions such as the so-called civil economy approach, i.e. the perspective of understanding the economy as a synthesis of efficiency, fairness, and solidarity, trying to establish an effective and efficient economic order respectful of human dignity. Theories rooted in the economic thought of Christian humanism, gave life to the "mounts of piety" (we would now call them banks) already in the late Middle Ages, especially in Italy, thanks to the Franciscan environment. They also produced important reflections on the purpose of money, exchange, and the market, as well as on the economy of gift. They brought into existence the idea of "the civil economy" through Abbot Antonio Genovesi in Naples in the mid-eighteenth century. In the following century, it was further developed by Giuseppe Toniolo, who refused to accept the positivist thesis of the separation of ethics and economy and placed the common good at the center of his theory. By doing this he stimulated the role of intermediate social bodies and encouraged the birth of the cooperative movement, well known to Chiara Lubich, as it was widespread in her homeland. In this way, principles such as solidarity, gratuitousness, and reciprocity found their place within economic activity and the market, creating new forms of enterprise, of sharing, and a growing appreciation of what today is called the non-profit or third sector.

One of the elements that has more recently become part of the reflection on the economy concerns the state of the planet and the impact of human activities, realizing that the future of the earth and its communities are closely linked and depend on the interaction of factors such as population growth, the availability of food resources, reserves and consumption of raw materials, industrial development and pollution. The more sensitive economists question the objective of growth at any cost, which has so far guided economic choices in both the advanced and the developing countries, and which was based on an ever-increasing consumption of resources and energy. Sustainable development is the only way to reconcile economic growth and social development. It requires a major change in the approach to production and consumption and needs a long period of transition. Quality of life, social equality, efficiency, sufficiency in production will be the new key words of this type of development and traditional economic models will have to engage again with the political world. At the same time, new forms of sustainable economy will have to be developed and implemented. Concepts such as green economy, sharing economy, circular economy, are entering the scientific lexicon.

As Amartya Sen, winner of the 1998 Nobel Prize for Economics, said "Development cannot be reduced to the process of increasing production, but the value of what is produced must depend on the effect it has on the living standards, freedom and equality of people."

COMING OUT OF THE TEMPLE

Ever since the beginning of her spiritual adventure, the solution of social problems has always been at the center of Chiara's concern and an intrinsic element of the charism of unity. This concern has evolved over time, from caring for the poor of Trent during the Second World War to considering the great global perspectives, with the growing and scandalous mass of discarded people in all the various parts of the earth. They are the result of unfair systems and a globalization in servitude to the powers of the world. This care draws on the basic choices and profound values that move the human conscience. It is inspired by the mystery of the Incarnation of the Word and of God sharing in our humanity. It draws on the model of trinitarian love, it believes in the dignity of every person as a child of God. These are the motivations that animate the social dimension of Chiara's charism and her thoughts and initiatives in more strictly political terms.

The prophets of the Old Testament, especially Amos and Jeremiah, aware that justice is the foundation stone on which everything is based, denounced it being subverted through a life where relationships are marked by domination and exploitation. Like Samuel, Ezekiel, and Isaiah, they also acted as watchmen, seers, and sentinels, capable of seeing further ahead regarding the good of humanity and without the filter of convenience. Just as Jonah took up God's invitation "Get up, go to Nineveh, that great city" (Jonah. 3: 2), Chiara understood she had to leave the temple, not waiting for someone to enter, but immersing herself in a pluralistic and secularized society which had lost its connection with Christianity. In place of temples, she proposed to set up tents as nomads on their way through human history, sharing their problems and hopes. Without giving in to the temptation to build fortresses or a promised land in the drama of history, she demonstrated in everyday life with simplicity, hospitality, mercy and with an awareness of what is limited and temporary, that the Gospel can be the leaven of a new society. It was necessary to avoid a model of faith that Tonino Bello criticized as being "...not very dusty on the shoes, not smelling of the streets, of the market squares or of condominiums, only smelling of the incense of our churches."

In the last decade of the century and of the millennium, Chiara seemed to perceive the direction in which the world was heading and the general impotence world-wide to understand and guide things in a convincing, unifying and pacifying way, so causing distrust, disunity and enormous dangers for humanity.

The principles of global solidarity were crumbling and new forms of conflict and terrorism were appearing whose political and cultural traits consisted in the denial of the concept and existence of the state and, indeed, of the entire international order. They made the legal conditions underlying the international institutions responsible for promoting peace and defending human rights (first and foremost the UN) inconsistent and inefficient. Although there was clear progress in its economic and financial sector, the ethical foundations of a united and democratic Europe were breaking down, as was confidence in the process of mid-twentieth century political integration, generated through the foresight of the leaders who had undertaken such measures. The center of gravity of the world was shifting towards Asia and models of "more or less" democratic regimes were coming forward. The enormous crisis in the Middle East remained unresolved.

The European model of democracy celebrated its triumph with the fall of the Berlin Wall and, for a short time, it seemed capable of governing the processes of globalization and dictating the rules for a new world order. Actually, it was facing a major setback, with the incipient crisis of neo-liberal ideology, which was incapable of guaranteeing economic stability, social justice and, in the case of the Balkan area, even peacekeeping. Europe was losing its identity and was no longer the laboratory of civilization and humanism as had been for at least two millennia. From Jewish culture to Greek culture, from Christianity to the Enlightenment, it had always been producing values based on the principle of the search for truth. Both the civil and religious dimensions now faced phenomena such as agnosticism and ethical fundamentalism, which caused destabilizing polarizations.

Even the Church, with its great potential derived from a universal vision based on faith and its capability to overcome localism and fragmentation, seemed to be directing itself towards forms of dialogue with politics and governments that provided for direct confrontation between the leaders. It seemed to be giving up investing with patience and far-sightedness to create occasions and places for reflection and to form a mature laity aware of their own spheres of action, in order to influence society and "what is Caesar's."

With the radical changes in the international political situation of the early 1990s, and with the disintegration of the Cold War scenarios and the collapse of twentieth-century ideologies, the conditions on which the Italian political system had stood for decades suddenly disappeared. With the collapse of traditional parties, huge investigations into political corruption and change in the electoral systems, we entered a long phase of transition, instability, and little influence on the international scene.

In this period, between 1992 and 1994, Chiara lived yet another dark night of the soul, characterized by a deep anguish and concern for the world. It was a night that, as usual, revealed great generative potential and preceded far-reaching intuitions and projects. One of these, which seemed to be a real sociocultural challenge, was the Movement for Unity in Politics. It was discussed and presented in Naples on May 2, 1996, before a large group of representatives of a variety of political forces, proposing the principle and the practice of fraternity in function of the common good. This "seed" was to be sown everywhere in the world, in the hope of finding fertile ground to germinate and so reform politics and institutions, but above all to have a positive impact on the destiny of humanity.

The spirituality of unity, in the same way as it contributed to the process of reconciliation between the Christian Churches and to dialogue between religions, would prove to be a powerful vector for renewing ties among people and between nations.

On the eve of Pentecost, May 30, 1998, in St. Peter's Square in Rome John Paul II called together the first great meeting of ecclesial movements and new communities. The pope spoke of rediscovering the charismatic dimension of the Church of which the movements were an evident expression, recognizing in the gifts of the Spirit that each one embodied a providential response to the dramatic challenges of the time, with hope for new "fruits of communion and commitment." On the same occasion, Cardinal Joseph Ratzinger, at the time prefect of the Congregation for the Doctrine of the Faith, gave a lecture entitled "The Ecclesial Movements and their Place in Theology," which became a point of reference for evaluating these new associative realities and inserting them in the Church. Taking as his model the Franciscan movement, born in the thirteenth century, he defined the new movements, usually born of a charismatic leading personality, as "concrete communities that by virtue of their origin relive the Gospel in its entirety and recognize without hesitation in the Church their raison d'être, without which they could not exist." Among the characteristics proper to the movements he pointed to a rediscovery of the missionary dimension of Christian existence and participation in the great social challenges of our time, while at the same time never considering these challenges simply as an alternative to developing their spirituality.

Chiara together with other "founders," such as Luigi Giussani, Jean Vanier, Kiko Argüello, and Andrea Riccardi, were asked to speak. They were entrusted with the task of deepening the path of communion between the various charisms and movements. This path found an almost "natural" outlet in an initiative called "Together for Europe." This initiative started in 1999 as a network of collaboration that developed and gradually spread to many European nations and Churches, involving over 300 movements and communities. It was both ecumenical and political, and aimed at giving a new soul to the old continent in the difficult process of integration and enlargement of the European Union. In November 2001, a large conference entitled "A Thousand Cities for Europe" was held in Innsbruck, where Chiara presented "the spirit of universal fraternity in politics as the key to the unity of Europe and of the world." On May 8, 2004 a great event with 10,000 participants was held at the Hanns-Martin-Schleyer-Halle, the roofed velodrome in Stuttgart, in connection with 163 other parallel events, where Chiara stated: "Fraternity in politics expresses itself by loving the country of others as one's own. Seeing and feeling ourselves as one people enriched by the diversity of each other, would be the highest expression of our human dignity, and this would become the guardian of the unity of our different identities."

At the same time, the European institutions were working on a constitutional text intended to amend and regulate the EU institutional structure, giving it greater powers and simplifying decision-making processes. It was a long and laborious debate, where downward mediation, secularist views and compromise solutions with Eurosceptic political forces prevailed. The requests made by countless religious and secular authorities to include in the constitution a reference to the Judeo-Christian roots of European conscience were not taken into consideration, depriving this important text of a basic reference to its identity. According to Ralf Dahrendorf's[155] words, "the wisdom of committed observation and of painful reason" have been passed over for a solution that highlights an obvious fact of our time: the progressive incommunicability and the breaking up of every form of alliance between intellectual elites and the political world. It is an interruption of the circuit between independent and critical cultural work and the mediation of politics for the pursuit of the common good.

Never has it been more necessary to engage in a powerful effort towards a redefinition of all the concepts underlying human coexistence and its future (human rights, democracy, peace, economy, environment...). As Mauro Magatti[156] wrote, to get out of the general crisis into which the contemporary world seems to have plunged itself[157] we need a total change of the

---

155. (1929-2009) A German-British sociologist, philosopher, political scientist, liberal politician, and member of the House of Lords.
156. Professor of Sociology at the Catholic University of the Sacred Heart, Italy and director of their Center for the Anthropology of Religion and Cultural Change.
157. Especially the European and Western world, after the economic and financial crisis that broke out in 2008.

whole framework in which we think and work (a paradigm shift). We need to change our rules and perspectives, adapt our vision to a new way of interpreting the world around us. And before a new paradigm, a new normality, is being established, there will be a time when all possibilities are open. This is the occasion when the new rules can be rewritten. But this demands that we identify the direction and follow it. For example, the renunciation of the blind economy of consumption, so that we can reach a sustainable form of exchange and propose a new phase for democracy.

From the era of great divisions, both ideological and political, we have passed to an era of fragmentation, even of the basic concepts of war and peace. The many frontiers of peace, and wars, if once they were under the control of international politics and energy sources, today they are under the control of quite different elements, such as the great computer networks. Climate change has begun to send us the bill. After years and years in which people and politics have ignored the consequences of human actions on nature, we are witnessing a series of unprecedented and devastating atmospheric phenomena involving ever larger areas and populations. Disputes traditionally resolved by diplomacy and on the battlefields are reverberating in many other spheres, such as religious cultures and institutions.

We increasingly live in a reality where everything is interconnected and correlated, and the definitions of "Anthropocene"[158] and "noosphere,"[159] once confined to philosophy and its vocabulary, are revealing all their political implications.

Towards the end of the millennium, for political, economic and demographic reasons, migratory phenomena began to take

---

158. Relating to or denoting the current geological age, viewed as the period during which human activity has been the dominant influence on climate and the environment.
159. Sphere or stage of evolutionary development dominated by consciousness, the mind, and interpersonal relationships.

on a global character, both from the point of view of the masses of migrants and from the point of view of the territories concerned. The trend towards globalization of migratory currents does not, however, exclude their geographical polarization (primarily southern Europe), linked both to demographic and economic as well as to political, internal, and international circumstances. Migration has various kinds of effects on societies, and it is extremely difficult to identify and assess all the consequences of migratory flows at the demographic, economic, social, political, and anthropological level.

But, beyond the data and surveys of the social sciences, migration also takes on an existential and spiritual dimension, prompting the conscience of every person to question themselves about their own membership in the human family. Christians are called to welcome people and to feel the presence of the other as a gift and a responsibility. The Acts of the Apostles (2: 9-11) speak of the birth of the Church in the plural, when at Pentecost the different peoples present in Jerusalem could hear the Gospel proclaimed in their own language.

The practice of hospitality, which in classical cultures and in many ancient civilizations had a character of sacredness, is well established in Christianity, despite the irony of this passage from the Letter to the Hebrews (13: 2): "Do not neglect to show hospitality to strangers, for by doing that some have entertained angels without knowing it."

Human civilization will have taken a decisive step forwards on the day when the foreigner, from enemy (*hostis*) becomes guest (*hospes*), and when a border will be understood as threshold (*limen*) rather than frontier and obstacle (*limes*). The day when the foreigner (*Xénos*) will recognize himself as a guest, or rather, a brother, something will have changed in the world indeed.

Memory, Communications and the Future

Visiting the central archives of the Focolare Movement, located in the basement of the Chiara Lubich Centre in Rocca di Papa, is an unforgettable experience. It offers the visitor a variety of ideas and impressions, allowing for a deeper understanding of who Chiara Lubich was as a person and of her work.

The installations and equipment dedicated to the preservation of all documents (in the broadest sense of the word): fire prevention, air-conditioning etc. are all the highest quality. The cleanliness is impeccable. The dusty smell typical of archives and libraries has no place here, nor do the mites and microorganisms that usually live and thrive among the ancient stacks of papers. The climate considered ideal for the conservation of paper and magnetic media (from 10 to 18 degrees Celsius and a relative humidity between 35 and 50%) is maintained by an efficient air conditioning system and carefully monitored for temperature and humidity. Paper, fabrics, films, tapes and audio and video discs may be well-preserved, but the same cannot be said for the health of those who work in or pass through, who must wear proper garments. Impromptu visitors who are unaccustomed to the dry, frigid temperature are provided with heavy jackets as they enter the facility.

Within the long series of metal cabinets that can be compacted and slide on rails, documents are arranged in a precise order, divided – according to archival practice and language – into "collections." The so-called "origins" of the collections can be summed up essentially in the person of Chiara Lubich and in the organization of the Focolare Movement. The first can be considered in all respects a personal archive, the second a collection of an institutional nature. The personal archive is subdivided, organized and classified by documentary typology and on a thematic basis (manuscripts, photographs, audio-visuals, travel, meetings, awards, etc.), the other one on the basis of the various (and complex) structures that the Movement has assumed throughout its history. The complementarity of the nature and shape of the two main collections is clear and can be summed up within the history of the charism of unity, initially as intuited and embodied by Chiara, and then transferred to the Movement as it developed throughout the world.

Substance and forms here differ in part from the traditional meaning of archives, which are usually made up of paper documents. It is a complex collection of records that, from its very beginning, shows a complex, composite, articulated, and multiform approach in all its aspects and organization. Equally interesting are the methods of storage of the documents over time.

Just as the founder never demonstrated that she had a precise and predefined scheme on how to structure the works that she would later create, so the archive was born and grew thanks to heterogeneous ideas and circumstances. Chiara's writings and correspondence were for the most part collected and ordered by Eli Folonari, her long-standing assistant. Her (particularly important) function as the organizer of Chiara's agenda was added to that of confidant, counsellor, translator, and editor of her most intimate intuitions and spiritual thoughts. She was the interpreter of Chiara's unexpressed wishes in order to give form to concrete projects; she was the intermediary between Chiara and the people (from the latest focolarino to heads of state, from simple citizens to religious leaders) who came to her for the most varied reasons. The ease and "instinctiveness" with which Chiara came up with ideas, concepts, reflections, meditations, letter drafts and notes, texts for articles, and speeches were inversely proportional to her care in preserving them. This function was fulfilled by Eli, with her practical sense and her innate organizational capacity, as well as with the foresight of those who are aware that they are in contact with a personality and an organization out of the ordinary, destined to affect the history of many people, of the Church and – in some way – of the whole of humanity.

Over the years, as studies and analysis about the life and spirituality of the Movement proceeded, and as the publicity surrounding the person of the founder increased, these archives were enriched with documents originally kept in other places, such as Chiara's letters to many correspondents (acquired in original or in copy), audio and video recordings of and about her apostolate in Italy and around the world, copies of papers concerning particular events that took place in very different times and under very different circumstances (for example, the documentation that made up the dossier on the Focolare collected by the Archbishop of Trent, de Ferrari, between 1945 and 1962). To this are added "material" testimonies of travels and meetings, reports of a personal and institutional nature, public activities and private interviews, including gifts, diplomas, honors, artistic works, costumes, maps, drawings, which together form a variegated mosaic of documentations, necessary to set up any narrative that has Chiara and the Focolare as its subject.

The archives related to Chiara's activity represent a first and fundamental step in understanding her charism and the nature of her activity. The imposing dimensions and the enormous variety of documentations represent a most eloquent clue as to the scope of her work, as well as to the foresight of her followers in adequately preserving the sources.

The archives, especially the private ones, are assembled and preserved because they answer the practical documentary needs of people and activities. They are, first, a memory in the form of documentation, as a "visible record" of concrete and preserved activities for immediate use. As time goes by, documents lend themselves to purposes quite different from those for which they were originally set up. The social and historical scenarios in which archives are immersed can transform their morphology, value, and meanings. In their becoming a memory of sources, archives and documents take on completely new functions, often far from the intentions of those who produced them. Drawing from the computer lexicon, archives can be defined as an interface or a relational database, which, with their potential and dynamics, condition the passage of information and the quality of knowledge, creating structures, questions and lines of research.

Over time, memory as transmitted through archives can be subject to manipulation and editing, to ever-new questions and requests, to ever-new points of view. The great historian Jacques Le Goff notes that "memory is an essential element of what is called 'identity" (individual or collective), the search for which is one of the fundamental activities of individuals and societies today." An ecclesial movement, born because of a particular charism and an experience of contact with the metaphysical, will continue to question its own identity as it develops throughout history. But the memory-identity is always changeable and full of a powerful subjectivity, emotionally involved and decidedly selective. Often memory does not need to prove anything, as it has, by definition, the "claim to faithfully represent the past" (Paul Ricoeur). Instead history is always provisional and never completed. As a form of critical knowledge of the past, it evaluates and analyzes the traces represented by sources to try to establish, argue, and prove some truths about the past. This is above all what the archives are used for. The archive exists to highlight and understand the true spiritual depth and the real historic and cultural significance of the person of Chiara Lubich and the works inspired and carried out by her. It also needs to set up, with faithfulness to the sources and foresight, the necessary updating of the interpretation of the charism and of the presence of the Movement in the Church and in the world. To allow people in every age to ask themselves always new questions, the correct preservation and critical reading of the archives and documents will be increasingly necessary.

This enormous quantity of audio-visual materials provides another key element in understanding Chiara's mission, which is strongly directed towards communication and the use of the media. With a well-chosen image Franco de Battaglia[160] defined these large collections of recordings as a "media crypt," naming it a "garrison of the Focolare Movement" and a depository of the "first relics of the new media age."

In English the term "medium," can also signify "means." For centuries, the medium on which the content of the documents and testimonies, that enabled the history of human civilization to be recorded has been paper, or at least physical media. The technological revolution that characterized the twentieth century and the entry into the "digital age," that characterized the beginning of the third millennium has led to a redefinition and an almost boundless expansion of this concept.

In January 1997, St. John's University in Bangkok, Thailand, awarded Chiara with an honorary degree in social communications. At the ceremony she gave an important talk on the subject of the media, which she repeated and expanded upon during a congress held in 2000 in Grottaferrata in a talk to media experts entitled "The Focolare Movement and the Media." In describing the links between the media and the Movement, she spoke of a "double affinity," especially as far as their aims are concerned. Speaking about the purpose and the collective vocation of these means, she said, "they too are made to help people to live together." She also identified another affinity, one in connection with its method:

> *The spirituality of unity, which is typical of the Movement, is not only lived in a personal dimension, but also in a communitarian dimension. The social theory that recognizes the birth*

---

160. Journalist from Trent.

and growth of the mass media as a new step in the evolutionary design of humanity is well known. It is almost like the formation, so to speak, of a nervous system that (similarly to what happens in the human body) introduces an unstoppable tension from the complexity to the one, from fragmentation to the search for internal unity in real time.

Further on in her talk, she recalled how the "desire to feel us all united" was the main reason for the explosion of a dense network of correspondence in order to "share among us the work that God was beginning to do among our people." God's work grew to the measure in which each person participated and communicated to everybody. News about the Movement had to circulate "like blood in a body" (an image that Chiara often used) because as long as blood circulates there is life. If not, we "regress and death sets in."

The first "medium" of the Movement was a leaflet containing a theological-spiritual commentary on a sentence taken from the Gospel, chosen to be meditated on and lived moment by moment. From the first mimeographed[161] copies of this "Word of Life," at the end of the last millennium it reached a circulation of 3.4 million copies in ninety-five languages, to which had to be added the numerous transmissions by radio and television stations all over the world, with an estimated audience of fourteen million people. Then, in 1956, the magazine "Città Nuova" (in the UK, "New City," and in the US, "Living City.") began to be published to "help those who felt an attraction and a desire for unity to achieve this ideal." This was an editorial adventure that would reach thirty-four editions in twenty-two different languages (European languages, as well as non-European ones like Mandarin, Arabic, Urdu, or Japanese). A dozen or so other journals would later begin, expressing the various sectors of the Movement. In 1959 a publishing house with the same name

---

161. The mimeograph is a form of stencil printing, an early device for duplicating.

came about, multiplied later into twenty-seven others worldwide, with books ranging from spirituality to biblical studies, patristics, various branches of theology and specialized studies together with a distribution and sales network. Although her encounter with the so-called "new media" was impromptu, Chiara immediately understood its importance and adopted a unique approach toward its use and development. In 1952 she was given a tape recorder as a gift and, sometime later, an amateur camera. That gift soon led to intuitions and purpose: "The spiritual step that we are taking here now, must be taken by all of us all over the world and at the same time." This desire to share everything, Chiara's great teaching ability and her undoubted talent for communication led the Movement to invest heavily in the field of audio-visual communication, always in step with current technological development, giving birth over the years to two production centers dedicated to St. Clare (a great mystic and communicator in her own right).

In 1980, there began a totally new way of using a traditional communication such as the telephone. As Chiara was often in Switzerland for shorter or longer periods, and taking advantage of the multi connection opportunities offered by the Swiss telephone company, the so-called "link-up" or "collegamento" was born: a monthly (and later fortnightly) conference call that reached all the focolare centers and communities around the world. The schedule was simple and basic: a spiritual reflection lasting five minutes and a conversation with news about the Movement taking up the remaining twenty minutes. There were eighty-three sites connected directly at the same time, to which were added many listening points. It was a moment of intense unity, in a very personal way, made up of sharing reflections and meditations, joys and sorrows, the need for spiritual and material support; it was an expression of the commitment to the ideal they had in common.

The Movement has kept up with advances in Internet and television communication. From the end of the 1970s – coinciding with the beginning (and maybe with the complicity) of the media-filled mission and authority of the pontificate of John Paul II – the great events organized by the Focolare Movement took advantage of increasingly advanced forms of transmission throughout the world, in collaboration with institutional and industrial partners at the highest level, all the way up to live broadcasts via satellite. The Familyfest organized in Rome in 1993 had connections with sixty-three national television stations and numerous local ones, with a potential audience of 500 million people. In the history of telecommunications, it was the first live broadcast with seven interactive connections and the simultaneous use of thirteen satellites. The 1995 Genfest[162] was broadcast through three intercontinental, fifty-three national and 288 local channels.

The satellite, a symbol of the greatest evolution of broadcasting and communication in the twentieth century, probably represents the pinnacle of Chiara's understanding and ability to information and the media. The following anecdote is revealing: in September 2004, while walking in the garden of a sanctuary full of sacred sculptures, Chiara commented: "here they have many statues; we in our garden have the antenna that connects the whole world." That antenna was a satellite dish, mounted in the green space in front of her house in Rocca di Papa where she lived and which she called "a monument to universal communion."

The process of transformation, often referred to as the "digital revolution," was breaking into human history. This revolution brought profoundly new characteristics and implications, not only in terms of technology, but also tremendously

---

162. Genfest is a festival for the young people of the Focolare Movement (Gen).

important cultural, social, political, and economic consequences. This revolution promised to change the way societies, as well as the lives of individuals and peoples, functioned. It triggered prospects for global improvement and, at the same time, fears, perplexities, and enormous problems. The programming languages, new grammars and new alphabets rewrote the way human relationships were structured (often replacing them with virtual ones). The digital revolution transported the globalized world beyond the borders and cultural frameworks of modernity into a dynamic and evolutionary phase, characterized by a strong degree of uncertainty. Humanity was grappling with relational, affective, hermeneutical, economic, and cultural instability. It was being organized in associations based on image and emotions, intertwined with uncontrollable movements of people, images, technologies, capital, and ideas. It was transformed by globalization and social fragmentation, made up of citizens bound by "liquid bonds" – as described by Zygmunt Bauman[163] – struggling with the difficulty of establishing solid relationships in a world of infinite possibilities and freedom, in which the representation of reality seems more real than reality itself.

During the last few years of Chiara's life, the Movement was also present in the vast open "media" square represented by the internet. We do not know how much she had the opportunity, or time, to reflect directly on the scope of this phenomenon, which is profoundly related to the ongoing change of epoch. She probably left this burden to her younger spiritual children and companions, but she did not hesitate to offer some hints as to how to investigate and interpret the signs of the times and the changing horizon that lie ahead for humanity. The origins, spirituality, and

---

163. *Liquid Love: On the Frailty of Human Bonds* is a 2003 book by Zygmunt Bauman which discusses human relations in the liquid modern world.

intimate organizational and relational structure of the Focolare provide some important indications.

A metaphor is a most useful means to convey the meaning to which it refers, and so clarifying it. One metaphor that best summarizes and represents the reality of the world and of contemporary societies, is certainly the Internet. With its almost unlimited network of connections and high level of complexity, it is one of the most powerful creations of the human intellect, even if it is easy to imagine and understand. The organization and growth of the net is highly "creative" and open to change. Moving from multiple starting points, it can progress without establishing internal hierarchies and is naturally suited to create productive communication through interaction between two or more points in any direction. Its system of nodes and connections, if well used, create relationships. Any point in the network is connected to each of the others through a multidirectional expansion. Just as the routes on a map seem already predestined, with an immutable geometry of streets, squares and alleys, there are infinite variations, following a series of forks and turns to arrive at the same destination. It happens in a similar way on the Internet, which allows for an infinite number of route choices to reach the same destination.

To compare the structure of a plant and the Internet, what appear as roots (the main nodes) are actually a real portion of the stem, constitute the buds from which flowers and new branches germinate, and are a deposit of nutrients. This image recalls the ways and dynamics of development, the articulation, and the lifestyle of the Focolare Movement, summarized so far in these pages. The net can therefore also be a place in which to experience the action of the Spirit, the passion to build communal bonds and relationships with the freedom that flows from the life of the Gospel, with the openness to be surprised by what is being created through each one's contribution.

Another comparison with the net can be found in a passage from the Gospel of Matthew (4: 18-22), when Jesus, walking along the Sea of Galilee, saw the two brothers Simon, called Peter, and Andrew, as they cast their net. He said to them, "Follow me, and I will make you fish for people," and immediately they left their nets and followed him. In the same way he called James and John, the sons of Zebedee, who were tidying their nets in the boat; they also became his disciples.

A conference in Grottaferrata in 2000 saw the birth of "NetOne – media and a united world," an international network of professionals, students, and communication professionals committed to telling the story of contemporary society, of the new phenomena and the challenges it poses to humanity. On that occasion Chiara also spoke about the nature of communication which is based on a method of dialogue and is attentive to the good of humanity, saying: "If every human relationship is a reflection of and has as its model trinitarian relationships, can then communication, the human relationship par excellence, escape these dynamics? These laws are inscribed in its very DNA!" There was a clear distinction here with respect to the prevailing logic of the world of the media: informing is different from communicating, just as data and bits of news are different from content and values. When you inform, you speak on behalf of someone else; when you communicate, you speak with someone else.

With regard to the principles and methods that should guide communication and its agents, she recommended: "Trying to live the Gospel in daily life, and the very experience of the Word of Life, have always been and still are inextricably linked to communicating it, to recounting its steps and fruits, since it is a law that we should love the other as ourselves. We believe that what is not communicated is lost."

And another suggestion regarding the relational aspect of communication:

> ... in order to communicate, we feel that we have to "make ourselves one" – as we say – with the listener. First we feel the need to know who we are dealing with, to know the listener or the audience, their needs, desires and problems. So we too should make ourselves known, explain why we want to make that speech, what drove us, what the effects of it are on ourselves and in this way create a certain reciprocity. By doing this, the message is not only intellectually received, but also participated in and shared.

She paid particular attention to "saying the good things," that is to underline the positive: *It has always been our style to highlight what is good, convinced that it is infinitely more constructive to highlight the good, to insist on good things and positive perspectives, than to stop at the negative, even if the appropriate denunciation of errors, limits and faults is necessary for those who are in a position of responsibility.*

In conclusion:

> *The person matters, not the media, which is simply a tool. In order to bring unity, we need first of all that indispensable means which is the human person, the new person, as in the words of St. Paul, who has accepted Christ's mandate to be the leaven, the salt and the light of the world.*

These thoughts are echoed, thirteen years later by the words of another great communicator—Pope Francis—in his apostolic exhortation *Evangelii gaudium*:[164]

> Today, when the networks and means of human communication have made unprecedented advances, we sense the challenge of finding and sharing a "mystique" of living together, of mingling and encounter, of embracing and supporting one another, of

---

164. *Evangelii gaudium* (*The Joy of the Gospel*) *is the apostolic exhortation by Pope Francis, issued in 2013, focussing on a new chapter of evangelism.*

> *stepping into this flood tide which, while chaotic, can become a genuine experience of fraternity, a caravan of solidarity, a sacred pilgrimage. . . . To go out of ourselves and to join others is healthy for us.*

Chiara called Jesus a great communicator ("Never has anyone spoken like this," Jn 7: 46) and focused on the way he died, an appalling torture marked by separation from the community, rejection, and even betrayal by his disciples (Mk 14: 72). To this was added the abandonment by his Father (Mt. 27: 46), the annihilation and loneliness of the cross:

> *Jesus crucified and forsaken, mediator (medium) between humanity and God, who, when the final curtain falls, when unity is accomplished, disappears and makes himself nothing. It is a terrifying mystery that fascinates us. It is an infinite void, almost a pupil of the eye of God, a window through which God can look at humanity and humanity in a certain way see God . . . So, can we ask ourselves, is his cry at the ninth hour the maximum expression of his being the Word? Is it, so to speak, the summit of communication? Yes, it is. It is in his annihilation in the abyss of his individuality, where every relationship has died, that he gives us the gift of himself as a person, capable of encountering God and all other creatures.*

EPILOGUE

The Final Night

In 2005, besides her physical illness, Chiara suffered what was defined as her "last internal night," one that spoke of "total darkness." God seemed to have "set like the sun on the horizon," as she described it. Confiding in those closest to her she said, "I seem to have lost my charism and have become just Silvia," no longer Chiara...like Jesus, who in his abandonment on the cross felt himself to be just a man and yet continued to love. Although she no longer felt the presence of God and spoke of "the death of Christianity" and "the cultural night of humanity," Chiara remained completely faithful to prayer, daily Mass, and the practices of devotion. Despite this terrible suffering she continued to pray. Weakened by her increasingly precarious state of health, she entrusted the messages and the writings of her talks to her focolarine and focolarini companions. She described the state of suffering of her soul and the feeling distant from the Father in her diaries, going so far as to speak of the "dark night of God," a stage that went far beyond the dark night of the soul.

Partial answers to the many anguished questions that oppressed her soul came from glimpsing an image of Mary who represented a light to follow and who reminded her of the words of the Roman deacon Lawrence, martyred in 258: "My night has no darkness, but all things grow bright in the light."

Her spiritual testament, addressed to her people born of the Gospel, was simple and summarized the charism of unity, referring to its origins:

Dearest everyone, I would like to emphasize the value of relationship, of relationships between us. When we started living the Word in Trent, both our relationship with God and our relationship with one another changed. Thus was born what we then called a "Christian community," that is, the Focolare Movement. Let us not forget these origins. Let us build the Movement on these foundations.

She concluded with a final exhortation: "Be a family."

March 14, 2008

At dawn on Friday, March 14, 2008, Chiara Lubich left this world to return to the bosom of the Father. A few days earlier she had been admitted to the Gemelli hospital for severe respiratory failure. The day before it was decided to take her back home, to the Movement's headquarters in Rocca di Papa so that she could die accompanied by her focolarini. Throughout the night, the gardens of the international center of the Focolare and the area around the small villa where Chiara had lived for thirty years became the scene of a sorrowful but serene procession, in an atmosphere of prayer and intense emotion, of adherents of the Movement from all over the world who came to greet the founder, so close to finally meeting her heavenly spouse.

In an interview in 1990 about death, Chiara said:

I may have been afraid of it, but right now, thank God, I'm not. Perhaps because so many things have become clear to me and above all because I have thought about it all my life. . . . St. Therese said that we are in exile here. Yes, an exile, but a very busy one. . . . Above all, what has become clear to me is that those who see death are those who see a person dying and are standing away from the dying person; but the one who dies sees life because death is the encounter with Christ. So, you close your eyes, so to speak, if you arrive in time to close them, or even better, you have opened them here, and then you open them there. You see Christ, the Christ who saved you, who loved you. . . . Now, if you have tried to do something for him during your life, he comes to you in that moment, I think, with all his benevolence.

Her funeral took place on March 18 in the Roman basilica of St. Paul-outside-the-Walls. From the early hours of the morning at the great esplanade in front of the basilica, the monumental four porticos and the five naves, an estimated 40,000 people gathered to greet Chiara and remember her in prayer. At 2pm the coffin, carried by six focolarini of different ethnic groups, entered the basilica to the sound of song and applause, accompanied by members of her family and representatives of the various vocations of the Work of Mary. Gen Verde and Gen Rosso inspired the congregation with the music that for years they had brought to churches, communities, and theatres around the world. The abbot of the Benedictine monastery of St. Paul, Dom Edmund Power, welcomed the coffin, interrupting a series of testimonies and prayers that were being offered for hours inside the basilica.

The coffin was placed in front of the Gothic tabernacle – the work of Arnolfo di Cambio – which overlooks the tomb of St. Paul, in the middle of the transept. In the background is the apse decorated with a large cycle of mosaics dating back to the thirteenth century, with Christ enthroned in the center holding the Gospel open in one hand, and with the other in an act of blessing. To the right we see St. Peter and St. Andrew, and to the left St. Paul and the Evangelist Luke. The figures are standing on an area covered in flowers, populated with numerous animals which recall the fullness of life in Eden. The scene is framed by two large palm trees that symbolically provide food and shelter in desert life. The other apostles are depicted in the lower register. In the center, between the figures, is the *Etimasia*,[165] the image of Christ's empty throne with the scroll and the cross flanked by instruments of Christ's martyrdom. The work's patron, identified by the inscription, completes the iconography of the apse: Pope Honorius III, clothed in white and prostrated at the right foot of Christ.

It was this pontiff who approved the rules of the two major religious orders of the Middle Ages: one founded by St. Dominic (1216), the other by St. Francis (1223). Many of the tertiary orders also came to life during his pontificate – the first of which was the one desired by the saint of Assisi – that particular form of life which allows any believer to be part of a religious congregation and follow its spirituality without abandoning their own state of life, for example that of a priest or of a married person.

The moment prior to the liturgy was full of symbols, starting with the three red carnations placed on the coffin as well as a copy of the Gospels. The flowers recalled the day Chiara consecrated herself to God in the Capuchin church of Trent. It was December 7, 1943, and before reaching the convent, Chiara had stopped to buy three carnations "for the crucifix waiting for me in my room, as a sign of this feast."

Among those who witnessed the event were many representatives of the universal Church, of ecclesial movements, of the different Christian denominations, of other religions, as well as numerous civil authorities. Seated in the front rows were the Metropolitan Gennadios Zervós, primate of the sacred Orthodox archdiocese of Italy and Malta (dependent on the Ecumenical Patriarchate of Constantinople), the German Evangelical bishop Christian Krause and the Anglican bishop Robin Smith, sister Anna-Maria aus der Wiesche, from the Lutheran community

---

165. The *Hetoimasia, Etimasia, prepared throne*, or *throne of the second coming* is the Christian version of the symbolic subject of the empty throne found in the art of the ancient world, whose meaning has changed over the centuries.

Christusbruderschaft of Selbitz. Catholic Action was represented by its national president Luigi Alici; then, Fr. Julián Carrón of Communion and Liberation, Salvatore Martinez of Rinnovamento nello Spirito, Andrea Riccardi of the Community of Sant'Egidio. Besides them, there were Lisa Palmieri, representative to the Holy See of the American Jewish Committee, Izak El Hajji Pasha, imam of the Malcolm Shabazz mosque in Harlem in New York, Yasutaka Watanabe, representing the Japanese Buddhist movement Risshō Kōsei-kai, Pra Tongrathana, monk of Theravada Buddhism, and representatives of the Sikh communities.

The liturgy was presided over by Cardinal Tarcisio Bertone, Vatican Secretary of State, representing Pope Benedict XVI and the whole Catholic Church, accompanied by many brothers in the episcopate and the College of Cardinals. His homily began with a commentary on the first reading taken from the book of Job, whose words evoked the ardent desire for the encounter with Christ that marked Chiara's entire existence, culminating with the last yes to the mystical spouse of her soul, Jesus forsaken and risen. The cardinal recalled Chiara's work in spreading love based on living the Gospel among people of different cultures, faith, and formation, summing up her life as a hymn to the love of God, to the God who is love. He referred to the model for living this love, to Jesus' prayer after the Last Supper, in his moving farewell to the apostles: "that they may all be one." It is this prayer that accompanies his friends in every age on their journey and it generates witnesses to the living Gospel.

Remembering the twentieth century, of which Chiara was a witness and protagonist, with its conquests and contradictions, he recalled how it was also the time when God raised up saints and pioneers of charity. It was the century that saw the birth of new ecclesial movements, animated by charisms that defined their features and apostolic action. Referring to the work of the founder of the Focolare Movement, he added:

> ... in her silent and humble way, she did not so much create institutions of social assistance and human promotion but she dedicated herself to kindling the fire of God's love in people's hearts; she created people around her who themselves are love, who live the charism of unity and communion with God and neighbor; people who spread "love-unity" by making themselves, their homes and their workplaces a "focolare" where burning love becomes contagious and consumes all that is near.

"This mission," he said, "is accessible to everyone because the Gospel is within the reach of everyone called to live the ideal of unity."

Referring to the last interview she gave which was shown during the period of her agony, he remembered how Chiara confirmed that "the marvel of mutual love is the lifeblood of the mystical body of Christ." The movement founded by Chiara was called the Work of Mary because Our Lady is "the precious key that lets us enter the Gospel." Referring to Chiara, he also mentioned "the prophetic intuitions that preceded and anticipated the great historic transformations and the extraordinary events that the Church experienced in the twentieth century," and he invited her spiritual children to continue the mission she had begun.

He ended his homily with the words Chiara loved repeating:

> I would like the Work of Mary, when it is waiting solidly at the end of time to appear before Jesus forsaken and risen, to be able to repeat and making its own the moving words of the Belgian theologian Jacques Leclercq: "... on your day, my God, I will come towards you... I will come towards you, my God, ... with my wildest dream: to bring you the whole world in my arms."

These words and this yearning completed the earthly story of this protagonist of the twentieth century whose thoughts and ideas continue to challenge people today regarding the great spiritual and existential questions with which they are confronted, starting with the meaning of life, transcendence, pain, and relationships. These thoughts and ideas are far from being fully understood. They constantly show those who approach them new complexities and dynamisms that can be applied to ever broader contexts and to the challenges to which humanity is being called, and not only in its relationship with the transcendent.

Chiara's remains were placed in the chapel of the International Centre of the Focolare, beside those of Igino Giordani (who died in 1980). In 2015, Pasquale Foresi (who died on June 14, 2015) was also placed beside them, reuniting the three persons who gave life, spirit, and form to the Focolare Movement from the 1940s onwards.

Facing these three tombs there is large mosaic by the Sicilian artist Paolo Scirpa, depicting *Mary Mother of the Church*. This title was attributed to the Virgin as requested by Paul VI in 1964 at the conclusion of the third session of the Second Vatican Council, but with ancient and deep roots, present in ecclesial thinking since the writings of St. Augustine and St. Leo the Great whose theological reflections were based on the Gospel passage (Jn 19: 25), where Jesus crucified and forsaken entrusted the disciple John to her. Our Lady accepted her son's will of love and welcomes all people, represented by the beloved disciple, as children to be regenerated to divine life, so becoming the loving nurturer of the Church that Christ on the cross, emitting the Spirit, generated. In turn in the beloved disciple, Christ elected all the disciples as representatives of his love for his mother, entrusting them to her so that they might welcome her with filial affection.

Paolo Scirpa, commenting on his work, which shows Mary surrounded by the people of God and the human activities inspired by the light and animated by the fire of the Holy Spirit, said: "It seems to me that I have had an intuition here of a central point of life to which all forces mysteriously converge in unity and from which they diverge successively as messengers of the evolutionary process, both of humanity and of the whole universe." These words are intricately linked to Chiara's thought: "The rays of the sun increase in intensity as they approach the sun. So it is with the soul of unity. It lives by letting itself be taken ever more deeply into God. So it draws ever closer to God who lives in its heart and ever closer to God who lives in the hearts of its brothers and sisters."

The adventure of unity promoted by Chiara Lubich began in her native Trent from a close and loving encounter with the words of Scripture, and ended (at least here on earth) at the burial place of the "Apostle of the Gentiles." Just so, let us close with some references to the letter St. Paul wrote from Corinth in the winter of 56 (or 57) A.D. to the Christian community in Rome. This text has challenged people of every age (we think of Martin Luther...) regarding their relationship with the Word and freedom, with faith and grace.

It describes a community composed of small groups that met in houses, to whom Paul presents himself as the herald of the Good News which reveals God's universal saving justice and sets faith in motion (Rom 1: 1-17). The baptism into Christ opens the way to liberation from sin and the law, thus permitting a positive response to our anguish (7: 7-25). Christian freedom and the life of the believer originate from the Spirit of Christ (8: 1-39). Paul exhorts the Christians of Rome to respond to the ethical imperatives deriving from the Spirit of the Master (12: 1-15) to exercise charity and a welcoming love towards the weakest, not to be lazy in zeal, to seek good and live in peace, not to be overcome by evil, but overcoming evil with good. In his final greetings, in Chapter 16, the apostle shows himself most attentive to the relationships and contributions of his various collaborators, and makes clear references to the substantial role of various women in Christian communities (beginning with the deaconess Phoebe), so much so that – according to the judgment of the biblical scholar Peter

Ketter – this passage is "the most honorable statement in favor of the apostolate of women in the early Church."

Maybe, as she read the Bible in the shelters of Trent, during the bombardments of the war (or as she wandered along the roads of the world), Chiara reflected on this specific passage while bringing to fruition all her activities.

It is a Word to fill a lifetime... both hers and ours.

BIBLIOGRAPHY

History of Christianity and the Catholic Church, encyclopedias, atlases, dictionaries

Bokenkotter, T.: *A Concise History of the Catholic Church,* Doubleday, New York, 2004.

Collins, M. & Price, M.A.: *The Story of Christianity,* Dorling Kindersley, London, 1999.

Duffy, E.: *Saints and Sinners, a History of the Popes,* Yale University Press, Los Angeles, 1997.

Dussel, E.: *A History of the Church in Latin America,* Wm. B. Eerdmans, Grand Rapids MN, 1981.

Fahlbusch, E. (ed.): *The Encyclopedia of Christianity,* Wm. B. Eerdmans, Grand Rapids MN, 2007.

Froehle, B. & Gautier, M.L.: *Global Catholicism, Portrait of a World Church,* Orbis books – Georgetown University, New York, 2003.

Hastings, A.: *The Church in Africa 1450–1950,* Oxford University Press, Oxford, 2004.

Herring, G.: *An Introduction to the History of Christianity,* Continuum International, New York, 2006.

Jedin H., Repgen, K. & Dolan, J. (eds): *History of the Church,* Continuum – Crossroad, New York, 1980-1982.

Kelly, J.: *The Ecumenical Councils of the Catholic Church – a History,* St. John University Liturgical Press, Collegeville MN, 2009.

Koschorke, K., Ludwig, F. & Delgado, M.: *A History of Christianity in Asia, Africa, and Latin America, 1450–1990*, Wm. B. Eerdmans, Grand Rapids MN, 2007.

Kreeft, P.: *Catholic Christianity*, Ignatius Press, San Francisco, 2001.

McManners, J. (ed.): *The Oxford Illustrated History of Christianity*, Oxford University Press, Oxford, 1990.

Norman, E. (ed.): *The Roman Catholic Church, An Illustrated History*, University of California Press, Los Angeles, 2007.

O'Collins, G. & Farrugia, M. (eds): *Catholicism – The Story of Catholic Christianity*, Oxford University Press, Oxford, 2003.

Perreau-Saussine, E.: *Catholicism and Democracy – An Essay in the History of Political Thought*, Princeton University Press, New York, 2012.

Schwaller, J.F.: *The history of the Catholic Church in Latin America – From Conquest to Revolution and Beyond*, NY University Press, New York, 2011.

Wilken, R.: *Christianity* in Hitchcock, S.T. & Esposito, J. (eds): *Geography of Religion*, National Geographic Society, Washington D.C., 2004.

Part i & ii
The beginning of a story
The finger of God

Carella, N.: *Silvia prima di Chiara. La ricerca di una strada nuova*, Città Nuova, Rome, 2014.

Casella, M.: L'Azione Cattolica nell'Italia contemporanea (1919-1969), AVE, Rome, 1992.

Droghetti, A. (ed.): *L'unità si fa storia. Pasquale Foresi e il Movimento dei Focolari,* Città Nuova, Rome, 2015.

Ferrandi, G. & Giuliano, W. (eds): *Ribelli di confine. La Resistenza in Trentino,* Museo storico, Trent, 2003.

Ferandi, M., Pacher, G. & Sardi, L. (eds): *Gli anni delle bombe. Trento-Bolzano 1943-1945,* Seta, Bolzano, 1973.

Lazzarin, P. & Massarotto, G.: *Gino Lubich, partigiano e giornalista,* Il Margine, Trent, 2017.

Leonardi, A. & Garbari, M. (eds): *Storia del Trentino. V. L'età contemporanea 1803-1918,* il Mulino, Bologna, 2003.

Leonardi, A. & Pombeni, P. (eds): *Storia del Trentino. VI. L'età contemporanea – il Novecento,* il Mulino, Bologna, 2005.

Leoni, D. & Marchesoni, P. (eds): *Le ali maligne, le meridiane di morte. Trento 1943-1945. I bombardamenti,* Temi-Museo storico in Trento, Trent, 1995.

Nicoletti, M.: *Il mondo cattolico trentino tra il fascismo e la guerra e le radici di Chiara Lubich* in *Comunione e innovazione sociale. Il contributo di Chiara Lubich,* edited by A. Leonardi, Città Nuova, Rome, 2012.

Riccardi, A. (ed.): *Le chiese di Pio XII,* Laterza, Rome-Bari 1986.

Tornielli, A.: *Pio XII, Eugenio Pacelli, un uomo sul trono di Pietro,* Mondadori, Milan, 2007.

Trinchese, S.: *Giordani Igino* in *Dizionario Biografico degli Italiani,* Vol. 55, Istituto Enciclopedia Italiana Treccani, Rome, 2001.

Trionfini, P. (ed.): *Per una storia dell'Azione cattolica nel mondo – Problemi e linee di sviluppo dalle origini al Concilio Vaticano II,* AVE, Rome, 2019.

Part III
A difficult journey

Alberigo, G. & Komonchak, J.A. (eds): *History of Vatican II,* Orbis/Peeters, New York/Leuven, 1995-2005, 5 vols.

Alberigo, G. & Sherry, M.: *A Brief History of Vatican II,* Orbis, New York, 2006.

Giovagnoli, A. (ed.): *Fra utopia e Vangelo. Contestazione e mondo cattolico,* AVE, Rome, 2000.

Iaria, R.: *Verso un mondo migliore. Riccardo Lombardi. Chiesa, mondo e regno di Dio,* Ancora, Milan, 2018.

Linden, I.: *Global Catholicism – Diversity and Change since Vatican II,* Hurst & Co., London, 2009.

O'Malley, J.: *What Happened at Vatican II,* Harvard University Press, Cambridge MA, 2010.

Orsy, L.: *Receiving the Council – Theological and Canonical Insights and Debates,* St. John's University Liturgical Press, Collegeville MN, 2009.

Riccardi, A.: *Il Vaticano e Mosca. 1940-1990,* Laterza, Rome/Bari, 1992.

Santagata, A.: *La contestazione cattolica – movimenti, cultura e politica dal Vaticano II al '68,* Viella, Rome, 2016.

Siniscalco, P.: *L'Est europeo, Chiara Lubich e Paolo VI in Siniscalco, P. & Toscani, X. (eds): Paolo VI e Chiara Lubich. La profezia di una Chiesa che si fa dialogo,* Studium, Brescia, 2015, pp. 86-110.

Walsh, M.: *The Religious Ferment of the Sixties,* in McLeod, H. (ed.): *History of Christianity, Vol. 9, World Christianities c.1914 – c.2000,* Cambridge University Press, Cambridge, 2006, pp. 307–328.

Weigel, G.: *The Final Revolution – The Resistance Church and the Collapse of Communism*, Oxford University Press, Oxford, 1992.

Zizola, G.: *Il microfono di Dio – Pic XII, padre Lombardi e i cattolici italiani*, Mondadori, Milan, 1990'

Part IV
Love in and for the world

Albarello, D.: *La grazia suppone la cultura – Fede cristiana come agire nella storia*, Queriniana, Brescia, 2018.

Alberigo, G. & Faggioli, M. (eds): *I movimenti nella storia del cristianesimo. Caratteristiche – variazioni – continuità*, in *Cristianesimo nella storia*, 24, 2003.

Balthasar, von H.U.: *The Christian State of Life*, Ignatius Press, San Francisco, 1983.

Balthasar, von H.U.: *Theo-drama – Theological Dramatic Theory, Vol. 3: Dramatis Personae – Persons in Christ*, Ignatius Press, San Francisco, 1992.

Bates, M.W.: *The Birth of the Trinity*, Oxford University Press, Oxford, 2015.

Beek, van H. (ed.): *A Handbook of Churches and Councils – Profiles of Ecumenical Relationships*, World Council of Churches, Geneva, 2006.

Briggs, J., Oduyoye M. A. & Tsetsis G. (eds): *A History of the Ecumenical Movement, 1968–2000*, World Council of Churches, Geneva, 2004.

Campanini, G.: *Il laico nella Chiesa e nel mondo*, Dehoniane, Bologna, 2004.

Centro di ricerche per lo studio della dottrina sociale della Chiesa: *Dizionario di dottrina sociale della Chiesa. Scienze sociali e magistero,* Vita e pensiero, Milan, 2004.

Coda, P. (ed.): *L'unico e i molti. La salvezza in Gesù Cristo e la sfida del pluralismo,* Mursia, Rome, 1997.

Colombo, G.: *La ragione teologica,* Glossa, Milan, 1995.

Congar, Y.: *Per una teologia del laicato,* Morcelliana, Brescia, 1966.

Dotolo, C.: *Teologia e postcristianesimo. Un percorso interdisciplinare,* Queriniana, Brescia, 2017.

De Fiores, S.: *Maria madre di Gesù. Sintesi storico-salvifica,* Dehoniane, Bologna 1998.

De Fiores, S. (ed.): *Maria. Nuovissimo dizionario,* Vol. 3, Dehoniane, Bologna, 2006-2008

Eilers, F.J. & Giannatelli, R. (eds): *Chiesa e comunicazione sociale. I documenti fondamentali,* ElleDiCi, Rome, 1996.

Fiddes, P.: *Participating in God – A Pastoral Doctrine of the Trinity,* Darton, Longman & Todd, London, 2000.

Goosen, G.: *Bringing Churches Together – A Popular Introduction to Ecumenism,* World Council of Churches, Geneva, 2001.

Harrison, S.: *Conceptions of Unity in Recent Ecumenical Discussion – A Philosophical Analysis,* Peter Lang, Oxford, 2000.

Hick, J. (ed.): *Truth and Dialogue – The Relationship between World Religions,* Sheldon Press, London, 1974.

Kasper, W.: *Harvesting the Fruits – Aspects of Christian Faith in Ecumenical Dialogue,* Continuum, New York, 2009.

Laurentin, R.: *Breve trattato sulla Vergine Maria,* San Paolo, Cinisello Balsamo, 1979 (2018).

Leahy, B.: *The Marian Profile in the Ecclesiology of Hans Urs von Balthasar,* New City (Press), London/New York/Manila, 2000.

Lossky, N. et al. (eds): *Dictionary of the Ecumenical Movement*, Wm. B. Eerdmans, Grand Rapids MN, 2002.

Moltmann, J.: *The Trinity and the Kingdom – The Doctrine of God*, Harper and Row, New York, 1981.

Momen, M.: *Understanding Religion – A Thematic Approach*, Oneworld Publications, Oxford, 2009.

Olson, R.E. & Hall, C.A. (eds): *The Trinity*. Wm. B. Eerdmans, Grand Rapids MN, 2002.

Perroni, M., Melloni, A. & Noceti S. (eds): *Tantum aurora est – Donne e Concilio Vaticano II*, LIT Verlag, Vienna, 2012.

Pontifical Council for Justice and Peace: *Compendium of the Social Doctrine of the Church*, Libreria Editrice Vaticana, Vatican City, 2004.

Rahner, K.: *The Trinity*, Herder and Herder, New York, 1970.

Ratzinger, J.: *The Theological Locus of Ecclesial Movements*, Libreria Editrice Vaticana, Vatican City, 1999.

Scaraffia, L.: *Donne, Chiesa e teologia*, Vita e Pensiero, Milan, 2015.

Valerio, A.: *Donne e Chiesa. Una storia di genere*, Carocci, Rome, 2016.

Valerio, A.: *Madri del Concilio. Ventitré donne al Vaticano II*, Carocci, Rome, 2012.

Visser't Hooft, W.: *The Genesis and Formation of the World Council of Churches*, World Council of Churches, Geneva, 1982.

Zamagni, S. & Bruni, L.: *Economia civile, efficienza, equità, felicità pubblica*, Il Mulino, Bologna, 2004.

Zanzucchi, M. (ed.): *Tutta rivestita di parola. Il mondo della comunicazione si specchia in Maria*, Città Nuova, Rome, 2004.

Books by or about Chiara Lubich

Cabetas, P.: *Chiara Lubich's Communitarian Way to Holiness – in the Light of John 17:11-19,* New City Press, New York, 2015.

Cerini, M.: God *Who Is Love – In the Experience and Thought of Chiara Lubich,* Theology and life series 1, New City Press, New York, 1992.

Gallagher, J.: *A Woman's Work – Chiara Lubich,* New City Press, New York, 1997.

Gillet, F.: *15 Days of Prayer with Chiara Lubich,* New City Press, New York, 2016.

Gillet, F.: The *Choice of Jesus Forsaken – In the Theological Perspective of Chiara Lubich,* New City Press, New York, 2015.

Lubich, C.: *The Art of Loving,* New City (Press), New York/London, 2010.

Lubich, C.: *A Call to Love,* Spiritual Writings Vol. 1, New City Press, New York, 1990.

Lubich, C.: *Challenges 99 x 4,* New City, London, 1987.

Lubich, C.: *Charity,* New City, London, 1981

Lubich, C.: *Charity Our Ideal,* New City Press, New York, 1977.

Lubich, C.: *The Christian Eye – Meditations,* New City Press, New York, 1966.

Lubich, C.: *Christian Living Today – Meditations,* New City Press, New York, 1997

Lubich, C.: *Christmas Joy – Spiritual Insights by Chiara Lubich,* New City (Press), London/New York/Manila, 1998.

Lubich, C.: *The Church – What Is It? Who Is It?* (edited by H. Blaumeiser and B. Leahy), New City, London, 2019.

Lubich, C.: *The Cry,* New City (Press), London/New York, 2001

Lubich, C.: *Diary 1964–65,* New City Press, New York, 1987.

Lubich, C.: *Early Letters – At the Origins of a New Spirituality,* (edited by F. Gillet and G. D'Alessandro), New City Press, New York, 2012.

Lubich, C.: *Essential Writings* (edited by M. Vandeleene) New City (Press), New York/London, 2007.

Lubich, C.: *The Eucharist,* New City (Press), New York/London, 1978/9.

Lubich, C.: *Fragments of Wisdom,* Mariapolis Trust, Bombay, 1992

Lubich, C.: *From Scripture to Life,* New City Press, New York, 1991.

Lubich, C.: *Gen Blueprint,* New City, London, 1972.

Lubich, C.: *The Gen Revolution,* New City Press, New York, 1972.

Lubich, C.: *God Loves You Immensely* (edited by M. Vandeleene and C. Ruggiu), New City Press, New York, 2010.

Lubich, C.: *God's Word to Us – Short Reflections on Living the Word* (edited by B. Hartnett), New City Press, New York, 2012.

Lubich, C.: *Heaven on Earth – Meditations and Reflections,* New City Press, New York, 2000.

Lubich, C.: *Here and Now – Meditations on Living in the Present,* New City (Press), New York/London/Manila, 2000 e.a.

Lubich, C.: *The Holy Spirit – The Unknown God* (edited by F. Gillet and R. Silva), New City, London, 2018.

Lubich, C.: *It's a Whole New Scene,* New City (Press), New York/London, 1970

Lubich, C.: *Jesus Forsaken* (edited by H. Blaumeiser), New City, London, 2017.

Lubich, C.: *Jesus in our Brother*, New City, London, 1982.

Lubich, C.: *Jesus in the Midst – the Essence of Every Relationship* (edited by D. Falmi and J. Povilis), New City, London, 2019.

Lubich, C.: *Jesus – The Heart of His Message – Unity and Jesus Forsaken*, New City Press, New York, 1985.

Lubich, C.: *Journey – Spiritual Insights*, New City Press, New York, 1984.

Lubich, C.: *Journey to Heaven – Spiritual Thoughts to Live*, New City Press, New York, 1997.

Lubich, C.: *Knowing How to Lose*, New City, London, 1981 (Rev. ed. 2015).

Lubich, C.: *A Little Harmless Manifesto*, New City Press, New York, 1973.

Lubich, C.: *Living Dialogue – Chiara Lubich on Christian Unity* (edited by G. Fallacara), New City, London, 2009.

Lubich, C.: *The Living Presence*, New City, London, 1997.

Lubich, C.: *The Love That Comes from God – Reflections on the Family*, New City Press, New York, 1993.

Lubich, C.: *Man's Yes to God*, New City, London, 1982.

Lubich, C.: *Manifesto*, New City, London, 1975.

Lubich, C.: *Mary* (edited by B. Leahy and J. Povilus), New City (Press), London/New York, 2018.

Lubich, C.: *Mary – the Transparency of God*, New City (Press), New York/London/Manila, 2003.

Lubich, C.: *May They All Be One*, New City (Press), London/New York, 1977/1984.

Lubich, C.: *Meditations*, New City (Press), New York/London, 1971 e.a.

Lubich, C.: *My Ecumenical Journey* (edited by M. Wienken and D. Goller), New City, London, 2020.

Lubich, C.: *Neighbors – Short Reflections on Loving the People Around Us* (edited by B. Hartnett), New City Press, New York, 2012.

Lubich, C.: *A New Way – The Spirituality of Unity*, New City, London, 2006.

Lubich, C.: *No Thorn Without a Rose – 99 Sayings by Chiara Lubich* (edited by J. Ciabattini), New City Press, New York, 2008.

Lubich, C.: *On the Holy Journey – Spiritual Messages*, New City Press, New York, 1988.

Lubich, C.: *Only at Night We See the Stars – Finding Light in the Face of Darkness*, New City (Press), New York/London, 2002.

Lubich, C.: *Our Yes to God*, New City Press, New York, 1982.

Lubich, C.: *The Pearl of the Gospel – Short Reflections on Reciprocal Love* (edited by B. Hartnett) New City Press, New York, 2013.

Lubich, C.: *Rays – Short Reflections on Living God's Will* (edited by B. Hartnett) New City Press, New York, 2011.

Lubich, C.: *The Secret of Unity*, New City, London, 1985, 1997.

Lubich, C.: *Servants of All*, New City (Press), New York/London, 1978/9.

Lubich, C.: *The Sun That Daily Rise – Short Reflections on the Mystery of the Eucharist* (edited by B. Hartnett), New City Press, New York, 2015.

Lubich, C.: *Unity* (edited by D. Falmi and F. Gillet), New City Press, New York, 2015.

Lubich, C.: *When Did We See You, Lord?*, New City Press, New York, 1983.

Lubich, C.: *When Our Love Is Charity*, Spiritual Writings Vol. 2, New City Press, New York, 1991.

Lubich, C.: *Where Two or Three*, New City (Press), New York/London, 1977.

Lubich, C.: *Why Have You Forsaken Me – The Key to Unity*, New City, London, 1985.

Lubich, C.: *The Word of Life*, New City (Press), New York/London, 1977/81

Lubich, C.: *Yes Yes No No*, New City, London, 1977.

O'Byrne, M.: *Model of Incarnate Love – Mary Desolate in the Experience and Thought of Chiara Lubich*, New City Press, New York, 2011.

Pochet, M.: *Stars and Tears – A Conversation with Chiara Lubich*, New City, London, 1985.

Povilus, J. M.: *United in His Name – Jesus in Our Midst in the Experience and Thought of Chiara Lubich*, Theology and Life series 2, New City Press, New York, 1992.

Proctor, W.: *An Interview with Chiara Lubich*, New City Press, New York, 1983.

Robertson, E.: *Chiara*, Christian Journals Limited, Ireland, 1978.

Schindler, D.L.: *An Introduction to the Abba School – Conversations from the Focolare's Interdisciplinary Study Center*, New City Press, New York, 2002.

Torno, A.: *Chiara Lubich – A Biography*, New City Press, New York, 2012.

Zambonini, F.: *Chiara Lubich – A Life for Unity*, New City (Press) London/New York, 1992.

Other sources for Focolare movement and its activities

Bruni, L.: *The Economy of Communion – Toward a Multi-Dimensional Economic Culture*, New City Press, New York, 2002.

Bruni, L.: *The Wound and the Blessing – Economics, Relationships and Happiness*, New City Press, New York, 2012.

Cocchiaro, M.: *Natalia – The first companion of Chiara Lubich*, Focolare Foundation, Melbourne, 2016.

Crepaz, P.: *Making the Ordinary Extraordinary – The Life of Domenico Mangano*, New City, London, 2019.

Daneo, S.: *My Life Across the Ocean*, New City Press, Manila, 2016.

Gallagher, J. & Buckeye, J.: *Structures of Grace – The Business Practices of the Economy of Communion*, New City Press, New York, 2014.

Gately, S.: *Like the Sunshine – Lieta Betono at the Dawn of the Focolare in Ireland*, New City Ireland, 2013.

Giordani, I.: *Diary of Fire*, New City, London, 1981.

Gold, L.: *New Financial Horizons – The Emergence of an Economy of Communion*, New City Press, New York, 2010.

Green, M.: *She Died She Lives*, New City, London, 1989

Green, M.: *The Vanishing Root*, New City, London, 1994.

James, M., Masters, T. and Uelmen, A.: *Education's Highest Aim – Teaching and Learning through a Spirituality of Communion*, New City Press, New York, 2010.

Johnson, F.: *Focolare Movement*, CTS, London, 2002

Masters, T. and Uelmen, A.: *Focolare – Living a Spirituality of Unity in the United States,* New City Press, New York, 2011.

Olsen, J. and Masters, T.: *The Family and Education,* New City Press, New York, 1989.

Robertson, E.: *The Fire of Love,* New City, London, 1989.

Zamboni, D.: *Glimpses of Gospel Life – The "Little Flowers" of Chiara and the Focolare Movement,* New City (Press), New York/London, 2004.

Zanzucchi, M.: *Chiara Luce – A Life Lived to the Full,* New City, London, 2007.

New City Press

New City Press is one of more than 20 publishing houses sponsored by the Focolare, a movement founded by Chiara Lubich to help bring about the realization of Jesus' prayer: "That all may be one" (John 17:21). In view of that goal, New City Press publishes books and resources that enrich the lives of people and help all to strive toward the unity of the entire human family. We are a member of the Association of Catholic Publishers.

www.newcitypress.com
202 Comforter Blvd.
Hyde Park, New York

Periodicals
Living City Magazine
www.livingcitymagazine.com

Scan to join our mailing list for discounts and promotions or go to www.newcitypress.com and click on "join our email list."

www.ingramcontent.com/pod-product-compliance
Lightning Source LLC
Chambersburg PA
CBHW051828230426
43671CB00008B/878